C000276512

"Attunement takes you to a place of seren_ want to stay there."

—Satisfied Attur

Healing is back. We are learning there is r use of medications and surgery, as valuable a_ Henderson is a healer, and she is showing the way.

—Larry Dossey, MD, Author of
Prayer is Good Medicine; Healing Words;
Recovering the Soul; Meaning and Medicine;
Space, Time & Medicine

Increasing numbers of scientists and lay people alike are finding that spiritual healing, energy healing, prayer, and laying-on-of-hands are demonstrably effectual. Of course, all of these methods are quite ancient; how ironic that modern technological medicine calls itself 'traditional', and brands these archaic, natural practices as 'alternative'! Jaclyn Stein Henderson's Attunement Chronicles is a valuable addition to the literature on the energetic healing revival — and an excellent introduction to a specific technique that effectively combines non-directed prayer, laying-on-of-hands, and energy balancing.

—Richard Heinberg, author of
Memories and Visions of Paradise,
Celebrate the Solstice, and
A New Covenant with Nature,
publisher of Museletter

Jaclyn Stein Henderson, LMP, RC and her work with Attunement will open your heart to powerful energy work that can be used to create harmony in body, mind and spirit.

—Audrey Harris, RN, Washington State
Coordinator for the American Holistic
Nurses Association, Therapeutic Touch and
Healing Touch Practitioner

I have found that the attunement current allows for an oasis of new life substance to be born out of what may have been a desert-like human condition. It is a most precious and significant gift on this earth and Jaclyn's facilitation is pure magic.

—Dr Lawrence Bakur, Chiropractor, and
Attunement Practitioner

For me, the experience of attunement is wholeness or oneness. I feel a strong mind-body-spirit connection at a cellular level, which leaves my body feeling loved, relaxed, sacred and coherent.

> —Diane L. Phillips, Ed.D.,
> Phillips & Associates

At last, a system that not only acknowledges the spiritual aspect of healing, but embraces and focuses on it... fills a void in healing literature and will be an important addition to every healer's library... The more I work with Attunement, the more self-aware and aware of energy patterns in others I become.

> —Martha Read, Licensed Massage Practitioner, in practice for 13 years

Your hands are magic. Very powerful and nourishing... I felt almost as though the energy around my head was gently rocking me... very comforting and relaxing... I was really able to feel energy flowing during the session. It seemed to come from your hands and to be awakening in me as well.

> —Participants in the Attunement
> Qualitative Research Project,
> Bastyr University, Seattle, Washington,
> January, 1995

Attunement Therapy is not only calming, balancing and healing, but also empowering: I use it as a great meditation tool to create positive change in myself, my community and the world.

> —Kaya McLaren, Elementary School Teacher
> and Licensed Massage Practitioner

You have a wonderful knack for saying the right words to encourage a trainee.

> —Judith Hurd, Attunement Trainee

I want to thank you for the caring you brought and the time you gave... You do have a special gift.

> —Martha Swain, Volunteer Coordinator
> Bailey Boushey House, Seattle, Washington
> (Bailey Boushey House is the largest AIDS
> out-patient and resident facility in the
> United States)

The Healing Power
of
Attunement Therapy

Stories and Practice

Jaclyn Stein Henderson, NCTMB, RC

with a foreword by Michael J. Moore, DC

FINDHORN
Press

British Library Cataloguing-in-Publication Data.
A catalogue record for this book is available
from the British Library.

Illustrations by Jill Frances Harris
Book layout and cover design by Findhorn Press
Printed on acid free paper and bound by Rose Printing Company, Inc., USA

Published by

Findhorn Press Ltd
The Park, Findhorn
Forres IV36 0TZ
Scotland, UK
TEL (01309) 690582
FAX (01309) 690036

Findhorn Press, Inc.
P.O. Box 13939
Tallahassee, Florida 32317-3939
USA
TEL (850) 893 2920
FAX (850) 893 3442

E-MAIL books@findhorn.org
URL http://www.findhorn.org/findhornpress/

A Note to the Reader:
Attunement is considered to be a viable form of alternative medicine,
and should not be used in place of sound conservative health care prac-
tice. The reader is advised to consult a licensed physician for all serious
health concerns.

Thank you to William Comer, BSc, HTP, Donald Henderson, Michael J.
Moore, DC, and Anthony Palombo, DC, for granting me permission to
include your stories.

This book is dedicated to all who reveal the pioneering spirit,
and is for Dick,
with a bushel and a peck,
and a hug around your neck.

Slow down...
and love will change
your fate.

—Uranda[1]

[1] Born Lloyd Arthur Meeker, see page 255

Also by the author:

Attunement Anatomical Charts

Energy Medicine Documentation Forms

The Attunement Therapy Training, Home-study and Certification Program

Contents

Attunement Charts and Illustrations   9

Acknowledgments   10

Foreword by Michael J. Moore, DC   11

Introduction   15

PART ONE   INVISIBLE ESSENCE

1. The Spiritual Landscape   21

2. Entering In   35
   Thankfulness Exercises

3. Spontaneous Remission and Inner Healing   41
   The Inner Healing Meditation

4. Non-Directed Prayer   53
   Radiant Energy Practice

5. The Invisible Guide   63
   Sanctification

6. Non-local Spiritual Attunement   75
   Long Distance (Non-Local) Attunement Practice

7. Ascension   81
   The Robe of Radiance Practice

8. Patterns of Agreement   91
   Creative Triangle Exercises

9. Manifestation   101
   The Paper Dot Exercise

PART TWO   VISIBLE FORM

10. The Cervical Pattern   111
    Cervical Pattern Attunement Practice

11. The Spiritual Path of the Endocrine Gland System   121
    Endocrine Gland Attunement Guidelines and Practice

12. Attuning the Digestive System   135
    Digestive System Attunement Practice

13. Attuning the Circulatory, Excretory and Respiratory Systems   143
    Circulatory, Excretory and Respiratory Attunement Practices

14. Attuning the Immune System 155
Attuning the Immune System

15. Holding Patterns — Attuning the Brain and 163
Spinal Cord
Brain and Spinal Cord Attunement Practice

16. Attuning the Skeletal System 173
Skeletal System Attunement Practice

17. Wound Healing 179
Injury Treatment Attunement Practice

PART THREE THE CREATIVE FIELD

18. The Life Process 193
Charting Your Own Stress Indicators Exercise

19. Terminal Illness 207
Foot and Hand Attunement Practice

20. Team Attunements 217
Team Attunement Guidelines

21. Representational Objects 225
Representational Object Practice Guidelines

22. Radiant Gatherings 233
Radiant Gathering Guidelines

Attunement Overview 241

Documenting Attunement Therapy Sessions 242

The Attunement Therapy Training, Home-Study and 243
Certification Program

Crossroads 247

About the Author 250

Appendix A — Histology Notes on the Endocrine Gland System 251

Appendix B — The History of Attunement 255

Appendix C — Attunement Pracititioners and Conference Facilities 259

Bibliography 265

Index 268

Attunement Charts and Illustrations

Balancing the Cervical Pattern Illustration 116

Balancing the Feet with Attunement Illustration 120

Brain – Central Sulcus Attunement Chart, Top View 166

Brain – Central Sulcus Attunement Chart, Lateral View 166

Circulatory System Contact Points Chart 149

Digestive System Contact Points Chart 139

Endocrine Gland Anatomical Chart 129

Excretory System Contact Points Chart 151

Facial Attunement Contact Points Chart 141

Foot Attunement – Endocrine Gland Contact Points Chart 213

Foot Attunement – Organ Systems Contact Points Chart 214

Foot Attunement Contact Points Chart, Dorsal View 214

Hand Attunement Contact Points Chart 215

The Human Skeleton – Long Bones Anatomical Chart 175

Lymph System Anatomical Chart 160

Radiant Energy Exercise #1 57

Radiant Energy Exercise #2 58

Respiratory System Contact Points Chart 153

Self Attunement Illustration and Chart 134

Spine and Nerve Chart 169

Acknowledgments

Deep love and thanks go to Dick Henderson, my husband and loving partner, who has supported me financially and otherwise for the past two and a half years, and by whose faith assisted me to complete this project. My love and thanks also goes to my mother, Harlene Stein, who continues to give me much love and support, and who encouraged me to write something commercial. My appreciation goes to Cliff Penwell, David Lesser, Charlene Hunter and the other Emissary Trustees, and to David Reis, Laurence Layne, Jude Repar, Paul Price, Laurence Bakur, DC, and Chris Jorgensen for their response to my work over the years which compelled me to finish this project.

Thank you Bill Comer, for your story. Thank you Don Henderson, Michael J. Moore, DC, and Anthony Palombo, DC, for granting me permission to share your stories with others. Gratitude and love go to Jill Frances Harris who, by her agreement in spirit, allowed this project to fill-out with beautiful form. A special thanks goes to literary agent Susan Schulman who first gave me the idea for this book. Thank you Susan Weinstein for your attentive listening ear. A big 'Thank you!' goes to Tony Mitton, LMT, who offered me expert editorial 'midwifery' assistance and spiritual sustenance through his suggestions, and for his love and light filled friendship. I also thank Thierry and Karin Bogliolo, publishers at Findhorn Press who were the first ones to show me the light of response to this project, and who stewarded this project to completion with patience, trust, finesse and care.

Continued love and thanks go to Rev. Roger de Winton, with whom I am deeply blessed to be associated for many years.

Many thanks go to my numerous students, clients, massage peers and friends who, through their open response to love, gave spirit an open doorway through which to move, surrounding me with light, and insight, and informing my creative field with love's perfect intent.

Foreword by Michael J. Moore, DC

I believe that each person holds within themselves a great potential and power to heal themselves and offer healing to others. This healing power is the life force which pulses through our bodies, assists us in our creative efforts, regenerates us, and can restore us when we are receptive to its inherent purpose. It is this life force that animates all living forms. Part of my job as a chiropractor is to assist others to take deliberate action for their own healing process, bringing themselves more fully into alignment with this inner healing power.

This book by Jaclyn Stein Henderson on the healing power of Attunement Therapy represents a significant step that attunement is now taking to influence and educate people about their own inner healing potential. Attunement Therapy is valuable work, and facilitates the path of awakening our own consciousness in powerful and creative ways.

When viewed with a larger perspective, attunement is not just a healing art offered by a chosen few but encompasses many natural healing tendencies which we express on a daily basis. Picture a mother holding the hand of a small child who has just fallen, or the hug of one person given to another to console or comfort, or a father giving his son a 'high-five' after a tough game on the soccer field. We all know that the same healing essence pictured above in each of those situations carries with it creative intentions which far surpass their routine nature. When these essences and their creative qualities are expressed in alignment with the life force that animates our universe, we greatly enhance the flow of healing energy that moves through our lives. This creative movement of life may be brought to focus through those who utilize attunement energy in their living.

I was first introduced to attunement shortly after I began my chiropractic training at Palmer College of Chiropractic in Davenport, Iowa. During that time I attended several 'Art of Living Workshops' on the East Coast, facilitated by Dr Bill Bahan, a pioneer in the attunement field, who was also a Palmer graduate chiropractor. Dr Bahan's contagious radiant personality brought focus and clarity of purpose to my study of the healing process. I recall one of my early attunement experiences. I was sharing one of my first attunements with an attunement practitioner. As the session began, I remember closing my eyes with the quiet, peaceful, feeling that came over me. Mid-way through the attunement, I opened my eyes quickly because I realized I could no longer feel my body touching the table. I wondered, was I levitating? What was happening? I opened my eyes to realize I was lying in the same position, and had not moved. There was an incredible feeling of warmth and relaxation within my mind and body — a feeling which I had never experienced before. This feeling became more familiar to me as I continued to learn more about the attunement technique in the years that followed.

Since the initiation of my private practice in Redding, California, 15 years ago, attunement, used in its various forms, has been an integral part of my service. Through my experience I have come to recognize the importance of the feeling of energy that continues to move through my hands. This awareness takes the work I do beyond the physical level to a place where my perceptions are enhanced and the flow of innate energy between myself and my patient is increased. Whether you choose to call this a vibrant bed-side manner, an atmosphere of healing, or simply an innate connection, this interaction is a vital ingredient to the healing process shared between people.

Over the last 10 years, besides providing Chiropractic care, I've also facilitated outdoor experiential healing workshops with my wife, Donna. Many of these workshops have utilized different forms of attunement technique. These techniques have proven to be subtle yet powerful ways to quiet the mind and emotions, thus allowing a clearer awareness of one's own divine identity to emerge while in the outdoors.

There have been many experiences that have provided amazing demonstrations of the power of attunement, including the finding that the movement of the attunement current does not require close proximity. Here is one story which portrays the healing power of love known and shared through close, personal friendship:

One day, a close friend of ours called and said that her son had been riding his bicycle and had just been hit by a car traveling 60 miles per hour. The ambulance was there getting ready to take him to the hospital and she needed someone to go with her. Donna arrived at the scene a few minutes later. As she ran past one of the Emergency Medical Technicians she knew, she asked how the boy was. The EMT replied, "It doesn't look good." He had a broken leg, massive facial injuries, and possible head and abdominal injuries. As Donna and her friend followed the ambulance to the hospital, not many words were spoken. They just held hands and prayed. When they arrived at the hospital, they were escorted to the Chaplain's private office where they were joined by the Sisters of Mercy support staff. At that point Donna called me at work to let me know what was happening. I immediately began sending attunement energy to the scene and joined them in person soon after. Donna also phoned a friend and spiritual teacher who lived in Oregon, and he began sharing in the attunement pattern with us. We also connected by phone with another attunement teacher who lived in Colorado. This attunement teacher was quite sensitive to long distance energy healing and after a few quiet moments working with the energy of the boy assured us by exclaiming, "Ryan is a strong boy. All will be well." Easy for him to say! He couldn't hear Ryan's screams coming from the emergency room down the hall!

As they waited, Donna shared an attunement with her friend, reflecting on the attunement teacher's words, "All will be well." After the attunement, Donna's friend remarked that her experience during this attunement was one of going from a state of shock to coming fully present in the moment. She said it was like being on a train that was switching tracks. One by one, her heart, feelings, and body clicked into a new track that brought clarity in her awareness of what was going on and what needed to happen.

Through this triangle of friends, there was a loving enfoldment that was undeniable and brought peace of mind and strength to this highly tense situation. The emergency technicians finally confirmed that Ryan had a compound fracture of his leg, but there was no serious internal or brain damage. He remained in the hospital for a few weeks while they attended his leg and multiple skin wounds. We continued with daily attunement work during his hospital stay and subsequent recovery. The doctors were amazed at the speed and extent to which he healed.

Another story comes to mind and pertains to how attunement and chiropractic technique work well together to assist in the healing process. One Sunday I received a phone call from one of my patients whose wife had delivered a baby at the hospital two days earlier. He asked "Michael, can you come? The baby is in intensive care and they are not sure she is going to make it." I arrived at the hospital a short time later and saw this tiny, premature baby in an incubator, attached to monitors and tubes. A mistake had been made and she was delivered via C-section one month early. She was 5 pounds 15 ounces at birth on the previous Friday, and by Sunday her weight had decreased to 4 pounds 10 ounces. This weight loss had the doctors concerned. The infant was having trouble taking a bottle so she was getting very little nourishment and would vomit up any fluids given to her. The doctor said that she was too pre-mature and the sphincter at the top of the stomach was closed, causing the vomiting, though it was felt that with maturation she would grow out of that deformation.

With that scenario, I scrubbed up and accompanied the mother and father into the baby's room. We removed her from the incubator and, knee to knee in a circle with her parents, I held her and checked her. The nurses looked on, curious, and somehow seemed to sense that I was there to help. I proceeded to gently re-balance her nervous system in the cervical and thoracic regions, freeing her body of nerve interference. I then shared an attunement with her, balancing the cervical region and endocrine gland system. During that time there was an amazing sense of warmth and energy moving through my hands and between the three of us in that circle. When I finally looked up, there was a circle of nurses and two doctors all around us. No one said a word, and at the end of the attunement those personnel went back to their tasks. Megan had fallen asleep so we put her back into the incubator with the feeling that she was going to be just fine. The father called me a couple hours later with the news that Megan awoke, started nursing and was not vomiting any longer. What great news! Four days later she was released from the hospital without any problems. I was so grateful to have the techniques and experience to offer healing to this tiny patient, who now, at the age of eight is so in tune with her body that she lets her mom know when she needs to go see 'Dr Michael' to receive a chiropractic adjustment. She brightens our office each time she comes in.

Just as these stories confirm, I am sure that you too can recall one or more people in your life who represented a steadfast, balanced and loving character, be it a mentor, teacher, or friend. You grew and were inspired by their example. As you continue to move along that same path, guided by the same spirit offered to you, you too may begin to be an example for others. As you open your life, free it of unnecessary manipulation, and instead offer a balanced alignment of heart, body, mind and spirit, you too may express life to your highest potential. Whether you choose to receive attunement from the hands of a health care provider, or practice attunement within the private confines of your own home, office, or private practice, you will undoubtedly begin to see attunement healing emerge within your own daily interactions with your children, loved ones, and friends.

I feel attunement is one of life's foremost experiences which offers the finest that we have to give. And I commend Jaclyn for bringing forward this handbook on Attunement Therapy. This book is a practical application guide for you to use as you move along your own journey, living your life to the fullest, and being of service to the greater whole of humanity.

Michael J. Moore, DC
Redding, California
February, 1998

Introduction

My many years of healing arts service informs me that the doorway to health rests in the realm of relaxation — relaxation of the mind, body, and emotions. Most clients who come to me for help do so because they usually have a full plate of stressful issues with which they are contending, and as these get sorted out, they begin to relax and heal. It's as if life were inviting them to change with their illness by saying, "Ah, excuse me, you've gone too far, maxed-out, and now we're going to stop and rest for a while. I'm putting on the brakes... it's okay, you're ready to change, so here goes..." Life always offers you this message if you listen for it, but if you're too busy to listen, then sometimes life *makes* you listen by putting you in a horizontal position for a while. This book on Attunement Therapy is an informational resource center for learning how to listen for life's messages, and then how to take action on the next creative impulse without having to spend your life in bed.

The true stories in this book demonstrate the fact that personal illness and life challenges provide people with radical shift opportunities. Oftentimes, complete transformations occur in peoples' lives when they open up to life in a new way. The creative purpose of life seeks to bring about change, in whatever ways it needs to, both torrential and with softer embrace, to bring people into alignment with its essential harmony. True healing of life illness brings with it an invitation to not be the same person you were, but to be the person life wants you to be, the person you know yourself to be in your heart, but are not expressing, to reveal yourself to yourself, to be the divine embodiment of yourself.

My own experience has taught me that when a life-threatening illness (or any illness) emerged, life was actually giving me an opportunity to change, and change at depth. I've learned that illness was life's way of enabling me to move forward along my own destined path towards my higher good, if I chose to accept this change for myself. Change was not about instituting a little variety into my life, not about shifting things around until the illness passed, not about sitting things out until I could get back on my feet again, and back to 'normal.' The deeper change that was offered was always a radical one, which shook the rafters of my heart until I relinquished my unhealthy hold on my world with a relaxing 'ahhhh....'.

Attunement service offers such a radical, relaxing shift. Attunement healing is not a mental exercise, but a change in one's life force vibration backed up by an open heart and mind to let this love vibration continue to express itself through the capacities. With gentle nudges, attunement energy (spiritual love energy) provides a rich spiritual provision for those who are willing to undergo creative transformation, no matter their state of health. The beauty of this healing practice rests in its capacity to relax the person at deepest levels of being so that the person may thereby let go, and let come a new life orientation. Attunement practice offers a softer awakening to the truth of oneself.

This book has been designed to take you on such a journey to serenity. Take a daily vacation by reading a little from this book and then practice the exercises for 15 minutes a day. After a few days you'll exclaim to your neighbor and/or family members, "You know, it works! I feel more relaxed! My life has eased up and problems plaguing my life just kind of drifted off and disappeared. I don't know why they ever seemed so important to me in the first place! You want to try it with me?" Pretty soon you'll have the whole neighborhood relaxing, sharing attunement, taking a daily vacation break together. And then watch for the serenity to emerge because your lives will never be in the same hectic, chaotic mess again.

What I present herein I gained over 17 years of learning and practice in association with the Emissaries of Divine Light Ministry (now the International Emissaries). This continues to be an enlightened journey of discovering how to offer my gifts and leadership talents within the healing arts. More information on the history of attunement therapy may be found in *Appendix B* of this book.

This book is a learning tool to teach you attunement from its simplest forms to its more complex styles. Each chapter contains a story about attunement healing, with some scientific explanation about how the healing works, and then offers an exercise for you to master by yourself, or with others. Practised consistently, and with an open heart to your own God being's purposes for you, these exercises will open and heal your life.

I present the exercises (and stories) in sequence, explaining invisible essences and how to master working with them, how to attune each system of the human body, through to working with larger patterns in one's life, and with others. With all of these exercises, you will learn how to creatively influence your own situation, and those situations and people around you and in the world. The exercises are offered in the same personable spirit in which they were originally taught to me — from a mentor to a single student or small group.

All of the stories presented in this book are true. Names of most of the people in the stories have been changed to protect the confidentiality of those concerned. The stories either came from my own personal attunement experience, or were told to me word-of-mouth from an attunement practitioner or client. Some stories are taken from my own private practice documentation with approval granted by the clients for their presentation here. All of the stories are verifiable. Given the same set of circumstances, all of the stories' healing effects are repeatable. The stories are recorded here to the best of my remembrance and are without exaggeration. Most of these stories have not had public exposure before — you are now witness to this portion of attunement therapy's public expansion.

As a whole, the stories and lessons in this book are cumulative — lessons should be followed in their order of appearance. By the end of the book, you will have learned all forms of attunement traditional to the practice. The avenues for practicing attunement are then endless — you may offer it to yourself and to anyone else at anytime, in any place, in any mood you find yourself (attunement will usually change your bad mood to a good mood), and for any creative purpose. One little rule though, this work is creative — you can't use attunement to harm anyone — spirit won't let you.

You need not worry or fear you will mistreat someone with attunement energy. That is an impossible task. Even if you feel like you don't know what you're doing to start, you can't hurt anyone with this work. You can only enhance the feeling of love you give to someone else and they to you. You cannot fix a problem with this work — you can only strengthen the life force flowing through the problem, imbue it with your own spirit, and enhance it with your own power. You cannot attune voids, dead energy, dead tissue or something that isn't present in form. You can only attune something in form which has the life force flowing through it (for living systems on earth, the life force moves along carbon-based molecules). You should also know, before embarking on this journey, that committing to practice this work without expectations is the hallmark of an attunement server. Sharing attunement with yourself and others, without expecting any kind of results, will creatively change your life.

Attunement has always been taught in a simple learn-as-you-do environment, so this book has many handy learning tools for you to use. You may wish to gather your friends together and practice the attunement lessons on each other. You may also wish to attend one of my attunement classes (see The Attunement Therapy Training, Home-Study and Certification Program section) or those offered by others (see *Appendix C*).

I believe that humanity is now closer to fulfilling its collective spiritual potential than ever before. Outer opportunities for unified creative action exist, and are as limitless in nature as is the personal inner urge towards union with Source. This book may then serve as a timely and practical spiritual tool to use towards that creative end. This book contains catalytic essence which may spark the fire residing within your soul, and compel you in the right direction as you abide in the awakening process. This book is a journey which may awaken both spiritual emergence and serenity simultaneously. It explores the release of your own spiritual authenticity and surrender made manifest. As you allow the magic of attunement practice to emerge, I rejoice with you to see the promise of love's return fulfilled in your own lifetime.

> *I am thankful, Lord, for the words contained herein, offered to me to give to others through the movement of your divine spirit. May all who read these words turn to you in absolute assurance. May Thy will be made manifest in the lives of all who read this book. May these lives know peace through attunement. May these lives bless the world as it turns swiftly in its cycles of restoration. You are glorified in my life now and forevermore. Amen.*

> *Jaclyn Stein Henderson, NCTMB, RC*
> *Port Orchard, WA, USA*
> *February, 1998*

Part One

Invisible Essence

There must be that secret place
within the heart of each one which is never penetrated
by the emotional storms of the outer world,
thus maintaining a place from whence spirit may flow
in dealing with those problems and situations which arise.

There must be an open door
in our hearts through which the Master may pass
when He comes to commune with us,
and through which the spirit of God's blessing
may flow forth into the world.

There is a secret place
from which the light shines forth
as we abide under the shadow of the Almighty.

—Uranda

1. The Spiritual Landscape

There is a universal similarity found in all spiritual encounters which is that much of what you feel or sense with spiritual perception is invisible to the eye, but common to the senses. This book is about teaching you how to acknowledge your own spiritual sensing in your emotional, psychic, mental, and physical realms, and putting several of these sensations together at once. The final destination point is for you to know how to harmonize yours and others' spiritual landscapes with the inner wisdom that is flowing freely from within. Step by step you will learn how to:

• sense spirit flowing through your body, mind and heart, while you

• connect a consciously loving intention in your mind, with the

• flow of energy moving through your finger tips, as it

• touches into a specific creative field or another person's etheric body.

That is quite a lot of sensation to recognize all at once! Too hard to do? Not at all! It will feel much the same as when you learned to walk as a toddler (not many of you will remember that event!). Now that you are an adult, the thought processes may seem more serious, but it is still just as fun with none of the spills.

In order to start you off on solid ground, I've included some introductory information about the sacred landscape upon which you are journeying, its purpose in practice, some essential vocabulary, ideas regarding your inner compass and self-care, what to take with you on your journey, information on how attunement is different from other forms of energy work, and thoughts about its therapeutic value. Bonne aventure!

The Layout of the Land

*There is a landscape
larger than the one you see.*

—*Anonymous*

All things in our world contain spirit — if they did not, they would not be. All things contain the spiritual essences of divinity, those invisible characteristics which make things particular to themselves, and as such, are a part of the spiritual nature of the kingdom of God, the kingdom of spirit. Divine components within you are your thoughts, feelings, spiritual awareness (intuition), and physical sensations which you feel from within (heat, cold, touch, pressure, etc.). It is through this invisible landscape that God or divinity acts in your life. As a divine associate of this planet you have the potential and opportunity to act with spiritual intention within this vital and invisible landscape called life.

The spiritual landscape is an intimate portrait of life's first creation. In it are deep and ancient memories, both of your life and of the lives of many other people. Your spiritual landscape contains within it the cultural and hereditary lines of force which make you who you are today — those issues of race, gender and family relations, as well as the glories and catastrophes the world's populations have faced. Both shadow and light reside in each person's spiritual landscape, containing invisible and compelling memory traces which work to conform your consciousness with numinous force.

Your spiritual landscape also holds rich beauty and is filled with the wisdom, memory, pathos and festivals of the human soul. In a day and age when society and culture yearn for spiritual nurturing, the living force which journeys through the spiritual landscape brings us home to our hearts. Attunement with Source guides our stressed lives to a resting place wherein that which eternally abides, soothes our ravaged emotional realms. Attunement within the spiritual landscape guides all chaos to a place of stability, a sacred space where deep harmony unifies and stills our being. The unity of spirit, when properly handled, may re-attune our destructive memory traces to the wellspring of health present within our core. Attunement is like a sacred ground point for all dis-ease, a silent beacon calling us home.

Learning attunement, you will be traveling through the spiritual landscape of your life, recreating life with the touch of radiant energy. Just as the massage therapist's hands contour to the physical shape of the physical body, so do the attunement practitioner's hands conform themselves to the natural subtle energy profile of the etheric body. And just as the healer's consciousness informs with healing intention the conscious surround of the client, so does the attunement practitioner's spiritual consciousness connect with Higher Power to inform the client's consciousness of her sacred intent. Healing touch both within the visible and invisible worlds carries significant meaning to those who work within these constructs, offering hallowed purpose.

Vocabulary Footholds

Spirituality: Your path through the spiritual landscape carries particular significance for you alone. This book does not intend to deter you from your own spiritual path, but enhance your presence upon it. Each reader brings to attunement their own background with regards to spiritual orientation; therefore I have included one definition of spirituality which we all may use as a guidepost in our attunement work together. These words may provide all readers with a bottom-line, basic context for what spirituality means:

> *Spirituality is the influence with which we take care of and nurture our human spirit to find meaning and richness in life happenings, as we cope with and enjoy the unpredictable, mysterious and uncontrollable aspects of life.*[1]

I like this definition because it engenders a healing, nourishing feeling to the idea of spirituality, which works well with attunement practice.

Service: Attunement Practitioners consider the practice of attunement to be a spiritual event. Offering private sessions, presentations, classes, writing, and other forms of attuned expression is a way for *attunement servers* to provide the public with a rich and sustaining current of radiant energy which will assist self and others to know union with Source.

Sharing an Attunement: From a historical perspective, attunement has always been shared between people, and more traditionally, between two people — one person serves as 'practitioner' and the other as 'client.' It does little good to say that one person gives while the other person receives since the reality of attunement practice is that both people give, by *sharing* in offering attunement outward. Here's a little story about what sharing an attunement means. I was once offering attunements during a health fair at a local health food store and a naturopathic doctor who was presenting her wares nearby heard me ask someone walking by "Would you like to share an attunement?" The naturopath turned to me and asked with subtle sarcasm, "You are *sharing* an attunement? What does *that* mean?" I quietly smiled, not reacting to her sarcastic tone, and continued sharing my attunement. The naturopath soon pulled up her wares and left the vicinity, telling the store manager that she wasn't getting any business. I saw things differently. I was sharing what I offered with others, and not looking to get anything. I saw a large creative field in front of me, with people eager to share in what I was offering. Offering a service to another is all about providing a quality of care, and the kind of quality you offer determines whether or not people are drawn to what you have to give.

Practitioner and *Client:* In this book, the easiest way to describe how people share attunement is to use the terms 'practitioner,' which will refer to the person who is sending attunement energy to another, and 'client,' which will refer to the person who is on the receiving end of attunement energy. If you are sending attunement energy to yourself, then you are acting as practitioner and client simultaneously.

Capacities: The capacities relate to your house of being, your faculties of body, mind and heart. While you read this book you will be asked on many occasions to be consciously aware of what kind of energy or thought form you see moving through your *outer capacities*. The outer capacities are what house your thoughts, feelings and actions, and surround your sacred inner chamber. Your sacred inner chamber is your *inner capacity*, which contains the presence of the *Wonderful One Within*, that power which radiates love through you to your world.

Expression: When moving through human capacities of body, mind and heart, attunement energy finds its focus through human expression. The term spiritual expression denotes any form of thought (either written, oral or silent), speech, emotion, movement, or action which is empowered by radiant energy, emanating from within. (More on this definition may be found in *Chapter 11*.)

Agreement: Agreement relates to spiritual accord between your capacities of mind and heart, or between yourself and another person. All attunement practice is based on spiritual agreement which is a quality of openness and trust that flows from one capacity to another. (More on agreement may be found in *Chapter 8*.)

Turning: Attunement practice asks you to incline your conscious faculties towards you inner higher power, to be open to the impulse from Source for your guidance and direction in living. You are asked to turn inward to see God, and to open your mind and heart in response to God's love. To turn is to *enter in*. (More on entering in may be found in the next chapter.)

Focus on the Feminine: Since I am a woman healer, and most of my clients and students have been female, I sometimes speak to and with a woman's tongue. My intention is not to ignore the masculine or dissuade men from learning attunement, but to present attunement within the context of its present day audience. Most hands-on healers, or healers who work within a nature-centered context are female (75% of all the students who attend Naturopathic Medical School are female).[2] This gender ratio may shift into balance as the human race becomes more androgynous with evolution. For now, my purpose is to offer pertinent information to my reader audience, and to convey that information which is realistically supported by my previous clinical experience.

Pneumaplasm and Morphogenetic Human Fields: Attunement practice clears energy fields found in yourself and all other living systems. Because much of our work together involves movement into someone else's subtle energy field, I will talk a little bit about what an etheric body or subtle energy field contains. (More on this point may be found in the other chapters contained in *Part I*).

Uranda entitled the subtle energy field which surrounds the physical body 'pneumaplasm,' meaning 'new substance.' Pneumaplasm is defined as 'first substance,' *that field of energy emanating from physical substance, through which subtle energies and the life force moves.*

This invisible etheric level of being is thought to harness the power of recreating physical form, and is a human blueprint, or human *morphogenetic field*, meaning that this field of energy gives birth to form.[3] Based on Rupert Sheldrake's scientific theories, morphogenetic fields are thought to be biologically-based information systems which do not lose their power after they are created, and which carry messages for the formation of physical forms. New morphogenetic systems contain within themselves seeds which resonate with older systems' seeds for the formation of similarly-based systems. You could say that the human body recreates itself through its own repository of morphogenetic information, and that the DNA of young seedlings (either tree or human) 'tunes into' the field of its predecessor, thus recreating a map of its forebears' genetic habits for its own use.

Other leading health care professionals see a similar view of the etheric body. Barbara Brennan, creator of the Barbara Brennan School of Healing, states that the etheric body is composed of radiant energy flows "like a sparkling web of light beams," having the same structure as the physical body including all the anatomical parts and all the organs and through it physical structure appears. "The field is prior to, not a result of, the physical body... this etheric structure sets up the matrix for the cells to grow, i.e., the cells of the body grow along the lines of energy of the etheric matrix, and that matrix is there before the cells grow."[4]

Lawrence and Phoebe Bendit, a physician and clairvoyant husband and wife team, also assert that the nature of the aura field is counterpart to that of the physical:

> *Actually, to speak of the aura as outside the body is misleading. In reality, it penetrates every particle of the body as well as extending beyond it... [it] is the matrix in which the body grows... it is filled with the energy counterparts of every organ, every cell, every cell-nuclear, molecule, chemical atom and subdivision of these atoms, in a series of energy levels.*[5]

Dr Kim Bong Han has completed many experimental studies into the nature of the meridian system, an ancient Chinese energy system carrying *chi*, or life flow, assumed to flow under the skin, and stimulated with acupuncture needles. Dr Kim concluded from the data collected during his embryological experiments that:

> *Spatial organization of growth from embryogenesis through adulthood is guided by a holographic energy-field template known as the etheric body... it would appear that the meridian system forms an interface between the etheric and the physical body. The meridian system is the first physical link established between the etheric body and the developing physical body.*[6]

Richard Gerber, MD, describes the etheric body as a physical-etheric interface or

> *...holographic energy template associated with the physical body... Within the etheric energetic map is carried information which guides the cellular growth of the physical structure of the body... also the structural data for growth and repair of the adult organism, should damage or disease occur.*[7]

From her many years researching neuropeptides, those biochemical components that are now believed to be the physical manifestation of emotion, Candace Pert, PhD, previous Chief of Brain Chemistry at the National Institutes of Health, states that there is a vibrational counterpart to the body, in that the body is only the outer manifestation of the mind: "The spirit, the subtle energy, which is the human body and the emotions can change the energies in it; that comes first and then things are manifested... Consciousness precedes matter."[8]

Placing your hands within this recreative field is a sacred trust you initiate between yourself and another, for when you touch someone's pneumaplasmic or morphogenetic field, you touch into a finely tuned aspect of the life force, and you are inspiring its physical counterpart to recreate itself along the new lines of force established at this invisible level.

   Anatomical Descriptors: To clarify any misconceptions pertaining to technical directions, follow these simple references: *anterior* – to the front; *posterior* – to the back; *superior* – above; *inferior* – below; *internal* – within; *external* – outside of; *lateral* – to the side; *medial* – to the center or middle; *sympathetic* – the excitable functions of the autonomic nervous system (ANS); and *parasympathetic* – the relaxing functions of the ANS.

Your Inner Compass

As you learn the attunement method of hands-on healing you will be learning how to facilitate the flow of energy moving through your life and that of another by focusing its release through your fingertips. Sometimes we use our palm chakras, but largely this system of training teaches you how to attune your sensing of energy flow through your hands, pointing the energy at specific locations on yourself or another. More is given on this technique later on.

   Since we are traveling through our own and other people's etheric bodies (the invisible landscape), we rely on finding direction for our individual progress by paying attention to intuitive sensings, which we know as silent messages from spirit. Personal intuition is a great source of truth for us, and this book seeks to strengthen your sensing of personal integrity, truth and honesty. All attunement practitioners rely on their personal integrity and their own sensitivities to spirit as main source points on their internal compass.

Journeyman's Day Pack

Since some of attunement practice includes travel through the etheric template of the human anatomy, you may find it useful to have a basic idea of how human anatomy is organized. I present the human anatomy here because in order to understand how the body heals, you need to have a basic concept of how it works, but its inclusion is not intended to scare you off. Most lay-people I have trained carry a keen willingness to know more about how the body works. If you happen to be a licensed health care professional, this should not present a problem to you either. As a basic guide, I present anatomical charts and basic anatomical information with all technical information so that all levels of readership may be primed with the same bottom-line understanding of how our vital organ systems work.

I also suggest that you keep your fingers primed on the contact point charts placed in Part II of this book, entitled 'Visible Form.' These charts are your keys to learning where the vibrational contact points are located on the human body. You may choose to order a separate, color-coded set of these charts to use during your sessions (please contact Findhorn Press).

Since the endocrine gland system is of vital importance to attunement practice, I also include endocrine gland histology notes in *Appendix A.* These notes were written immediately following my histology course at Bastyr University while I was in attendance in Naturopathic Medical School.

Traveler Self-Care

When practicing the exercises in this book, it is best to have your 'client' lay down on a massage table, sofa, bed or couch. If you share attunements with your client sitting in a chair, make sure it is a big comfy chair. The best kind of chairs are fold-out chairs which allow your client to lay back and relax instead of the straight-up kind (see *Chair Attunements* in *Chapter 21*). A massage table works best. Bolster underneath your client's knees for added support to their spine.

You will want the height of the table to be at a comfortable distance between yourself and your client. You need to be able to place your hands above the top of your client's body without touching, and without needing to strain your arms and hands in any way. If you are shorter in height, have your client slide over the left edge of the table so that you do not strain your arms trying to reach over your client. Since you will be holding hand positions for 20 minutes or so (at one time) you will also want to make sure that your arms, hands and wrists are loose.

Some of my previous students have commented to me that at times they felt that their client's energy pattern had entered their own vital energy field, and had affected them with dissonant energy. Some students complained of feeling cranky, moody, sick or dizzy for no apparent reason. If this occurs in your experience at any time during your attunement practice, you need to stop what you are doing and clear your own field. Here are several ways to clear your own energy field, and protect you from other people's intrusive patterns:

- Enter into any attunement or energy work relationship with clear intent to serve another, free of your own life problems. Before you begin, affirm with your client that you are there to give and receive only positive energy.

- Visualize that you are wearing invisible protective gloves which do not allow another person's energy pattern to touch you. Always put on your gloves before attending to another person's energy pattern. (Those experienced with other ways of deflecting another's negative energy pattern may practice their own form of protection.)

- Practice daily Sanctification sessions, morning and evening, every day (see *Sanctification* in *Chapter 4*).

- Vibrationally brush yourself off following each energy session to dissipate any vestiges of another's energy field on you.

- In a spray-bottle, mix a few drops of some of the following flower essences with pure water, and spray your session area after each client: Self-Heal, Lavender, Yarrow, Walnut, Crab Apple and Mountain Pennyroyal. Evening Primrose is especially useful to cleanse the air of any toxic psychic emotions surrounding feminine distress associated with abuse and self-recrimination (which may manifest in the form of transference and counter-transference).[9]

Attunement and Other Energy Practices

As a healing arts technique, attunement is a specialized form of therapeutic touch and mind-body therapy which shares many similar features with other energy medicine techniques. Even though some of these other techniques may share the same kinds of ideas presented herein, and they may use the word 'attunement' within their own vocabulary (i.e. Reiki) and practice technique, please be advised that there are important differences between Emissary-based attunement practice and other forms of energy work. The following points clarify how attunement is similar to other techniques:

- Reiki practitioners channel Universal energy and call Reiki initiations 'attunements,' (but this should not be confused with the form of attunement practice presented here).

- Therapeutic Touch therapists sweep away vibrational distortion patterns related to the etheric body energy field.

- Qi Gong providers use an undulating wave motion with their hands while working with the Qi, or life force.

Attunement employs none of these methods, and instead incorporates the following:

- *Attunement views each person's in-dwelling Source (God Being) as the central power and positive force in the healing process.* Practitioners view their clients from this vantage point, and work with the purposes of inner intelligence for best results.

- *Attunement practitioners stimulate the release of radiant energy flow* by encouraging expression of love-based attitudes, and through a specific non-touch modality. The energy moving through the practitioner's hands is thought to originate from within the client, and is focused to allow its release during sessions. Also, through simple attitudinal counseling practices, clients are invited to release negatively-based expressions of resentment, guilt, blame and accusation (to name a few), and focus their expression in a radiant, love-based approach, expressing positive attitudes such as thankfulness, contentment, forgiveness and joy. By expressing outwardly that which naturally dwells internally, the radiant power of love is then allowed to flow freely through the client's inner and outer worlds, creatively touching and influencing all in its path.

- *Attunement Therapy seeks to clear vibrational distortion patterns by holding an energy flow pattern* at various sites in the body, and allowing the energy to balance, clarify and intensify in and of itself. A 'vibrational distortion pattern' or dissonant pattern mentioned in this book is defined as any feeling the practitioner senses through the hands which does not fall under a still, warm, even pulsation. Dissonant patterns are actually responsive needs, and include:

  - •• electrical jumps (small or large) which are also called tingles,

  - •• an uneven flow of energy between the hands (one hand feels more energy than the other),

  - •• hot spots (as opposed to warm spots which are okay), and may include

  - •• energy draws (the practitioner feels energy being taken away from the hands).

  The practitioner may also feel 'flat energy' which is simply an area of the etheric body which needs to be stimulated in order for it to hold a stronger radiant flow of energy.

- *Attunement Therapy bases the non-touch modality on a system of Vibrational Gateway Points,* which are similar, in most cases, to reflexology points, and which may be synonymous with the Chinese Meridian System points (this question needs further research). With these vibrational gateway points, one need not touch the body to elicit the energy flow characteristic of attunement. For clients and patients who are touch sensitive or where non-touch is indicated, Attunement Therapy offers to promote deep, long-lasting and healing results without touch.

- *Attunement Therapy recognizes Seven Levels of Spiritual Expression* which find their corresponding source points in the endocrine gland system. Due to its western heritage, attunement views the endocrine gland system as a positive point system in relation to its negative or responsive point system represented by the chakras. (See *Chapter 11* for further information on this point.)

Attunement Therapy

Attunement's therapeutic effects include and are not limited to:

- deep parasympathetic response (relaxation response),
- meditation state with accompanying increased alpha wave generation,
- clearer awareness of internal stillness,
- increased sense of purpose and identity,
- stress reduction,
- increased willingness to release negative attitudes through attitudinal healing, and
- faster wound and surgery healing rates.

Attunement sessions may also include specialized attention to the lymph and immune systems, skeletal system, and spinal column. During spinal attunement, the practitioner's attention is drawn to providing increased energy flow at points on the spinal nervous system which have correspondence to specific organ systems. Attunement practitioners may also accompany their clients into hospitals and day surgery centers, sharing on-site attunement before, during and after surgeries. In cases where practitioners are not allowed in during surgery, long distance attunement is provided for the client and family in the waiting room of the hospital.

Attunement Therapy works effectively with those clients who have a hard time releasing negative attitudes, and also those who suffer from a multiple diagnosis including: recovery from drug, alcohol and codependent behavior patterns, incarceration, sexual abuse (victims and perpetrators), post-traumatic-stress-disorder, cancer, immune dysfunction,

HIV/AIDS, geriatric, pregnancy, rheumatoid arthritis, etc. Attunement service provides specific benefit to those who are touch sensitive or whose condition warrants them as contra-indicated to touch, either by locality (rheumatoid arthritis in specific joints) or entirety (AIDS).

For those clients who present with psychological and/or emotional challenges, attunement therapists may elect to counsel these clients using a variety of attitudinal healing techniques, or may refer these clients out to other licensed professional counselors. If a client elects to follow other kinds of counseling, bodywork, standard or alternative health care services, attunement therapy may provide complimentary therapeutic benefit. (Since the attunement flow works within the body's own natural healing systems, attunement practitioners usually refer clients to naturopathic, chiropractic, acupuncture and/or other licensed health care providers who serve the public with natural healing systems.)

Attunement has been successfully offered to clients at the Adult Day Health Programs at the Denver Nursing Center for Human Caring, Denver, Colorado and the Bailey Boushey House, Seattle, Washington for the treatment of HIV and AIDs, and is also offered at several health centers in the United States and Canada.

Attunement Research

A small research protocol was completed at Bastyr University's Naturopathic Physician program in January 1995, within the school's Sacred Space program. This protocol tested for anxiety levels in medical students, and showed positive subjective results. Following one attunement session, positive results in 88% of the participants included increased subjective feelings of relaxation, alertness, wholeness, acceptance, at one with life, in touch, gentleness and tranquillity. Larger and more extensive research is needed. If you represent a research facility and have an interest to pursue dialogue regarding attunement therapy research, please contact the author.

Chapter 1 Notes

[1] Defined by Dr Gordon J. Hilsman, Supervisor, Clinical Pastoral Education, St. Joseph Medical Center, Tacoma, WA.

[2] This information comes from my personal medical school experience.

[3] Based on the work of Rupert Sheldrake, and found at web page: http://www.context.org/ICLIB/IC12/Sheldrak.htm

[4] Barbara Ann Brennan, <u>Hands of Light,</u> (New York: Bantam Books, 1988), p. 49.

[5] Lawrence and Phoebe Bendit, <u>The Etheric Body of Man,</u> (Wheaton: The Theosophical Publishing House, 1977), p. 22.

[6] Richard Gerber, MD, <u>Vibrational Medicine,</u> (Santa Fe: Bear & Co, 1988), pp. 125-126.

[7] Gerber, <u>Vibrational Medicine,</u> p. 121.

[8] Candace Pert, PhD, 'Candace Pert, PhD: Neuropeptides, AIDS and the Science of Mind-Body Healing,' *Alternative Therapies*, July, 1995, Vol. 1, No. 3, p. 72.

[9] Patricia Kaminski and Richard Katz, <u>Flower Essence Repertory,</u> (Nevada City, CA: Earth-Spirit, Inc., 1986), p. 241. (Phone number to The Flower Essence Society: (800)548-0075.)

2. Entering In

A man whom I will call Richard tells this story about his experience during the Vietnam war.

During the 1960's Richard was drafted into the military to serve in Vietnam. Knowing his hatred of war, yet also knowing he was required to serve his country, Richard went to visit the Attunement Master Server and spent some time with him learning how to share attunement with himself and others. He also worked to establish a foundation of peaceful intent in his heart before he left for war.

Once enlisted and trained for battle, Richard was sent overseas and stationed at an outpost near the North Vietnamese border. At one time during his stay, he was posted on top of a bunker, overlooking a valley. A tall mountain loomed across the valley and he noticed that the North Vietnamese who came to attack him came from the direction of that mountain. Heavy artillery shells and rapid gun fire pounded his senses, and he was ordered to shoot the North Vietnamese who came into his range.

Richard felt a compulsion to send radiant love energy towards the mountain, but did not understand why. He realized that the attunement he shared with the mountain brought him feelings of peace amidst the high death intensity surrounding him. So to balance with love his feelings of guilt and despair, the man kept his left hand on his canon rifle, guiding the bullets of death, and with his right hand he sent out radiant attunement energy to the mountain.

Later on, his post was bombed and Richard was forced to go underground, into the bunker. All around him lay injured men. Richard was not injured himself, and there were few medical supplies to meet the needs of the wounded. While they waited to be air lifted out of the bunker, Richard spent time sharing attunement with the men who were lying surrounding him. He reported that during that waiting time he may have helped to save these lives. It is probable that his sharing of attunement also served to save his own life in that menacing situation.

Years later, Richard came across a photo of the valley and mountain where he had been stationed. The photograph revealed something he did not know during the time of the war, namely that there was a hospital stationed at the foot of the mountain, hidden from his view on top of the bunker. He had been sending out radiant love energy to other men in need, compelled by a power greater than his conscious mind. He had been compelled to share radiant healing energy with those he was supposed to hate, not even knowing that this was what he was doing. Love from within, bounded by larger borders than the mind, knew only the needs of its own kind.

Richard also reported that following his enlistment, he continued to share attunement, and that this energy had helped to heal his post-Vietnam stresses.

Thankfulness and the Holy Place

In all things give thanks.

—*Uranda*

Attunement practice, much like other meditation-based practices, suggests that responding individuals turn inward to a sacred space within, and through the process of entering into the Holy Place, have opportunity to share union with Source, and awaken with spiritual enlightenment. Joining the presence of the Lord, or Source, allows one's focus of attention to rest in harmonious knowing of one's true purpose in living.

We all carry an inner ecology which is filled with a multitude of personal and collective patterns, and which subconsciously compels us to make choices based on previous memories, cultural and familiar expectations and personal longing. Tied into our longings are our own assumptions for success and determinations to seeing our successes come to fruition. Entering into the Holy Place through meditation and attunement energy sessions initiates a clarification process whereby one is allowed to place upon the altar of awareness one's deepest longings and desires, thoughts, words and deeds. All that is brought before personal divinity then moves with divine intelligence through a purification cycle where that which is of pure intent and purpose for one's life is received with blessing while that which is not pure is rejected. When received by inner divinity, those desires which are inviolate and of true purpose are returned to the person's awareness and subsequent lifestyle with manifold blessing and infinite abundance. When rejected, those impure desires are burned by the eternal radiant flame to nothing.

The fire upon the inner service altar burns eternal within each person's divine presence. It is from this fire that each person's radiance comes. Through this process of entering in, opening up and then offering out what has been clarified, each person is able to share radiant enlightenment with their world.

The Holy Place is the internal home of each person's divine Source where nothing unclean nor that which makes a lie, can enter in. One cannot maintain one's own expectations or demands for success within the Holy Place. No feeling of resentment or jealousy, nor thought of criticism, blame, complaint or judgment are allowed in. Each person who enters into this meditational sanctuary space is required to leave behind all of their earthly identification with the outer world. Within an attuned space, all is sanctified and one is able to bless one's world with peace and tranquillity.

The only way whereby one may enter into the Holy Place is through thankfulness. Attunement practice confirms one's active participation in expressing daily attitudes of thankfulness, in every situation, circumstance and with each person one meets. No matter what happens, positive or negative in nature, people are invited to respond to the event by sharing in continual thanksgiving with Source, thereby blessing their world with radiant energy.

Oftentimes, if a thankful attitude is present within what seems to be a conflicting or crisis situation, that radiant flow of energy brought through thankfulness provides a calming and catalytic grace when received into the minds and hearts of those present. Usually the person who offers a thankful stance within an emergency situation is applauded with additional thanks, which increases the harmony between all involved.

Practicing thankfulness creates a protective hedge within and throughout your world. Think about it. No two differing attitudes can express through your heart at once. People choose to either express attitudes with thankful, loving intent or not. And with every positive or negative intent, one receives back the same energy only now with ten times more strength than its original expression. With our increasing world pace, it behooves us all to practice thankfulness in and for every situation, no matter how crazy that situation appears to be. Here are some everyday examples of how and why thankfulness practice works. These examples might seem mundane in nature, but by imbuing them with meaningful thankfulness, we may enhance the ordinary with extraordinary flow:

1. If you return home from a busy day at the office and find that your dog has tinkled on the rug, expressing an attitude of demand and disgust will not only mis-train your pooch with negative connotation, but will also send conflicting signals to the animal. Instead, if you express a

gentle yet firm attitude of thankfulness while teaching him where the backyard is, this will send positive multiple memory traces into the animal's behavior patterns.

2. If you are grocery shopping one day and are surrounded with disgruntled shoppers due to the frenzied pace and crowded setting of the store, expressing a harsh critical view of the setting with your neighbor at the check-out stand will only increase the negative energy and stress. Rather, if you express how thankful you are to be finished with your shopping and how you are looking forward to returning home, this conversation will probably open up a fun conversation with your neighbor, sharing stories and recipes. I've ended up handing out many a business card (with subsequent return client visits) under these very circumstances.

3. If someone takes your favorite parking space within your parking structure, you can choose to complain about this or simply give thanks that this person now has easy access into the building. Expressing this kind of giving attitude may be hard, but as you let go, you let come something new. Giving thanks for someone else's good fortune opens the door for good fortune to return to you. You might find a better space waiting for your car around the next turn. If not, go on your merry way, knowing that you blessed someone for their good fortune.

4. If you return home one day and find the place a mess once again, and feel within yourself a gathering rage towards your children, take a pause before you speak a word to remember your thankfulness for them and for their life learning cycles. Other circumstances which guide their lives may surface through your own quiet contemplation of the larger picture and vibrational pattern present in your home (e.g. you might ask yourself, "What is the quality of cleanliness in my own work space?").

Uranda sums up this first lesson by writing,

> *Give thanks in all things. Praise the Lord at all times, under all circumstances, without a single exception. As thou shalt let thy heart sing praises unto the Lord within thee, thou shalt begin to know the will of the Lord for thee… The only way whereby thou shalt begin to depend fully and completely upon the strength of thy Father is through constant thanksgiving to Him. So long as thou shalt depend upon thine own strength in any way, thou shalt fail in fully entering in.*[1]

Uranda's reference to one maintaining one's own strength refers to the strength of one's outer mind's wanting or its identification with earthly affairs, which tends to detract one from experiencing union and inner harmony during attunement.

Thankfulness Exercises

Thankfulness exercise is just what it sounds like — a vigorous spiritual expression workout whereby you actively express thanksgiving for all that you think, say, do, see and share. Practicing thankfulness will pump up your creativity, activate your lifestyle with new thought processes, and bring you manifold blessings in return for the positive energy which you send out. Staying within the Holy Place while you express a thankful attitude will open up your awareness with a continual stream of new found understanding regarding your life purpose and direction.

Thankfulness exercise also produces the following therapeutic effects: increased joy, connection to people and living systems, sense of well-being, stillness, clarification of personal direction, and ability to make right choices. Thankfulness exercise also decreases tension, by producing stillness from within. Sharing similar therapeutic effects as that of laughter therapy, prayer and visualization practices, thankfulness exercise is felt at the vibrational level within the solar plexus, when both receiving and giving thankful attitudes to oneself and another.

For optimum health benefits, practice these simple thankfulness tasks each day:

1. Place small reminders (little colored post-its work well) on your bathroom mirror, dashboard of your car, and computer monitor which read, "Be thankful." You might opt to create your own design layout for these words, adding to their positive energy flow with your personal artistic flair.

2. Take one minute out of every waking hour of each day to practice private thankfulness for one thing in your life. Your one minute may soon spill over into more time, but one minute per hour is a good way to initiate the thankfulness current and maintain the process of entering in.

3. Begin a daily habit to express your thanks about something or for someone at least once a day. Tell your wife, partner, mother, sister, boss, co-worker, neighbor, gas station attendant, etc. something about them or something that happened around them for which you are thankful. Tell them to their face, write a note, give a phone call or e-mail. The list of people is endless, as are the possibilities.

4. Get into the habit of sending thank you notes to people who do kind deeds for you.

5. Teach this practice to your children and family. Instill thankfulness in those you love. Speak of it at night, with them, at bed time. Inform

your nanny, if you have one, of the new 'thankfulness' routine, to ensure proper carry-through of your wishes during the day. Offer your thanksgiving teaching gently, with open invitation for others to join you in it, and without demand.

6. When family and/or friends come to visit, and the conversation turns to the 'bad news' about Uncle Fred who is again in the hospital, or who died, or the 'terrible' thing that happened to so-and-so, you can try praying to Source to enlighten the episode in the mind of the beholder speaking about it. Or, you could try offering an enlightening comment to those present, changing the focus from something negative to something positive. Take a chance that your enlightenment will not be rejected, and offer a loving change. Speak of how you could bring to the ill person some of the beautiful flowers that were growing in your garden to cheer him on his way. Offer a thankful prayer for those in need. Hold fast to your silent thanksgiving by sending thoughtful blessings of hope, love and charity to those spoken of in need. As you stay attentive to the uplifting need at hand, you will silently inspire a current of thankfulness which will usually appear at the right time.

7. If your mind begins to insist that it knows better than this thankfulness practice, tell it to be quiet (discipline of the outer mind capacities is usually necessary when beginning thankfulness practice). Most humans are raised to believe that their outer mind activity rules them, controls them and indeed is them. It is not! The outer mind is not you, but was created by your spirit as one of your capacities, and was created to be open and receptive to that which governs it, namely your inner divinity. As Uranda says, "The outer mind vibrates to *what it thinks*. The inner urge vibrates to *what it knows.*"[2] That loving presence which dwells within governs your life and brings to you what you need. It heals your wounds and activates your living with vibrant energy flow. At this beginning stage in your attunement process (and whenever necessary) show a backbone. Be disciplined. Be thankful. And do it.

These words can only offer you the way. Mere words cannot make you be more thankful nor activate into expression that which rests as potential in your heart. Only through your thoughtful response and active participation in this thankfulness program will you unlock the door that allows the entering in. Begin it now and see. Peace be yours as you enter into the presence of the Holy One who dwells within.

Chapter 2 Notes

[1] Uranda, The Triune Ray, Teachings of the Third Sacred School (Loveland: Eden Valley Press, 1938), pp. 63–64.

[2] Ibid., p. 59.

3. Spontaneous Remission and Inner Healing

One day, during my first attunement training intensive, the Attunement Master Server shared with me this story about how one of his clients healed from breast cancer by following a strict attunement program.

Some time ago, a woman arrived on Sunrise Ranch, the international Emissary headquarters, in Loveland, Colorado. She had developed breast cancer and she moved to the Ranch to begin a new life. She had a vivid Type A personality and held rigid thought patterns as to how things in life should be done. She kept herself to an inflexible daily routine, had few friends and was a workaholic. Without daily recreation, this woman had worked herself into illness.

Although her body was in a weakened state due to her illness, the woman was determined to work herself well. She took on a responsible leadership position inside the Emissary business office and began to work long hours. She thought that by ignoring her disease and expressing her fervent attitude to serve others, her disease would just disappear. She was trying hard to be a 'good' person, but to her detriment.

Without hindering her natural instincts to be of service to others and be creative, the Attunement Master Server began sharing daily attunements with her and keeping track of her progress. He also invited one of the office workers to take the woman on long walks after lunch each day. These two women struck up an immediate friendship and shared many long hours of pleasant chit-chat among the beautiful and luscious Rocky Mountain scenery.

The woman's intense vibrational pattern slowly began to change as she learned about life from the standpoint of loving it instead of having to do it. She learned that she loved her long walks with her friend, and she began to see herself anew within this relationship. Her daily attunements stilled her racing mind and began to vibrationally change the nature of her body's response to healing. The woman spent long hours outdoors, away from the office, becoming attuned to the rhythms of the earth. Her office tasks were easily encompassed by others who were as interested in her healing as they were in their own work of service.

Not only did her workday change, but her social life changed as well. She began having weekly parties in her new home on the ranch, and became well known for her flamboyant soirees. Moving out of her old constricting life patterns, the woman unveiled her flamboyant personality to the delight of her neighbors and family.

Having been diagnosed with breast cancer, and with little chance for recovery, the nurse on Sunrise checked her one day and reported to the Master Server that she was free of any visible signs of cancer, and that all signs and symptoms had slowly receded and disappeared. When the Attunement Master Server told me this, his eyes lit up, he made a soft moving gesture with his hands, and said smiling, "She was clear!"

The woman healed herself of breast cancer by changing her inner and outer lifestyle patterns. By allowing her response to life to change from one of 'having to' and 'shoulds,' to one of willingness, loving to and letting, this woman re-learned how to live according to her own abilities and within normal boundaries of giving. She changed from being a 'workaholic' to a 'work-a-love-it,' doing what she loved to do. And this change was a process that took time, patience, deep inner questioning and meditation. She had to discover herself anew within her current surround and lifestyle, and had to realize what life meant to her in fact, not just as habit. She had to make a new start in consciousness, away from her previous way of being and behaving. Personal healing was, for her, a process of remitting, of giving back, of forgiving one's debts, of returning to one's natural place of being, and of doing what was natural for one to do. Therein lay her secret to cancer remission.

Defining Remission

> *Let not your heart be troubled, neither let it be afraid,*
> *because fear is faith in the power of destruction*
> *rather than faith in the power of creation.*
>
> *—Uranda*

Webster's definition of 'remiss' or 'remission' includes the following pertinent phrases:

> *[from the Latin remittere, to send back, remit] …the act of remitting; …a natural feeling, releasing, resigning, relinquishing, surrendering; … forgiveness; pardon, as of sins or crimes; …cancellation of or release from a debt; …a lessening of tension; relaxation [Obsolete]; …the act of sending back. [Rare].*[1]

One 'sends back' one's sin(s) to be forgiven with remission. This understanding is very resonant with the attunement process of entering into the Holy Place within to view one's personal internal environment, and to seek to change one's direction through humility and forgiveness. Scott Miners, Editor and Publisher of the *Well Being Journal,* in North Bend, Washington elucidates this definition further by commenting that sin means 'to be out of a state of awareness of the consciousness of being connected with a supreme, omnipresent source of life,' which can be 'changed by free will at any time...'[2] Certainly, to remiss of our previous conscious state is to simply turn towards the source of wholeness in our lives.

Over the last twenty years several cases of spontaneous remission have been studied to discover if there were any correlates present within each case which could begin to define how spontaneous remission worked. One spontaneous remission study, completed in 1975 by Dr Yujiro Ikemi and his colleagues in Japan, is worth noting. This study followed five patients with diagnosed cancers, confirmed with biopsies. Within this study, one particular patient, Y.H., stands out as a good example for our discussion.

Y.H. was a teacher and spiritual leader with the Shinto religion. At age 64, after many years of completing difficult and stressful administrative duties with his church, he developed cancer of the right maxilla (upper jaw) which was surgically removed that year. The following year diagnosis confirmed the presence of a laryngeal tumor affecting his vocal chords. Doctors prescribed removal of his vocal chords, but this male church worker declined. "This is God's will and I have no complaint about it.... Whatever should happen will just happen."

Ten days later, after receiving stimulating reinforcement from his church elder for the invaluable work he was doing for the church, Y.H. began to get better, and after two months, could speak again for up to thirty minutes. He then lived for thirteen years, clear of any form of cancer. After repeated evaluations, no cancer was known to be present. He died at age 78 from unrelated causes.[3]

The useful points to consider from this brief case synopsis relate to the attitudes expressed by Y.H. in relation to his terminal illness. He refused to believe he needed to die, just because a physician told him so. As Larry Dossey, MD, explains:

> *Y.H. showed no tendency to lapse into depression, despair, lack of motivation and fear of death, which is typical of many patients. He did not engage in specific prayers in which he pleaded or bargained*

with God to 'change the diagnosis' and grant him a cure. He did not 'fight' cancer in any ordinary sense of the word, as doctors and others often recommend today. His attitude was rather one of renewed commitment and gratitude to God, combined with the belief that God's will was being done, no matter what happened.[4]

Dossey further notes that the key found in these spontaneous remission studies points to the patients' abandonment of all formulas to rid self of disease, or to bargain with God for a cure, or to adopt a spiritual life with a hidden agenda as to outcome. By simply being true to oneself and expressing an attitude of increased joy and thankfulness, the Ikemi Study patients extended themselves beyond any notion of formula for any kind of outcome.

Dossey notes that *"Often a prayerful, prayer-like attitude of devotion and acceptance — not robust, aggressive prayer for specific outcomes... precedes the cure,"* and that "cancers sometimes regress spontaneously, not when some specific formula is followed, but when all formulas are abandoned."[5]

Neither did the successful ones take on spirituality from the outside, but instead they remained true to themselves, honoring their own inner emergence. In these cases, the patients in question let their own inner divinity guide their belief system and energies to health. They allowed their inner divinity to emerge in a more powerful way by letting go within. This experience even overrode all hopes or notions of the cancer disappearing. They simply 'gave up' (a good description) into their higher power. In these cases, identity with, awareness of, and emergence of in-dwelling God presence proved right the theory that 'one's authentic, higher self is completely impervious to the ravages of any physical ailment whatever.'[6] They became themselves 'at the most essential level,' and realized that they were 'untouchables — utterly beyond the ravages of disease and death.'[7]

As Dossey indicates, letting go of all hope of recovery through a recognized 'formula,' spiritual or otherwise, led these particular cases to an endpoint of their individual journeys. All that was left for them to do was to identify with higher source, which then led them to experience a sense of completion with their healing. Giving up, letting go, and relaxation experienced at the deepest level ignited the spontaneous working of an inner healing mechanism. Apparently this 'unformulated' prescription for new health is not as popular as the formulated or prescribed kind, given that there are not more examples of spontaneous remission on record.

The Inner Healing Mechanism

In a landmark study funded by the Institute of Noetic Sciences and Fetzer Institute, Brendan O'Regan and Caryle Hirshberg compiled ten years worth of spontaneous remission research into one large annotated bibliography entitled *Spontaneous Remission*. This bibliography represented the largest published database on the subject in the world to date, and was commissioned as part of the Institute of Noetic Science's *'Inner Mechanisms of the Healing Response Research Program.'* In *Spontaneous Remission*, O'Regan and Hirshberg accepted the healing response premise in its entirety by assuming that there was/is an inner healing mechanism operating within each person:

> *which appears to contain at least three components:*
> 1.   *A Self-Diagnostic System*
> 2.   *A Self-Repair System*
> 3.   *A Regenerative System....*
>
> *The evidence suggests that this kind of healing can be triggered by a variety of stimuli, diverse in nature, including signals, suggestions and guidance from the physical, mental and/or spiritual realms of every individual.* [8]

Although the authors of *Spontaneous Remission* refer to the inner healing mechanism as 'the mind's ability to alter or influence the body,' attunement practice considers their reference to 'mind' to include a much larger context than simply mental energy. Entering in, one visits the holy seat of wisdom wherein one's inherent creative force offers radiant energy to all conscious, subconscious and environmental influences.

When the capacities of mind and heart remain open and yield to the movement and purposes of spirit, then spirit's radiant force of energy quickly attunes the capacities to its own nature. Attunement of mind and heart with spirit results in a new spiritual alignment which brings about a therapeutic effect to the human capacities which were previously stressed from misalignment. When the capacities are open and receptive to divine presence and flow, then people experience ease, contentment and well-being. When the capacities are closed due to feelings of resentment, guilt, shame or an accusatory attitude, then spirit is halted in its pathway through one's being and illness usually develops. The following chart illustrates this point:

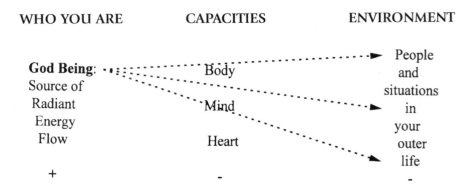

WHO YOU ARE	CAPACITIES	ENVIRONMENT

The arrows in this chart indicate whence divine energy emanates and whither it goes, moving through the capacities into one's world. Radiant energy originates from divine presence within, which is seen as a positive, absolute point in each person's world. The capacities of body, mind and heart, however are 'negatively' charged (negative refers to a responsive nature), and are created to be yielded and opened to let spirit flow through them.[9] When the capacities of heart and mind decide to be in control and resist the flow of spirit, they act as if they were positive in nature, and as two positives repel each other, the capacities begin to move away from their own spiritual focus, thereby opening themselves up to disease and illness.

Inner attunement with Source may account for another medical mystery, namely the *placebo effect*. The term 'placebo', from *to please*, was originally used as a prayer form within the Catholic Church, a Vesper for the dead. Today, placebos are used within medical systems as innocuous medications or therapies given to patients with the intention of satisfying them or soothing their illness symptomologies. Interestingly enough however, mounting clinical evidence suggests that giving a patient a sugar pill (whether or not the patient consciously knows it is a placebo), still produces the desired therapeutic outcome, sometimes resulting in spontaneous remission, hence the term 'placebo effect.'

Clinical research supports this evidence. One controlled study using *active placebos* (i.e. patients knew they were only getting sugar pills), revealed that 13 out of 14 psychiatric outpatients who received placebos for their somatic symptoms reported relief, including objective reduction.[10] Another recent chemotherapy experiment cited "30.8% of those patients who received placebos (as a control group), lost their hair!"[11] Harnessing this active process within human beings may make obsolete many medical practices. As Norman Cousins states: "An understanding of the way the placebo works may be one of the most significant developments in medicine in the 20th century."[12]

Studies in the placebo effect indicate that the potential residing within each person has the power to heal far beyond invasive operational treatments or even chemically-based therapies. Dr Ronald Pero, an ecogenetic toxicologist from the Sloan Kettering Memorial Hospital Cancer Research Center believes that all medical research should focus on human's inherent power to heal themselves by stating that:

> ...*human beings operate at ten to the minus seventh of one percent of their genetic potential. In studies they have determined that a single cell organism which operates at .0000002 percent of its genetic potential does not experience disease as we know it... [Dr Pero came] to the conclusion that cancer research is futile and that cancer is a natural phenomenon of the level of expression in which human beings now operate. [He believes] that research or investigations should be centered in those things which increase human potential.*[13]

Given the mounting research evidence, further therapeutic analysis of prayer and inner meditation practices warrants our attention.

The Healing Power of Meditation

As a powerful form of remission and prayer, meditation practice enables us to realize union with Source by stilling the mind, body and emotions in order for us to hear inner wisdom's direction. Just as O'Regan and Hirshberg recognized, we have the opportunity to meditate within, and work with Source to self-diagnose, self-repair and regenerate our own bodies, minds and hearts. Meditation is one leading therapy designed to allow us specific time for us to enter into a state of tranquility, as the following scientific studies demonstrate.

During the late 1970's and early 1980's, many research studies focused their testing on natural ways to decrease trait anxiety levels in various populations of people, without using drugs. Four studies reached identical conclusions that out of all of the relaxation-based treatments offered to their participants, meditation and specifically transcendental meditation figured most prominently in decreasing trait anxiety levels.[14,15,16,17] Other positive therapeutic effects from transcendental meditation were: decreased levels of neuroticism/stability, extraversion/introversion and drug use, and decreased state anxiety disorders.[18] Besides these positive psychological effects, meditation also showed therapeutic effects at the physical level with decreased respiratory rate, blood pH, blood pressure and blood lactate, and increased levels of alpha wave generation. In this study, transcendental meditation induced 'a wakeful hypometabolic state' different from that elicited during sleep, hypnosis and autosuggestion.[19]

The interesting point about transcendental meditation in relationship to attunement is that this particular practice seeks to allow the practitioner and client to reach a state of effortlessness, usually recognized during an enjoyable activity such as playing music or creating art. The act of achieving an effortless world seems to contain within its nature an 'intrinsically attractive quality' which allows the practitioner and client to feel freedom within levels of consciousness not attained through normal or mundane activities.[20] Transcendental meditation and attunement meditation both seek that transcendent place in consciousness where one realizes peace and mystical union with Source.

The Inner Healing Meditation

The following meditation is an exercise to free up your outer mind from its attachment with the outer world, and instead focus its direction within. This healing meditation is intended to empower you with self-healing energy. Gently relax yourself into a meditation pose, either lying on a meditation mat or bed. You'll want your body to be supported and as comfortable as possible, so lie flat on your back and bolster beneath your knees to support your lower back. Place a blanket over you for added warmth. Wear loose clothing. During this time, remember to turn off your pager, phone, cell phone, and computer, and post a 'do not disturb' sign on your door.

You might want to pre-record this session and play back the tape for your listening convenience. Or, you might wish to gather some friends around and have one person read what follows for a group practice.

> *Focus your thoughts on your breathing. Simply watch your breathing in and out and feel its flow through your body. (Pause) Watch how your breath circulates through your body with each intake of air, how it wafts through your lungs and arms and reaches your neck and head, settles back down inside your stomach and hips, and nestles within your womb space before it departs. (Pause) Watch how your breath is like the wind, moving effortlessly through your body space. Each breath taken in and out frees up your stresses, worries and fears. Take in a few deep breaths now, hold them for a*

few seconds and then release. (Pause) Feel how the air follows a path deep into your chest cavity. Feel your stress wash away inside with each inflow and outflow of air. Each breath brings you increased peace, stability and contentment. The air inside your body eases your pain, disengages your discomfort and rids you of anxieties. They are gone now, leaving you with clean, fresh space. (Pause) Slowly now take in a few more deep breaths. (Pause)

Notice now that there is a change in the nature of your body. You no longer feel any stress points or hold any negative thoughts. Your worry is gone, as are your fears and expectations. Your new breath brings in contentment, security and peace. Your exhalations offer that same delight, assurance and tranquillity to your world. Take in a few more deep breaths now. (Pause) You see your breath as one unified system. With each breath in, give to yourself and receive from your world freely, without restraint. Each breath in nourishes you and fills you. Each breath out nurtures your world with that which has filled you. (Pause) See how your body responds to the love within you and around you. All is well. All is one. All is warm, bathed in your radiant light.

Drawing your attention within, follow the warm light where it leads you. (Longer pause) You have entered into a still place, with a light emanating from beyond, in an inner chamber. The inner chamber beckons you and you are drawn to it. Entering in, you see only an altar with one single flame that burns upon it. See the altar now. Define it for yourself, and see the radiance of the candle. (Pause)

You recognize this chamber and feel at home here. You have been here before — it is a familiar place which you've carried with you for many years, even before this life time. You know this place because it reminds you of your inner longings. You feel the energies of perseverance, strength, assurance and honor. Trust is here, as is respect and gratitude. You recognize these qualities as your own character. They welcome you with open arms and enfold you, cherish you, care for you as they always do. You greet each one as an old friend. They stand with you now as your trusted allies within your chamber space. Greet each one now. (Longer pause)

The fire shines like a star and sends shimmering rays of brightness into your awareness, filling your body with light and color. The brightness and colors are so rich you can touch them with your hands. Touch them now. With each gentle touch, you send pulsations of light waves into your being. These colors and their pulsations harmonize your being with their radiant light.

The candle flame upon the altar is bright and it beckons you. The light is small but it is so bright that you must raise up your hands to shield yourself from its radiance. This fire is the light of God, and the flame sends a message to you asking for absolute obedience. You cannot proceed to the altar or move closer to the flame until you clear your thoughts of any remaining fears or doubts. And yet the flame beckons. You know that you have entered the inner chamber to commune with God, and you do not fear God's presence now, but yet you are not ready. You realize that you need to make yourself ready first — to discard any vestige of impure thoughts or emotions. Quickly, scan your consciousness for any present negative emotions or thoughts, and give them to the flame. That is what the flame is beckoning you to do. Offer each offense to the flame and watch it burn to nothing. Your envies, striving, fears and blames. Your accusations, mistrust and impatience. Bring all of these forward from within yourself now, and let them burn away. Their burning does not cause you pain or grief, only relief and release. Continue until you are clean. (Pause)

With your heart clear, you move closer to the flame and stand face to face with your own radiant countenance. The altar is waiting for something — it is waiting for you to ask your questions — that is why you've entered the inner chamber. You seek divine guidance from the One Who Dwells. The One who Dwells is a radiant force, and does not exist in human form. The One Who Dwells never dies, but lives forever within the radiance of the flame. This One represents all wisdom, all power, all knowing, and is your constant source of truth in your life.

In emptiness and humility, you move close to the flame. Its light and warmth are soothing to you. With gentle innocence, you ask your questions to the flame, and without assumption as to the answer, you await the response. (Long pause)

The flame has responded with absolute truth and clarity. You see with new eyes the answers to your life questions in this moment. You know that this flame burns continually, and is ready to serve you at any moment of your life. You bow down with gratitude and humility before your light, thanking it for its compassion, its healing strength and purity. You turn and leave this place, taking with you the silence of this sanctuary space as your own. (Pause)

Slowly, gently, you emerge from your sacred space within, and look towards the earthly world where you dwell. You carry with you a remembrance of the sacred splendor of the inner chamber, and know that you will hold this space inviolate and sacred from now on. Carrying your light with you, you bring forward all that you have witnessed during this time. Your stir quietly, awakening to your earthly life. Awaken now, refreshed, renewed, rejoicing. Your light is with you always. Awaken now.

Take an Attunement Break

You can utilize the ideas within the Inner Healing Meditation to take a short 2-3 minute attunement break. Follow these few short steps for a rejuvenating pause:

1. Sitting quietly, enter in by focusing consciousness on a still place within yourself.

2. Free-up your mind and heart from any worries, doubts and fears. Clear your mind of any self-willed ideas or purposes you think you have for yourself by simply being open to receive what your inner wisdom will tell you.

3. With an open facility, ask your question to Source, and wait silently for the answer.

4. Do not seek to guide the answer with your own self-will or determination.

5. The answer from Source may take a few seconds (Source sometimes needs to process how best to approach your consciousness!), but it will come. Hold yourself open, in patience, for the few seconds it takes to receive your answer.

6. Trust this answer — it is your key to enlightenment in the moment.

7. If you have a hard time getting your will out of the way, simply practice this exercise a few times. In time, you will learn the difference between self-willed answers and those offered to you from Source.

Chapter 3 Notes

1 <u>Websters Seventh New Collegiate Dictionary</u>, (Chicago: G. & C.Merriam Co., 1965), p. 725.

2 Scott Miners, 'Comments on the Nature of Prayer Research,' Alternative Therapies, July, 1997, Volume 3, No. 4, p. 20.

3 Larry Dossey, MD, <u>Healing Words</u> (New York: HarperCollins Publishers, 1993), p. 31.

[4] Ibid.

[5] Dossey, Healing Words, pp. 31–32.

[6] Dossey, Healing Words, p. 36.

[7] Ibid.

[8] O'Regan and Hirshberg, Spontaneous Remission, An Annotated Bibliography, (Sausalito: Institute of Noetic Sciences, 1993), Introduction, unnumbered.

[9] Positive and negative terms may be viewed within the context of an electromagnetically charged field, like north and south poles of a magnet. Each of the poles operates with an opposing force to the other, but neither is thought of as less perfect than the other — they each simply carry a different and complimentary nature to each other, balancing each other with equal and opposite attraction.

[10] Thomas J. Hurley, III, 'Placebos and Healing: A New Look at the 'Sugar Pill,'" *Noetic Sciences Collection*, Summer, 1985, unnumbered.

[11] Ibid.

[12] Brendan O'Regan, 'Placebo — The Hidden Asset in Healing,' *Investigations, A Research Bulletin*, Institute of Noetic Sciences, Vol. 2, No. 1, p. 4.

[13] Michael and Nancy Burghley, The Rising Tide of Change, (Loveland, CO: Foundation House Publications, 1986), p. 21.

[14] Robert Keith Wallace, Herbert Benson, and Archie F. Wilson, 'A wakeful hypometabolic physiologic state,' *American Journal of Physiology*, Vol. 221, No. 3, September 1971, p. 30.

[15] Kenneth R. Eppley and Allan I. Abrams, 'Differential Effects of Relaxation Techniques on Trait Anxiety: A Meta-Analysis,' *Journal of Clinical Psychology*, November, 1989, Vol. 45, No. 6, p. 957.

[16] David C. Zuroff and J. Conrad Schwarz, 'Effects of Transcendental Meditation and Muscle Relaxation on Trait Anxiety, Maladjustment, Locus of Control, and Drug Use,' *Journal of Consulting and Clinical Psychology*, 1978, Vol. 46, No. 2, p. 264.

[17] D. A. Throll, 'Transcendental Meditation and Progressive Relaxation: Their Psychological Effects,' Journal of Clinical Psychology, October, 1981, Vol. 37, No. 4, p. 776.

[18] Ibid.

[19] Robert Keith Wallace, Herbert Benson, and Archie F. Wilson, 'A wakeful hypometabolic physiologic state,' p. 795

[20] Kenneth R. Eppley and Allan I. Abrams, 'Differential Effects of Relaxation Techniques on Trait Anxiety: A Meta-Analysis,' p. 972.

4. Non-Directed Prayer

To Pray Without Ceasing

Whatever arises, let me dwell in the Secret Place
of the Most High.
Let there be a place of stillness in the midst of turmoil.
Let there be a place of ease amid disease.
Let there be a place of order in the chaos.
Let there be a place of love and beauty
in the midst of fear and ugliness.
Let my presence be a beacon of enfolding radiance
in every circumstance.

—Martin Exeter

I shared my first attunement on Wednesday, November 22, 1981. I was living in Los Angeles at the time and had started attending Emissary mid-week services on Wednesday nights. During my first attunement session I could have sworn that the practitioner was using strings beneath the table to sway the energies I felt balancing my head and neck. When I asked my practitioner about this afterwards, he just laughed softly, and then I began to cry. I recall that I felt an up-welling in my heart, and an accompanying feeling that I did not deserve to receive this attunement, that I wasn't worthy enough. When I confessed to him the reason for my tears he commented that my response was sweet, and that most people felt that way about receiving something beautiful for free. It would be many years before I fully understood the meaning behind those words.

About six months later I was walking down a country road with this same man, my attunement server, as I called him. Along came a bee, and while I swatted at it furiously (I was afraid, which only incensed the insect), the bee proceeded to sting me on my left arm, above the elbow. My attunement friend took a moment to assess the situation, and then proceeded to share an attunement with my upper arm, clearing away the vibrational distortion pattern that the sting had caused. My friend knew that as he cleared away the distortion, and allowed a new, clear vibrational pattern to once again settle into the site, that the skin and underlying layers of fascia associated with the wound would heal. He worked to establish a clear vibrational resonance at the site of the injury.

For ten minutes or so, he focused his attention on sending to my arm an attunement current, utilizing several contact points at nearby joints. My arm began to swell at the site of the sting, and I also felt intensified pain for the first few minutes of the attunement. But this pain was a 'good' kind of pain, like the kind of pain one feels during a deep tissue massage session. I knew that the pain meant that something was healing at the site where I hurt.

At the close of our session, the swelling had stopped and was receding, and disappeared altogether later on that evening. I returned home to brag about the healing incident to my friends. I wished that I could carry this practitioner around in my back pocket and take him out whenever I needed him — that I had this magic tucked under my coat and hidden from the envy I imagined my friends felt for me. I decided then and there that this attunement business was something not to take lightly, that it really worked, and that I should receive as much attunement during my free time that I could.

This session also inspired me to look further into the healing arts as a vocation. A short time later some friends suggested that I become a massage therapist, and soon after, I found myself enrolled in a small massage apprenticeship class near my community home.

Prayer Healing

Part of the energy that went into dissolving my bee sting came from the practitioner's use of non-directed prayer — a specific form of prayer utilized by all attunement practitioners. With non-directed prayer, the practitioner experiences a profound personal transformational shift by connecting with Higher Source. This shift welcomes a power beyond Self to move through Self to another. Non-directed prayer practice is an experience of spiritual transcendence which may find an inspirational home in your consciousness as you move through the spiritual landscape of interconnected needs with another.

You will note that there are different kinds of prayer which serve different needs. Some forms of prayer seek supplication from an invisible deity outside oneself, and others utilize worship activities and include reading from books of prayers. Jeffrey S. Levin, PhD, MPH, notes four "...independent dimensions of prayer." These were described as ritual or recitational, conversational or colloquial, petitionary or intercessory, and meditative prayer.[1] Non-directed prayer may use any one of these prayer methods as long as the practitioner frees up the mind for no outcome.

The Spindrift organization of Landsdale, Pennsylvania spent a decade performing laboratory experiments trying to determine which prayer strategy was most effective: directed prayer for a specific outcome, or non-directed prayer, having no specific outcome. Directed prayer participants sought to 'direct' the system they were praying to, and held an outcome in mind, such as to rid a person of cancer or heal someone of heart disease. Non-directed prayer, on the other hand, was viewed as an "open-ended approach in which no specific outcome was held in the mind. In non-directed prayer, the practitioner did not attempt to 'tell the universe what to do'."[2]

Larry Dossey, MD, noted author and public speaker, informs us that the Spindrift research experiments has given us much evidence to show that non-directed prayer works better than directing prayer for a specific outcome. In one experiment, the Spindrift researchers tried to grow mold on the surface of agar plates used routinely by bacteriologists. After stressing but not killing a patch of mold, directed prayer was used to encourage growth on one side of the plate while non-directed prayer was used on the other side of the divided glass surface. Directed prayer produced no results. Non-directed prayer produced multiplication of the mold into concentric growth rings.[3]

These and other experiments conducted by Spindrift give indications for the best prayer method to use in situations when we don't know what should happen. For example, with a heart attack patient, do we pray for increased tissue formation or for increased blood flow? Do we pray for successful bone growth for a bone fracture patient, or maintenance of the proper bone alignment? When under a cloud of uncertainty, the Spindrift researchers suggest 'letting go and letting God':

> *(The Spindrift experiments) suggest that it isn't necessary to know which way the body ought to go. One need only pray... asking only for what's best — the "Thy will be done" approach... These experiments suggest that non-directed prayer moves organisms toward those states of form and function that are best for them and that the practitioner need not know what 'best' is.*[4]

In another non-directed prayer experiment which lasted over ten months, 393 Coronary Care Unit patients were randomly selected and included in a double-blind study testing the efficacy of Intercessory Prayer.

While they were hospitalized, the group being prayed for received Intercessory Prayer from a group of born-again Christians who remained outside the hospital setting. After randomizing each patient with three to seven intercessors, each intercessor was given the instruction to pray for their individuals' rapid recovery, but specifics as to how this needed to happen were omitted. The control group did not receive any form of prayer. Summary results confirmed that "the prayer group had less congestive heart failure, required less diuretic and antibiotic therapy, had fewer episodes of pneumonia, had fewer cardiac arrests, and were less frequently intubated and ventilated."[5]

Dr Dossey notes 130 scientific studies on the therapeutic effects of prayer. "In more than half the studies, prayer does something remarkable under laboratory-controlled conditions... repeated studies have shown that prayer after surgery will lead to faster healing."[6] Dossey, author of *Healing Words, The Power of Prayer in the Practice of Medicine*, predicts that someday prayer will be routine protocol in all medical proceedings, and that absence of prayer on the part of practitioners will constitute grounds for malpractice. Hospitals already note that "regular chaplain visits shorten the patient's average stay by one to two days on average — a potential annual saving of millions of dollars per hospital."[7]

Prayer and the Client-Practitioner Relationship

Non-directed prayer also shows significant healing potential for the practitioner as well as the patient. In a research survey conducted with nurses, Carol Leppanen Montgomery, RN, PhD sought to discover the nature of caring from the caregiver's perspective. She noticed that among the nurses questioned, there emerged a theme which stated that the art of caring for another included an experience of spiritual transcendence. Spiritual transcendence was defined to mean "experiencing oneself in relationship as a part of a force greater than oneself... [Spiritual transcendence served] as an important resource for self-renewal and motivation for the caregiver, so that caring [was] associated with profound fulfillment and growth rather than burnout."[8]

Montgomery found that within the care-giving relationship, there was a distinct difference between relationships connected at the ego level and those connected at a higher or greater level. Her nurses sought ways to simply connect with their patients, without maintaining an achievement-oriented focus. When our agenda is to fix or to cure, the focus is on the self as the 'ego-hero,' but when the energy used for caring was seen to 'come from a greater source beyond the self,' then nurses felt they were 'pulling from abundance,' feeling the existence of a greater force beyond themselves, nourishing their caring encounter:

> [*This research suggests that*] *in the caring encounter, the caregiver and the client experience union, but that this union occurs beyond the level of self, at the level of spirit. Spirit can be understood as a common humanity, the fundamental sacredness and unity of all life.*[9]

Accessing an energy source which is limitless and encompasses the needs of everyone simultaneously may seem implausible, but the idea is gaining ground within mainstream medicine. Dr Dossey finds that many physicians who suffer from 'spiritual malnutrition,' find value in identifying with a spiritual source during practice, and wish they could more accurately express their spiritual feelings 'without fear of censure.'[10]

Radiant Energy Practice

Radiant energy is the descriptive term applied to all attunement energy work. 'Radiant energy' implies that this quality of energy originates from a positive point, like what we see to be present in the sun of our galaxy system. The sun is a fire ball, sending forth continual beams of radiant energy far beyond itself. The power of the sun warms millions of miles of universal space far beyond the body of the sun. Just so, the radiant power of your Source of energy lights and warms your world beyond your own body, influencing your world with creative force. This idea of a radiant energy flow which emanates from each person's Source of being is specific to attunement work, and is one of its hallmark, distinguishing characteristics.

> *The best way for you to begin to recognize your own radiant energy field is for you to bring your hands together, mirroring each other, as the illustration shows. Hold this position for a few minutes. You should begin to feel energy moving through your hands towards each other. You have placed both hands into each other's etheric body flow, and that is why you feel a slight tug between the hands. This energy flow felt between the hands is a natural part of our human make-up. We use it all the time,*

and never notice that in shaking someone's hand or doing the dishes that this part of us is being touched. This is something to be aware of now that you are beginning to practice attunement.

Now, move your hands apart slowly, so that you can still feel the energy moving between them as you move them apart. Move them far enough apart so that your hands are resting comfortably in your

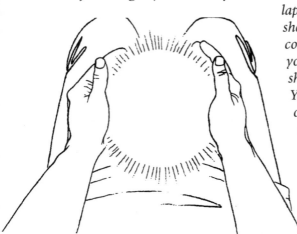

lap. Shoulders, arms and hands should all be relaxed, like limp, cooked spaghetti. Gently cup your hands, mirroring their shape like you see in the picture. Your conscious focus should be on maintaining the flow of energy moving between your hands, like you were holding a little energy vortex. Some energy practitioners view this as an 'energy ball.' Although we're not particularly interested in doing anything with this energy ball (like moving it to another person), the fact that this 'ball' feels like it has a spherical shape and mass is important to your recognition of its qualitative nature.

Now that you have consciously connected with the energy flowing through your hands, you are ready to begin working with it. The following exercises teach you how to send radiant energy from yourself to yourself or to another person. The steps of this exercise are cumulative and should be followed in order. You may find it useful to tape yourself reading this exercise, and play back the tape during your initial sessions.

Find yourself a quiet place. Light a candle and perhaps play soft ocean music. Keep a journal handy.

Begin by surrendering your consciousness to higher power in a nonintrusive, heart-felt way. Still the capacities of mind and heart into a rhythm slower than the usual speed with which you move during the day. Free your heart of any harsh, negative or ill thought or feeling onto which you may be holding. Still your heart and mind with a quiet peace which you feel emanating from within yourself. Focus your attention on this energy flow moving through you heart and mind.

Slowly become aware of the vital energy moving through your being — your physical body, mind, emotions and spirit. Thoughts and feelings may still be moving through your being quickly, and you want to tell them to be still and quiet. As they become still, remember to maintain your conscious focus with the slower rhythm you have already established. Gently tell your thoughts to hush and your emotions to cool. Simply watch the thought forms enter and leave your world in an easy, relaxed fashion.

*Tell yourself that you are not your mind or emotions, but you are the divine presence behind them, giving them life. You are the power that animates the capacities of mind and heart. Tell them to **be still and know**.*

As you slow down, begin to send love energy to every thought and feeling you are experiencing. Send your radiant energy to whomever or whatever passes through your mind, being gently aware that your offering is creatively influencing the lives of those whom you are consciously touching. If thoughts and feelings about yourself arise, then send yourself love energy too.

Continue alignment with higher power and begin to breathe deeply, feeling your breath move through your whole body, enlivening your arms, rejuvenating the chest area, filling your lower body sections. Feel the depth of breath fill your whole body as you envision its movement through each body section. Envision your breath as golden light. Now this golden light passes through your chest, arms and hands and exits through your finger tips.

Continue to envision the energy of light exiting through your fingertips as you finish each breath. Your fingertips should begin to tingle with new life force after a few deep breaths and visualizations. As you continue on with this exercise, feel the warmth of the radiant breath move through your being and out your hands.

Now focus your attention on the energy pattern between your hands. Remember to keep arms and hands loose throughout this session — check now that they are relaxed. The fingers of each hand should be together, without spaces between. Because your hands are enlivened with radiant energy flow, you should soon feel a pulse flow through your fingers, from one hand to the other. As this is so, bring to mind someone, a situation, or yourself. Feel the pulse of energy enfold this person you are thinking about. The energy pattern flowing through your hands is called a 'creative field' in attunement terms. (Attunement practitioners bring many different people and situa-

tions into their creative fields to allow their spiritual bodies to relax, rejuvenate and replenish with vital life energy.)

You may feel little electrical jumps in one hand or both. This is called a vibrational distortion or dissonant pattern, and you don't need to worry about it or do anything with it because the flow of spirit will clarify it. This distortion pattern may have come from a thought you've just had, or may be associated with someone you are thinking about. What you need to do with this dissonant pattern is to hold it while letting radiant energy move through it. Spirit will clear the distortions by itself — you don't need to fix anything.

Remember to keep your thoughts focused on the energy field between your hands and send love to whomever you are working with. Don't let your mind wander. If you find your mind drifting off, then bring it back without recrimination. If you feel a dissonant pattern, hold the pattern and wait. It will usually clear away or become less intense within a few minutes. If it doesn't, then that signifies that this particular thought form requires more time and/or additional sessions to clear.

Envision your hands as an electromagnetic charger, and that each hand represents a positive and a negative point which serves to balance and clarify the electromagnetic energy held between them. (Electromagnetic energy is also called etheric or subtle energy when used in this context). If you are right-handed, then your right hand will likely be the positive hand, and vice-versa if you are left-handed. (Later on when you learn how to focus and relate attunement energy with sites on the body, your hands will switch from positive to negative and back again, but for now, learn to feel comfortable with holding electromagnetic energy this way).

As you hold this pattern, you may feel more energy in one hand than the other. That's okay. Holding the pattern will balance these energies. Enjoy feeling a single pulse moving through your hands when energies are balanced.

Work for only five minutes at a time when you first begin attunement practice, and build up to 10 – 15 minutes per day.

Realize that the creative field between your hands is a holy and sacred ground for creative action and transformation. Once you have initiated a creative field for attunement work, you have established a safe container for the life force to move freely, to do what it will to change forms associated with the vibrational energy.

The Returning Cycle

As you send love energy out, listen for what comes back to you. Oftentimes, upon first starting to share attunement energy, there appears in your consciousness personal habit patterns related to the people and places upon whom you are focusing. These may or may not be of creative intent. If this happens, the first thing to do is to realize that these thought processes came to you through the movement of spirit — they did not necessarily originate from within you at this moment. They are part of the returning cycle — having touched someone, they come back to you, brought back on the carrier wave of energy which originated from your work.

If your returning cycle contains something of a negative psychological nature, dissuade yourself from reacting to it — don't succumb to any personal pressure to retaliate, resent or fear (to name a few negative responses). Uranda clearly states that whatever a practitioner receives back in the returning cycle, "depends upon the quality and quantity of his giving in true service."[11] While you learn to purify and clarify your giving energy, utilize this main attunement adage: *judge not by the form of things.* Don't be quick to judge how you feel about what you sense is present in your returning cycle, or about the form of whatever it is that comes back to you — good or bad. In maintaining your integrity with love, you will allow spirit to purify your capacities of mind and heart. Let the radiant energy that is returning to you fill you with humble knowing and nurturing vitality.

Be mindful that what is coming back to you is carried on the wave of love you just sent out. This is not practice — you are doing it! And it is easy! This is not an imagined fantasy of what you think may be happening — it is actually happening! You have actually sent out love energy to someone else or to yourself. In time, what comes back to you will be of a pristine nature — you will be sending out clear life force energy and receiving the same kind in return. Practice daily *Sanctification* (see *Sanctification* section in the next chapter) to maintain the clarification process.

Perform this radiant energy exercise for a few minutes each day, slowly increasing your time and focus until you can share radiant energy sessions for 10 – 20 minutes each day. Record any significant findings which surface and be clear regarding your personal purification process.

Receiving Attunement Energy

If you are on the receiving end of a long distance attunement session, you will feel a tangible sensation of receiving love at a vibrational level. This vibrational impact will revitalize you at deep levels, below the conscious line. Repeated sessions will restore your inner stillness to such a degree that you will be aware of it consciously, and thereby provide this gentle vibration for yourself.

While the pattern shifts, and if you are healing from an illness or injury, you may experience concern about what is happening. If this is so, hold your heart still with faith. Just as the Biblical Centurion knew that when the Master "gave the word" that healing would take place in a far-away location, so too you may know that when your life force is held by another with sacred intent, that healing spirit is working its magic in and through you with restorative intent.

Chapter 4 Notes

1   Jeffrey S. Levin, PhD, MPH, 'How Prayer Heals: A Theoretical Model,' *Alternative Therapies*, January, 1996, Vol. 2, No. 1, p. 67.

2   Larry Dossey, MD, 'The Science of Prayer,' *Natural Health*, March/April, 1994, p. 104.

3   Ibid.

4   Larry Dossey, MD, 'Prayer, Old Approach, New Wonders,' *The Quest*, Summer, 1990, pp. 43–44.

5   Randolph C. Byrd, MD, 'Positive Therapeutic Effects of Intercessory Prayer in a Coronary Care Unit Population,' *Southern Medical Journal*, July, 1988, Vol. 81, No. 7, p. 829.

6   Gurney Williams III, 'The Healing Power of Prayer,' *The American Legion*, August, 1994, p. 20.

7   Ibid.

8   Carol Leppanen Montgomery, RN, PhD, 'The Care-giving Relationship: Paradoxical and Transcendent Aspects,' Alternative Therapies, March, 1996, Vol. 2, No. 2, pp. 52–53.

9   Ibid.

10 Bill Thompson, 'Doctors Want This to Be True,' *Natural Health*, March/April, 1994, p. 75.

11 Grace Van Duzen, The Vibrational Ark, (Loveland, CO: Eden Valley Press, 1996), p. 160.

5. The Invisible Guide

While I was a Clinical Pastoral Intern at a nearby hospital, I was privileged to assist a family with the passing of their loved one. This is my story about that event.

As part of my pastoral class requirements I was required to stay in the hospital one night a month as an 'on-call' pastor. My on-call services included the possibility of being woken up in the middle of the night for any emergency pastoral needs which included prayer needs, birth christenings, last rites, and early morning pre-surgery prayers. I was scheduled to attend my first overnight stay about six weeks after my training had commenced. Before that time, I listened eagerly to the other ladies in my class tell of their uneventful nights. As yet, no one had been woken up by the hospital supervisor to take care of any emergencies. As each week passed by, each student reported their boredom with the quiet evenings, and I listened to their complaints thinking that something was missing on their part, namely an invitation to serve in crisis situations.

I entertained a different agenda for my training. I wanted to be a part of the action during an emergency. Having spent six months in Cadaver Dissection laboratory in medical school, I was not afraid of blood and guts. I wanted to be in the thick of the drama. I wanted to be on hand when someone was brought into the emergency room with gunshot wounds and stand near to where they were being treated. Maybe I regretted not becoming a physician, and this was my way of still being able to serve during crisis. When it came time for my overnight experience, I was pumped full of adrenaline. It took awhile for me to fall asleep, but I dozed off somewhere around 11:00 p.m.

I heard the code sound at 3:30 a.m. and at 4:00 a.m. received a telephone call from the supervisor. I was to report to the sixth floor Neurological ICU. With my mental faculties intact, I dressed and quickly made my way to the sixth floor, ready for the challenge.

When I arrived, I counted eleven hospital nurses and technicians huddled into one hospital room. A woman, who had developed Guillian

Barre (a debilitating neurological disorder) had apparently suffered a lung aneurysm. They had been applying cardiopulmonary resuscitation for 45 minutes before I arrived and when they found out that the Chaplain was now present, they told me that the family had been called, and that they didn't see much hope for reviving the patient. Most of them looked despairingly at the woman. The head nurse informed me with saddened eyes that this was her fourth death in a month. I made a mental note to check-in with her later to see if she wanted to talk about her own issues.

The family arrived a few minutes later, accompanied by the hospital supervisor. I was introduced as the Chaplain, but they didn't seem to register this information. They were in shock. After a few minutes, I motioned to the supervisor that I would take over from here. She left the scene shaking her head.

The family consisted of the deceased patient's husband and daughter-in-law. They both loudly exclaimed their shock and disbelief that she had died, because just that day the doctor had given her an 80% chance of recovery. Without registering my presence through verbal word or gesture, they walked in circles through the ICU ward for the next ten minutes, acting as if I wasn't there. I didn't say a word during that time, but followed them. I watched how the blow of the news traumatized their senses, sending any hope for rational thought processes to the back burner. Deep grief set in and I followed them now with a box of Kleenex, ladling them out like an invisible hand. I watched myself glide through the situation like a ghost, acting like an unseen guide. I felt as though I was a spirit, shepherding them across the dark expanse they had just begun to cross.

The supervisor had announced before leaving that they could stay in the ICU waiting room, so when they walked there, I followed them without saying a word. They acted as if they were ignoring me, but I knew that somewhere they had registered my presence, and it didn't matter anyway. What was important was their grief, that they had it, owned it, opened to it, felt it. The grieving husband ranted and raved, screamed and cried, and paced the room. The daughter-in-law spoke continuously about seeing her mother-in-law just a few hours ago. She spoke into the thin air in front of her. I sat and listened, receiving all that was going on, some distance away from them. I began to share radiant energy with them, having established a radiant field between my hands, holding the pattern of their life force with care.

After about fifteen minutes, when the pattern had cleared somewhat in my hands, and their voices had died down, I moved to sit near the girl. I introduced myself to her, and asked her a few questions, getting a better idea about their family relationship. The man overheard our conversation and screamed his own responses. I received his response without a break. His noisy expression seemed perfectly natural to me.

After a little while (time seemed to stand still), the head nurse entered the waiting room and informed us that they had stopped the CPR and had pronounced the woman dead. More ranting, raving and tears. The nurse looked at me in horror and disbelief, as if to say, "How can you possibly handle this?" I told her quietly that all was under control and everything was fine. She mentioned to me that in a few minutes they could enter the wife's room for final viewing. They acted as if they hadn't heard her and demanded to see the doctor, to see if there were something else that could be done for the wife; they didn't believe she was dead. The head nurse then left, shaking her head.

I sat with them again, re-entered their radiant pattern, felt their grieving waves crest and subside through my hands, and then mentioned quietly to them that they could go be with her in the hospital room if they wanted. The husband flatly refused, saying there still was something that could be done for her, that she wasn't really dead and questioned why the doctor wasn't there. After this outburst, he started moving towards the ICU ward where his wife was located. His actions were guided by some unseen power, and I knew that at a deeper level he knew she was gone, but his outward action didn't match that understanding. I doubted he even knew what he was doing because all the time he moved he denied what he was doing. Something told me, however, that everything was okay, that he was doing what he needed to do, that even though his grief and movement patterns seemed disconnected, they somehow made sense, and I silently followed.

Outside the ICU chamber, he seemed to change his mind, and started for the waiting room again, saying that he couldn't face her, that it was all his fault. I looked him in the eye, pressed his hand and spoke with a clear, gentle voice, "You may regret your decision later on." Those words, cutting through the fog like clean steel, registered in him, and he stumbled with the daughter into his wife's room. They stayed with her for the next 40 minutes, holding her hand, rubbing her body, cooing and loving her.

By the time the man and the girl left the hospital, their denial was over. They had signed the autopsy forms and expressed openness to receive my call in the next few days regarding bereavement support. I continued my morning shift with a heart-felt conversation with the head nurse.

Reflecting on my actions later on, I was thankful to spirit for giving me the wisdom to handle this situation. What I was guided to do was to move myself out of the way in order to let their grieving take center stage. I knew that the man's grief would eventually find its own way through the darkness, healing his harsh feelings and purifying his shattered life. I realized that this time was a proving for me, a test from spirit to see how able I was to keep my integrity in spirit when others seemed to doubt spirit's ability to handle the situation. For me, this time was about my learning how to be an invisible guide, a silent spiritual beacon, shining light into a dark situation by attuning my capacities to the spiritual needs of the moment. I connected with the depth of the family's grief through the power of spirit, and knew that as I kept my hand gently on the pulse of the family's response pattern to life, that spirit would open their way into the light. Touching these lives I learned about my own needs by trusting the process and listening to spirit's gentle wisdom. I learned about their needs by allowing spiritual peace to emerge in its own time.

The Inner Guidance System

> *Let your soul be your Pilot, Let your soul guide you upon your way.*
> *—Sting*

Inside each of us there is an inner guidance system, an intricately interwoven and complex system of invisible human energies which synchronously influence human activity. During times of sorrow, we intuitively know that something greater than our mere minds is holding us up. Our inner healing occurs because we each are endowed with special human attributes that are blessed with divine character. Collectively, I call these attributes an *Inner Guidance System* and view them within the context of O'Regan and Hirschberg's Inner Healing Mechanism.

This guidance system is fueled with radiant power from within, and is empowered by the presence of inner divinity. To the extent that human capacities are open to its power, this great pathfinder directs all human qualities of life, breath, will, faith, imagination, passion, drive, intuition, empowerment, belief, and attitudinal release through life channels. During times of sorrow and grief, as described in the story above, the inner guidance system 'kicks in' with subconscious focus, escorting us through the darkness to the dawn of a new day. I see these inner guidance system components directly linked to our inner healing potential by reason of their creative potential within us. Inner components have the power to help bring about a positive healing result through our conscious identification with them and revelation of them in our living.

Inner Guidance System Components

> *Each patient carries his own doctor inside him.*
>
> —*Albert Schweitzer, MD*

There are many inner guidance system components which compose and influence the nature and quality of each person's expression and activity through powerful conscious and subconscious means. These components include but are not limited to the quality of each person's:

- will or willingness;

- self esteem and subjective belief about that quality;

- inner child health and inner-connectedness;

- belief patterns (i.e. how we each hold resentments, grudges, jealousies, prejudices, and negatively based thoughts regarding personal power and authority);

- processing system (whether one is or is not 'in touch' with one's emotions);

- vitality or vital energy, and libido;

- resiliency in meeting daily challenges (may be hampered by chronic illnesses and accidents);

- personality; and

- habit patterns.

Negative qualities for each of these components include expressions of complaint and criticism, over-use of limits and boundaries, trust issues, high stress behavior patterns (i.e. being a 'workaholic'), patterns of limitation and learned behavior patterns such as family of origin and survivorship techniques. Obviously, one's psychological profile plays a significant part in assessing the qualitative health of one's inner guidance system. Positive counterparts to these negative traits include hope, faith, belief in Self, Other and Higher Power, feelings of joy, contentment, trust, assurance, happiness with one's life pursuits, achievements, and fulfilling lifestyle, etc.

Christiane Northrup, MD, makes several interesting points in relation to our inner guidance system components and how they work together. First, she notes that the Body-Mind connection functions on a learned behavior approach in that "...our central nervous system and sense organs function in such a way as to choose and process *only those stimuli that reinforce what we already believe about ourselves."*[1] She suggests that we re-think or seek to purify those 'tried and true' yet limiting beliefs about ourselves which keep us locked into lower energy patterns of behavior and expression.

Second, because consciousness is a universal, non-local medium, and is located within our body everywhere at once, Northrup contends that our subjective sensing of our inner guidance system comes to us through the subconscious level — that place which contains automatic physical processing (such as heart beat and digestion). Therefore, all memory traces of who we know ourselves to be first come through the subconscious level, and take time to reach the mental, conscious level. When we 'soul search' or stretch to access higher power intelligence, we utilize components of the inner guidance system which are not solely part of the conscious human intellect. We reach the light by traveling through unseen, unconscious territory. Northrup states that the "intellect works best *in service* to our intuition, our inner guidance, soul, God or higher power..."[2]

Attunement philosophy asserts that as one 'rises up' into belief about inner wisdom, one may begin to identify its power with one's own power, and that this transaction produces a harmonizing effect at the mental, emotional and physical levels of being. Union with Source produces a healing effect in one's living. Being at one with God's loving nature allows one to more easily express natural God-like qualities which helps one not be distracted by or react to the busyness of the outside world. By practicing daily attunement therapy exercises and other forms of Mind-Body connection activities, one may be able to free up one's inner guidance system to work more efficiently, in harmony with spirit, and centered in radiant activity.

Inner Guidance System Models

Natural forces within us are the true healers of disease.

—Hippocrates

All human interactions occur in two distinctly different ways: (i) those interactions which occur subjectively — within oneself alone, that is between the inner guidance system components themselves, and (ii) those interactions which occur objectively — those which we internally process but which occur outside ourselves, as in those which occur between ourselves and another person. We may watch the TV and have our own thoughts about what we see, but this kind of internal dialogue is vastly different in scope than if we spoke about that TV program to our neighbor.

Seemingly simplistic but having dramatic ramifications for our world, our choice as to how we process inner and outer actions is entirely dependent on the quality of our inner worlds — how we choose to keep house within us. One may harbor shadows which pertain to one's personal selfhood, and by expressing these dark moods, color the true potential of any interaction. Darker patterns of behavior and personality play into one's subjective view of Self in a powerful way, often with self-defeating outcome.

To enlighten our deeper selves, we may align with the movement of radiant energy flow which emanates from within our divine being. There follow three models which illustrate how divine energy flows through being. These models show how divine energy initiates and fuels the inner guidance system, and how this energy moves within oneself in relation to human function, behavior, interaction and expression. These models may assist you to understand how inner divinity may be used more efficiently in your life. When your consciousness is identified with the radiance of love, a higher unified experience may be allowed to flow from you, influencing your world with light.

INNER GUIDANCE SYSTEM MODEL *I*

1. Your God Being naturally expresses **Radiant Love Energy,** which

2. animates your **personal identity and belief system** (learned through family-of-origin and social educating circumstances), which

3. utilizes **mental/emotional guidance, intuition and memory** input to validate, process and act upon identity and belief system thought patterns. We then

4. **experience and perceive the outside world**, which

5. **challenges us to choose, interact, and enact response.** Here, individual strengths present at various inner guidance levels will be tested and explored (i.e. those areas which are weak and lacking in vital energy may be assisted by radiant attitudes of faith, passion, thankfulness, forgiveness, compassion, willingness, etc.). Next, we

6. perceive our own response to our outside interaction as positive or not, which **establishes and/or strengthens a memory trace** of how we view ourselves in the outer world. This perception (positive or negative) either empowers or dis-empowers us from the initial radiant love energy seeking to fuel this interaction. If one meets the outer circumstance in a similar way as before, memory of that interaction is retraced — strengthened and embedded. We then see a

7. **transformation of the outer personality based on new and/or strengthened memory traces. Transmutation at our Four Levels of Being (mental, emotional, physical and spiritual) occur here.** Transformation and transmutation are synchronistic, simultaneous events. Disease patterns may begin to manifest here through poorly maintained etheric openings associated with biological processes.

8. **The initial radiant love energy from Source**, having traveled through inner and outer realms, now **returns to Source**. Radiant love energy has empowered the entire process and changes have occurred. Hands-on attunement session work intercedes and clarifies radiant energy's return to Source at this and any other point in the process.

This model indicates that maintenance of an accurate identity with love presence throughout, challenging outer circumstance, avoids negative memory imprints which then need to be cleared, processed, and integrated. If negative memory traces are laid down, a personal practice of daily sanctification and attunement may negate their settling into psychological and physiological processes. Maintenance of a correct spiritual identity with Source throughout each day's events allows for a consistent radiant energy to flow from within and outward through the capacities of body, mind and heart. One may then clear the energy pathways through one's life with creative and healing success.

When spiritual energy is mis-aligned, more energy must be poured into the system to correct, process or realign mental and emotional capacities back to Source. Attunement sees that these oftentimes cumbersome processing requirements may be easily circumvented through an open, forgiving and thankful heart. Thankfulness expressed in the most mundane or crucial of situations will often open the floodgates of spiritual flow into one's world, circumventing the need for lengthy cycles of outworking and/or illness which often serve to bring the person back again into correct spiritual alignment.

There are two other models of how the Inner Guidance System works. (The third and final model follows a figure eight energy circuitry, which relates to the lemniscate, a symbol of universal energy.)

These models show that when one aligns oneself with divine energy flow through open-hearted response from oneself to spirit, this flow will open conscious and subconscious doorways. Free spiritual movement through the individual is a healing event which maintains inner health or may bring positive change at all levels of being according to one's response to spirit. If one's response to spirit is closed, then negative changes (including illness) manifest in the person's life.

INNER GUIDANCE MODEL II

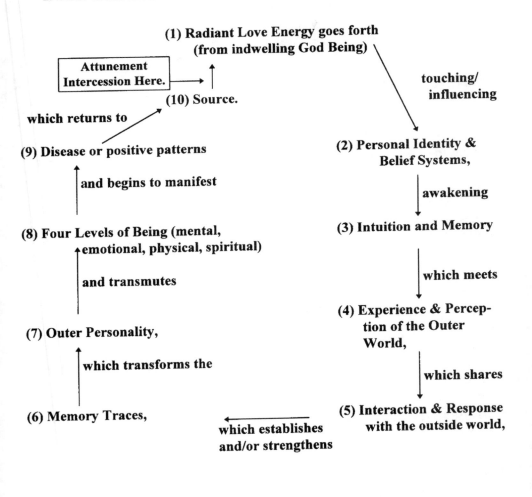

(1) Radiant Love Energy goes forth (from indwelling God Being)

Attunement Intercession Here.

(10) Source.

touching/ influencing

which returns to

(9) Disease or positive patterns

(2) Personal Identity & Belief Systems,

and begins to manifest

awakening

(8) Four Levels of Being (mental, emotional, physical, spiritual)

(3) Intuition and Memory

and transmutes

which meets

(7) Outer Personality,

(4) Experience & Perception of the Outer World,

which transforms the

which shares

(6) Memory Traces,

which establishes and/or strengthens

(5) Interaction & Response with the outside world,

INNER GUIDANCE SYSTEM MODEL III

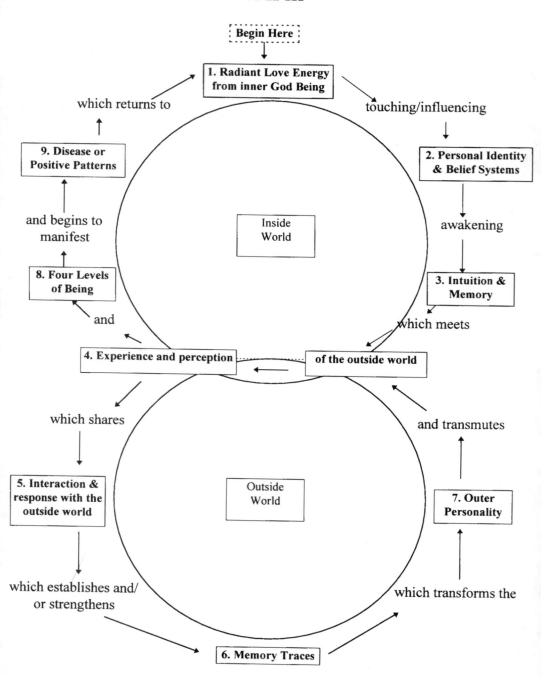

Many spiritual activities help to strengthen personal connection to Source and have been shown to be healing in nature. Besides practicing the many attunement exercises in this book, I highly recommend daily practice of many of the following activities for personal enjoyment, relaxation, personal growth and healing: creative visualization, affirmations, meditation, yoga, massage, exercise, acupuncture, Reiki, Shiatsu, Shen, Joh rei, Qi Gong, Feng Shui, aromatherapy, art therapy, art activities, counseling, music/sound therapy, privacy, retreat time, journal writing, eating healthy and nutritious food, sex, worship, spiritual practices, and other forms of human work and play which creatively enhance the synchronous movement of spirit through the physical, mental, emotional and spiritual areas of life.

Sanctification

Sanctification is a traditional attunement practice taught to all interested attunement students and clients. You may want to include sanctification as part of your morning and evening ritual, and nurture Self and your daily encounters with this simple, short exercise.

Morning: After awaking and before rising from bed, gently bring to mind the events you know are coming to you this day — places, people, meetings, shopping, lunch with a friend, dinner with your family, quiet time with family. Bring to mind each activity one at a time. Open the door for spirit to flow through your day's events by giving thanks for these circumstances before they arrive into your life. Picture yourself walking through these situations with joy, expressing attitudes of thankfulness and blessing. Visualize success, fulfillment and prosperity, setting in motion the movement of positive energy into your world. See divine presence opening up the possibility of creative outworking in any negative situation before or after you arrive. When you've visualized your day (should take 5 – 10 minutes), then move about with your normal morning routine.

Evening: At day's end, it's time to put your day to rest. Just before dropping off to sleep, bring to mind the day's events. Recall the way you felt about each encounter — waiting in traffic, attending a boring meeting, talking with a friend, offering comfort to a needy neighbor, hugging your spouse and children before bedtime. Ask yourself, "Was I expressing an attitude of thankfulness, compassion, and helpfulness?" or were there moments of impatience, arrogance and accusation? Gently forgive yourself for any defensive posturing or mistrust of Self or Other. Recall each occurrence with a larger, compassionate understanding which now sees with forgiveness, humility and respect. Silently ask all you have harmed to forgive you and re-sanctify your relationship with purifying honesty. Give thanks for your day. Putting your day to rest before retiring clears your heart of all wrong doing. Sanctifying your day, you are setting the stage for restful sleep.

Realizations: Maintaining a daily practice of morning and evening sanctification brings many benefits: increased clarity of thinking, easier personal processing time, decreased personal down time, and conscious connection to your personal purification cycle. You may not need lengthy time to process unfinished business because you will be sanctifying each day's negative events on a continual basis. Personal depression may fade because you will not longer be carrying around yesterday's emotional baggage. As you sanctify each day on a continual basis, you will see the content of your consciousness rapidly purify. Filling your days with blessing, you will know a richer attunement with spirit. Let love radiate without concern for results.

Chapter 5 Notes

[1] Northrup, Christiane, MD, <u>Women's Bodies, Women's Wisdom</u>, (New York: Bantam Books, 1994) p. 28.

[2] <u>Ibid.</u>, p. 31.

6. Non-local Spiritual Attunement

The following story was sent to me by Anthony Palombo, a Chiropractor and attunement practitioner practicing in Louisiana, USA. I will call him Tony for short.

Late one afternoon, two of Tony's clients, an elderly couple, came into the health center with heavy hearts and tearful eyes. "We would like you to help our little great grandson," the elderly gentleman implored. "He's going to have his kidneys removed in the morning at a hospital in New Orleans. Our granddaughter is going to give him one of her kidneys. They are both going to be prepped for early morning surgery tomorrow. Can you help him?"

Tony immediately answered that he would love to help but being a Chiropractor he was not allowed inside the hospital to administer Chiropractic or attunement assistance.[1] "No, we mean from here!" came the quick response (they were eighty miles from the hospital).

Tony had been sharing attunements with this elderly couple on a weekly basis for some time in conjunction with their Chiropractic care. He didn't recall ever having mentioned long distance attunement practice to them. They were absolutely sure that he could help their great-grandson even though distant from the hospital. With their faith in the power of spirit to heal this little boy, Tony knew that his attunement would work. He also felt assured that the healing process had already begun due to their absolute agreement with him that it be so. They were carrying that little boy right in their heart of hearts with a spirit of victory. "Yes, we can do this!" Tony told them as he lead them to the session room.

Tony started to ask the great-grandmother to lie down on the Chiropractic table, but she was in such a state of turmoil that he felt it best that she go into an adjoining room and rest while he worked with her husband, who seemed much more contained emotionally. Moreover, the elderly gentleman was in absolute agreement with Tony. He did not express the slightest shadow of turning from his faith in spirit to heal his great-grandson. Tony knew instinctively that a healing energy could be sent through his client to the boy.

Tony had him lay on his left side on the treatment table. After the man was comfortable, Tony sat down behind him and considered how to approach this session. He was going to be sending radiant divine energy to the boy in the hospital through the boy's great-grandfather's kidneys. The great-grandfather and his kidneys were going to act as contact points into the life of the great-grandson. Tony began the session by lifting up his heart in thanksgiving to the Father within for the opportunity to serve, and for the healing current of love he was going to extend through the pattern of agreement brought to him. He then extended his right hand and held it over the area of the back where the kidneys were located. He extended his left hand over the crown of his client's head (at the site of the pineal gland). Within a minute Tony felt a tremendous turmoil of energy, in contrast to the still focus of love energy he felt present in the room. Working to bring a balance to the energy pattern in turmoil, Tony started moving his left hand toward the right hand, radiating into the spine as he came down the body. As he approached the kidney area, with one hand on the spine and the other over each kidney, one at a time, he began to feel a ball of erratic energy, spherical in shape. As he moved his hands toward one another and then apart, Tony felt as if he were massaging a balloon between his hands, the energy pattern was so strong. He continued with the massage motion over his client's kidneys, back and forth between his hands, for about five minutes before he felt a shift in the pattern of energy.

Slowly the ball of erratic energy began to dissipate, and it felt as if air was being released from the balloon of energy he held. After a time, the entire pattern shifted into stillness, leaving only a peaceful pattern over the kidneys. Immediately Tony lifted his heart and gave thanks, saying to the elderly gentleman, "Ok, it's done."

As he was leaving the session room, Tony asked his client to call him at any time, night or day, just as soon as they heard from the family in New Orleans. His client agreed, thanked him and then left with his wife. At 1:30 a.m., Tony received a phone call from the man. He was choking back his tears of deep joy. The little boy had wet his bed in the hospital, a sure sign that his illness was receding, and he was on the mend. The doctors didn't know what to think. They said that it looked like a miracle. A few days later the doctors took the boy off the dialysis machine and held him over in the hospital for observation. His kidneys continued to function normally and they sent him home three weeks later.

The next time Tony saw the elderly couple he visited them at their granddaughter's home where he had opportunity to meet the little boy. The boy was a bright child, exuding lots of light and bouncing with energy. Tony knew then that anything was possible with people who shared unwavering agreement, and he looked further into carrying out more long distance attunement therapy within his practice.

Non-local Agreement in Action

*Faith is a love response to, even as
love is a realization of the sense of oneness with.*

—*Uranda*

What the Chiropractor in the preceding story experienced was the absolute agreement extended to him by another for a third person. This absolute energy flow did not attempt to fix the body of the little boy from the outside in. Rather, radiant energy moved with synchronistic effect from the great-grandfather to the Chiropractor to the little boy simultaneously because spirit is non-local (i.e. is present in all places at the same time), and the great-grandfather's personality was in perfect alignment with his inner divine character. This non-local alignment, known by both the Chiropractor, great-grandfather and child, was what allowed spirit to flow freely and heal the child.

Attunement Therapy resides on the leading edge of new scientific thinking, aligned with many other scientists and medical specialists who advocate the concept that consciousness is a non-local event. Larry Dossey, MD writes, "…consciousness is *infinite* in space and time, bridging between distant individuals and other conscious creatures."[2] Asserting a similar view to that of Dr Dossey and also Depak Chopra, MD, Candace Pert, PhD, previous Chief of Brain Surgery in the Neuroscience branch at the National Institute of Health, states that "There's a wisdom in every cell… the mind is non-local. It's throughout the body and moves around in the body." Dr Pert also suggests that "…on some level, all the information in the universe is available to all the other information in the universe."[3] The idea that conscious energy exists in all places simultaneously would account for a number of unexplainable phenomena including prayer and distance healing, psychic impressions, near-death experiences, extra sensory perception, out of body experience and Shamanic trance and travel.

Long Distance (Non-local) Attunement Practice

Long distance attunement practice rests at the heart of all attunement service and consists of one or more attunement practitioners sending radiant energy (previously presented in Chapter 4) to one or more clients. Later chapters cover how to set up and administer *Team Attunements* and *Radiant Gatherings* (long distance and on-site attunement sharing between a group of people), so this chapter's guidelines will just present one-on-one long distance attunement therapy practice.

To begin, follow the Radiant Energy Practice Guidelines presented in Chapter 4 when setting up your energy field between your hands. Follow these guidelines, and when you have created a radiant energy field, bring to mind the person with whom you wish to share radiant energy. It is always good practice to keep photos of those to whom you send radiant energy, so that when you share a long distance attunement, you are able to bring them to mind clearly. Place the person's photo close by and refer to it often.

It is also a good idea to pick a time and date together with your client, and share conscious agreement of the time you are sharing together. Since you may share attunement with anyone, anywhere, at any time, plan ahead for time changes between shores (Pacific Standard Time v. Mountain, Central or Eastern Standard Time), and countries. Choose from among the following different long distance attunement session types:

1. Radiation list, long distance attunements. Radiation list attunements consists of you writing down the names of those people with whom you want to share long distance attunement, and sharing radiant energy with each one of them, one at a time. Spend a few minutes with each person on your list, moving from one to another in an easy fashion. Hold each person's pattern long enough to allow a balance of their energies to come into your hands. Remember that when first encountering someone else's energy pattern, one of your hands may feel warmer, or more of a spiritual energy flow than the other. Simply hold the person's pattern without trying to fix anything, letting spirit bring a balance in its own time. This should take only a few minutes.

Practitioners usually keep three or more names on their radiation list, and set up their radiation session at specific times during the week (i.e. Mondays, Wednesdays and Fridays from 9 a.m. – 10 a.m.), inviting others into their energy field at those times. The beauty of this type of practice is that the practitioner gains valuable experience maintaining a long distance practice on a consistent basis. This is usually the first kind of long distance exercise administered by a beginning attunement practitioner.

2. Contact point long distance attunement. As presented in this chapter's story, you can choose to share an attunement on-site with someone who acts as contact point for another person or group of people situated far away. As described, it is best to keep clear and maintain your lines of conscious agreement between all parties concerned for best outcome.

3. Long distance attunement with full body attunement technique. After you have learned full body attunement with its corresponding contact points (Chapters 10 – 16), you may utilize this technique when you share any long distance attunement. Simply set up the radiant energy field between your hands, bring to mind your client, and begin sharing a full attunement long distance. Without directing the outcome of your session, visualize your client resting between your hands as you begin to work with the energies moving through the cervical pattern, endocrine glands, organ systems, lymph and skeletal systems. Feel free to get up and move about the area while keeping your client in mind and maintaining your client's energy field between your hands. Sharing full body attunements through long distance technique feels much the same as if your client were in front of you, and is very soothing for the client who receives the attunement.

Long Distance Attunement Guidelines

You should practice long distance attunement 10 – 15 minutes each day. With consistent practice, you will develop a personal affinity to specific people's energy fields, as well as a greater vibrational sensitivity to a wide variety of illnesses. Ask people with whom you share long distance attunement about their illness — this will increase your own ability to receive and clarify specific patterns. However, you should be careful not to let your mind control the session — let spiritual discretion be your guide.

Remember that each person's vibrational pattern is a sacred entity. You are actually holding their life force in your hands, so learn to handle this force with patience, perseverance and humility. Always ask permission first, and inform the people on your list or in your field that you are sharing attunement with them at your given time so that they may be more consciously aware and receptive to the flow of love energy which you are providing.

As you share long distance attunement every day, you will begin to establish your own creative field, or sphere of vibrational influence, in a specific way. Slowly, you will begin to develop and strengthen your perceptions and sensitivities to subtle energies flowing between yourself and another. In time, your ability to hold a radiant energy flow will increase to a point where you are able to handle multiple energy patterns at once and share attunement energy for long periods of time. These are valuable and necessary talents which most attunement practitioners need to possess for group work, and for on-site hospital and professional attunement practice.

Car Attunements

You can share long distance attunement in your car while you're driving to work, both as a beginning meditation for your day or when coming home. Simply establish your radiant field of energy between your hands by placing your hands in their natural places on the wheel, facing each other. Then begin to radiate love energy through your hands to someone you love, or to a situation needing your loving focus. Send some radiant energy to the driver next to you too! If you need to shift gears or use the turn signal, simply use one of your hands to do so while maintaining the energy current with the other hand, and then bring both hands into the field again when finished.

Car attunements are a great way to spend your time wisely, and often provide a comforting and protective energy pattern within and outside the car, as long as you remember to drive first, and attune second. It is the perfect choice for when you are driving along long, boring stretches of highway. They also work well when you are stuck in traffic jams, or when you or someone else get cut off on the road by a rude driver. In that case, just let the rude driver pass without getting caught up in his erratic behavior. Stay stable within, and offer him some radiant energy as he passes you by. Erratic drivers are accidents waiting to happen, and need TLC to thwart the unstable energy seeking to land them in one.

Of course, if you're a passenger, you can practice long distance attunement without having to stop to switch gears or use the hand signal. Car attunements can be great fun and relaxing ways for the entire family to share creative time together, healing, sharing insights, and focusing loving attention on each other.

Chapter 6 Notes

[1] Laws at that time, and in that state, restricted Chiropractors from working within hospital systems.

[2] Larry Dossey, MD, 'The Healing Power of Pets: A Look At Animal-Assisted Therapy,' *Alternative Therapies*, July, 1997, Vol. 3, No. 4, p. 15.

[3] Candace Pert, PhD: 'Neuropeptides, AIDS...' pp. 72–76.

7. Ascension

I shared my first four day Attunement Intensive with the Master Attunement Server in 1994, just prior to moving to Seattle to begin medical school. Over the previous 13 years I had learned attunement cosmology and some of its associated techniques but I had not yet learned the full body attunement technique prior to this time.

The Attunement Intensive took place on Sunrise Ranch, birthplace of attunement therapy, and home of the Master Server. Our time together was split between our offering team attunements in the morning to residents of the community, and afternoon lessons in the Master Server's study. During the intensive I stayed in a nearby guest room and ate my meals with the residents. In the late evening I perused the Attunement Sanctuary's library, and read many services offered by Uranda and Martin Exeter which spoke about the specific attunement principles which had arisen during the day. I spoke with Ranch residents about their knowledge of living in attunement and in community. It was a 24 hour experience of complete saturation in the healing touch of attunement.

Vibrationally, this intensive time was the most profound I have ever felt. Since my heart was completely open to move higher in consciousness, this is what occurred. At times I felt as if I were lifted up onto an elevated plateau, where I was given the opportunity to look down upon myself and my interactions with others, seeing them for what they were, aligned with truth or not. Attunement intensity brought with it a higher vision coupled with a concentrated and objective scrutiny of the quality of character I was bringing to my life at that time.

My last session with the Master Server was particularly significant. We decided to focus our attention on the principles of long distance (non-local) attunement. At 10:00 a.m., he drew forth from his pocket a photograph, and started sharing long distance attunement with the person pictured in the photo. He explained that he didn't know the person in the photo, and actually wasn't sharing an attunement with the person in the photo. He was sharing an attunement with someone that he did know quite well, who was consciously connected to him at that time, and who was also consciously connected to the person in the picture. The Master Server was utilizing a triune contact point configuration of agreement connection to send radiant energy to the man in the picture, who was undergoing kidney surgery at that time. The Master Server explained that he shared an absolute spirit of agreement with his friend about the right outworking for the man in the picture, who was under anesthesia at the time. Since the man in surgery had no conscious connection to the spirit of agreement while under anesthesia, these two men were holding that pattern for him — a specific kind of intercessory skill.

At a few minutes past ten o'clock while the Master Server was speaking to me about long distance work, he paused to comment, "Oh, they're deep within him now." He could feel the invasive pattern of the surgery within his long distance client. He showed me the picture. It was of a little boy. The man was now fully grown, and the photo was taken when he was just a boy. The age of the person in the photograph didn't matter because the Master Server's technical expertise was so well developed that he could connect with the figure in the photo no matter how they had grown or changed.

A few minutes later, while we were still sharing long distance attunement, he received a phone call from someone else asking to receive an attunement (the Master Server received a lot of phone calls of this nature). Without breaking the pattern of response of the three people with whom he was already working (myself, his friend and the surgery patient), he sat further back in his armchair, allowed deeper serenity to enfold the proceedings and answered, "We are well into an attunement current right now, and you are most welcome to join in." All were welcome into this Master Server's expansive energy field. Needless to say, this long distance learning session far surpassed any of my expectations.

Following the close of the intensive experience, I returned to my guest room to rest. It was only then that I realized I was covered in a thin film of sweat. All of my clothing was saturated with water and salt. I felt physically exhausted and wanted to rest, but instead my body was urging me to expel unwanted matter. During the next two hours I went to the bathroom seven times. I felt as though I were moving through an intense cleansing at the physical level. The physical form was following after the vibrational changes which had ensued from the previous three days. I wasn't surprised at my body's physical reaction because I was consciously aware that I had moved across a great expanse — I had crossed the line of wanting to love God and was actually at one with God. My consciousness had lifted, and I was lifted up with it. Spirit moving through me had allowed me to come into union with Source in a very specific way, moving me forward through the ascension process.

How Ascending Energy Works

The radiance of love and the response of love
sets up the creative cycle of the flaming fire.
Where love is actually manifest,
those who respond to love will be drawn.

—Uranda

As presented previously, attunement healing energy clarifies the morphogenetic/etheric body field (or informational genetic blueprint field) surrounding and interpenetrating all physical substance. This clarification process allows life (prana, Qi, whatever you wish to call it) to move upward and onward in its creative process. Over my many years of learning attunement with the Emissaries I was told many times to trust the life current and its associated creative process because its ascending movement was absolute. And this lesson is true. From a scientific standpoint, the life current is governed by equal and opposite forces directly mirroring that which drives physically-based substance. These forces compel life to move upward in an ascending motion as Professor William Tiller, PhD asserts:

> *Physical substance manifests itself in the positive space/time frame (meaning you can see it) — it is electrical in nature, has positive mass, travels slower than the velocity of electromagnetic light, [and] gives rise to the gravitational force… Etheric substance is postulated to manifest itself in the negative space/time frame (meaning you cannot see it) — it is magnetic in nature, has negative mass, travels faster than the velocity of electromagnetic light, [and] gives rise to the **levitational** force.*[1]

Eastern schools of spiritual insight know that the etheric plane of being contains higher consciousness, capable of moving the physical body with it during an ascension process. Many eastern schools of thought speak of "rising up in consciousness," through meditation and elimination of all physical influences which cloud the mind of clear blissful thought. Alongside eastern thought are many modern mystics who observe humankind traveling along a evolutionary spiral, rising up, out of our past state, into a new world, a new age, the age of enlightenment.

One of the more noteworthy authors in this field is Ken Wilbur who recently simplified all universal processes into one basic structure, the 'holon.' The holon, according to Wilbur, is an entity that is whole while still maintaining its part within a larger whole. Holons share two horizontal tendencies: *agency and communion*. This means that all holons (all things) maintain their own identity, autonomy, and wholeness, while at the same time they seek communion with a larger environment. Holons also share two vertical characteristics: *self-transcendence* and *self-dissolution*. This means that all things move to a higher level of existence while simultaneously losing something of itself in this process, thereby allowing a piece of itself to move to a lower level of existence. Wilbur says that all holons have these four pulls working on them at the same.

Moreover, holons emerge, and not only do they emerge from within themselves to an outward area beyond themselves, but they emerge holarchically, meaning that holons emerge into increasing levels of wholeness. Each emergent holon transcends and also includes its predecessors. Wilbur associates universal and human cycles of existence as holonic movements, including the rise and fall of civilizations, psychological trends in consciousness (especially relating to masculine and feminine purpose within the species), and all universal processes. The life impulse is to transcend and include, and humans move along this spiral axis towards their ultimate destiny.[2]

Dr Tiller asserts that human beings move upward in the ascending process of life because *negative entropy* moves through etheric energy, and affects physical substance with an integrating force. Negative entropy brings together physical substance in resonant and harmonizing ways, natural to its design and structure. Negative entropy does not affect etheric energy, but is the prime motive behind this energy's vital force. *Positive Entropy*, which is the Second Law of Thermodynamics, works upon physical substance in an equal and opposite fashion. Positive entropy, which is the force associated with physical matter, moves physical matter in random motion, moving physical substance further into chaos. Positive entropy, when working on physical matter, requires more energy to be poured into the system in order to organize it into a manageable coherency (which is the Third Law of Thermodynamics). Seeing the difference between the laws which work on physical substance and those that work through etheric substance, one may see that the very nature of etheric energy (which is life) is intended to organize, cohere and harmonize that physical substance which houses its vital force.

To illustrate the theories presented above, let's look at an example. When a person dies, we see that physical tissue begins to decay. Why?

What was it that animated and kept alive the tissues while the person was alive? It was the life force, the Qi, the integrating energy behind the physical form. To illustrate this point further, I refer you to a research study completed by Dr Justa Smith. Dr Smith measured the effectiveness of energies emanating from healers' hands on test tubes containing enzyme tyrosine. Those tests showed that the "...activity of the enzymes affected by the healers always seemed to be in a direction that was toward greater overall health and balanced metabolic activity of the organism."[3] This research also showed that

> *...healers' energies caused variable changes in the reaction rates of different enzymes, whereas magnetic fields could only cause a non-specific increase in activity. **The direction of change in enzyme activity always seemed to mirror the natural cellular intelligence.**[4]*

Attunement Ascension Theory: Five Phases of the Attunement Process

In order to move fully with the ascension process, human beings need to be consciously connected to its presence and its uplifting movement in their living. Consider the recorded ascension process which occurred in the life of Jesus Christ. Here was a man who maintained his conscious connection with the Father throughout his entire life process.[5] Being one with the Father upon the moment of his conscious passing, he then moved into an intensive ascension process whereby the record states that he took his body with him when he left this world. A very necessary step for us to take while moving through enlightenment is to take our consciousness with us along the way.

Uranda taught that as one's consciousness maintains unity with one's inner radiance, then one will express outwardly with the same kind of transforming power that one recognizes within. Outer world activities and people are drawn to each person's radiant expression, and this expression comes from within. As people and situations respond to one's inner radiance, they are lifted up through the power of light transformation, and this is how we move along together in the ascending process. Think about it — you read a book or attend a lecture given by a radiantly expressive and consciously awake person and those new thoughts and light-filled moments attract you to respond with your own inner light. As you come into conscious agreement with this teacher, you then express outwardly into your own world with the same radiance given to you before. At the end of this process, all who responded to the original radiance share in a unified, larger expression of that original light. Uranda elucidates this point:

> *The [inner] Christ radiance of God Being goes forth and creates, and that which is created is drawn to, and absorbed by, the Christ radiance so that it may take part in further creative action. Radiation, response, attraction, union, unified expression, which is radiation — thus is the creative cycle completed.*[6]

Let's look at these five steps, one at a time:

- **Radiation:** Radiation is the central core of inner light which shines through a person and extends out into their worlds. Radiation refers to that light-filled aspect of love which seeks to furnish and impart a division of itself to something outside itself, for the sole purpose of creative transformation. Love radiation seeks response from that which is willing to be changed by love. When you express radiant love energy through yourself to another, you then receive back response from willing conscious hearts and minds who wish to share in that same radiant flow.

- **Response:** Response relates to the returning aspect of love. Those life forms which respond to love seek to be changed or transformed by love. We see evidence in nature of the working of these two principles together, for you can't have one without the other. Yin and Yang commune together as do the masculine and feminine expressions. Likewise, the planets orbit around the sun, in response to its power and light.

An important point to remember about response is that it brings light into human consciousness. When you respond to a person who expresses themselves with radiant authority, something within you wakes up. You experience the 'light being turned on' when the penny drops or you hear words of inspiration. Expressing response to a radiant force reveals light — that is what the new age of enlightenment is all about.

- **Attraction:** The light compels attraction back to Source. Within this attraction phase, responding substance either ascends to the next level, or it dissolves out of sight, into nothingness. That which leaves the cycle is not needed further in the ascending process. That which continues onward is pure in nature, and is capable of blending into union with the radiant source. In other words, the attraction phase separates out the wheat from the chaff or the dross from the gold, leaving only pure substance to carry on in the ascending process. That which is drawn by love because it is of love, will continue on in the process. That which carries the love substance along, but is not of love itself, will leave the process and pass away. Now the creative process contains only love substance.

- **Union:** During this step, the purified aspect of responding love comes naturally into union with radiant love, thereby expanding love's creative force and field.

- **Unified Radiation:** Love's larger radiant force again goes out seeking response to itself, for the sole purpose of expanding its creative force and field into the natural world.

These steps outline what happened to me during my attunement intensive experience. The physical changes which occurred following the intensive experience were a result of the action of the attraction phase flowing through me. That which was within me of pure love substance ascended to a higher plane, blending with the radiant aspect of love from within, while that which was not useful to the purposes of love in my life at that time passed away. Thus it is with all people who share in attuning themselves to their inner radiance. Life moves on and we move with it, higher in consciousness and feeling compelled to offer outwardly that purified aspect of love which we now know.

The Robe of Radiance Practice

Recall from the *Entering In* chapter that the first step to entering into union with Source is through expressing a thankful attitude. By establishing a daily meditation and radiant energy flow in your life, you will take on what Uranda referred to as a 'Robe of Radiance.' This robe is an invisible shield which will appear in your consciousness. The radiant robe is a kind of conscious morphogenetic field which contains new information for your outer mind consciousness regarding divine purposes in your life which may not have yet been revealed to you. Most times when people strive to attain inner conscious awareness about their own divine destiny, the wanting compulsions of their outer mind prevent them from entering in, thereby denying the very thing that they want to receive. It's like trying to open the door in front of you by pulling on the doorknob, but the door won't budge because you have your foot on the bottom edge of the door, preventing it from opening. By following the Robe of Radiance guidelines, you will learn how to leave behind your outer mind's wanting and striving and instead follow your inner knowing. Uranda speaks on this point by saying,

...only the Spirit of your Lord and Master, which is your Robe of Radiance, can reveal the Secret Things of God unto you. As you are drawn of your Master into rhythmic and harmonious coordination with His Expression of God-Being you will act as He acts, speak as He speaks, and think as He thinks... Within your Robe of Radiance your understanding is full, and your Vision is perfect... As you minister in the Temple, before your Master, the Sacred Truths will be revealed to you, and the Secrets of the Sacred Service will be released through you...[7]

To increase your inner attunement with Source practice the following *Robe of Radiance Guidelines* on a daily basis. These guide points work well with the *Inner Healing Meditation* found in Chapter 3.

Robe of Radiance Guidelines

1. Give thanks for all things in every moment.

2. Act in accordance with your inner God-Being, recognizing that divinity is within you and is perfect, full of wisdom and power.

3. Be receptive to every inner urge that comes to you from your inner divinity, and act only when you are urged to do so by God-Being. This will allow your inner radiance to flow freely in each moment.

4. Pay attention to the force of love being expressed through you from within, as it expresses itself through every thought, word and deed. Thoughts, words and deeds are each person's temple services which may be purified in season, according to the will of the *One Who Dwells*. Paying attention to each of these three services, you will begin to see a divine direction appearing in your consciousness.

5. Realize that your flow of love, emanating from within, is a positive force in your world and allows all that it touches to be transmuted and transformed within its creative influence. Offering your world a consistent, positive radiant energy flow will set up a protective shield around you through a robe of radiance. This will dispel any evil or damaging energy from entering into your sphere of creative activity.

6. Become aware of the different vibrations which distinguish conscious thoughts and inner urges. The outer idea vibrates to *what it thinks*. The inner urge vibrates to *what it knows*.

7. Realize that the inner urge is not interested in judging other people, places or situations as being better than others. The inner urge knows

that all that is needed for your life and the lives of others is provided for you by inner radiance. Judging outer things is a waste of time and a useless endeavor. As you continue to express through the oneness you have found from within, all that you will need will be drawn to you according to your own drawing power expressed from within. Judging other things outside of this field only stops the flow of energy from moving out.

8. As you continue to turn in response to the *One Who Dwells Within*, turning away from any outer striving or wanting, being obedient only to the inner urge under the control of the Father within, all things shall follow after you, and you will realize that the *One Who Dwells* has already provided all that you need to live a full life here and now.[8]

Chapter 7 Notes

[1] George Vithoulkas, The Science of Homeopathy, (New York: Grove Weidenfeld, 1980), pp. xii-xiii.

[2] Ken Wilbur, A Brief History of Everything (Boston: Shambhala Press, 1996).

[3] Gerber, Vibrational Medicine, p. 149.

[4] Gerber, Vibrational Medicine, p. 150.

[5] Rudolf Steiner states that when Jesus was on the cross, and was offered vinegar laced with the medicinal hyssop, he denied it, for it would have deprived him of his full conscious awareness during those crucial moments.

[6] Uranda, The Triune Ray, pp. 14–15.

[7] Uranda, Letters to You, (Loveland, CO: Eden Valley Press, 1941), pp. 36–38.

[8] Abridged version of Uranda, The Triune Ray, pp. 58–59.

8. Patterns of Agreement

One day, a massage student came to me to learn attunement. I will call her Peg. Peg was thin, pale, had already experienced one surgery for breast cancer, and was an anorexic/bulimic. She signed up for an individual seminar day, wherein I taught attunement technique one-on-one, giving personalized attention to the needs of the student. When she signed up for this intensive day, I knew that I was going to be meeting a challenge due to the many apparent distortions in consciousness which she carried. But I was rock solid in my agreement with Source to extend a helping hand to her in order to give her the possibility to let creative changes occur in her life.

For a private one-on-one training intensive, I always began the day by sharing an attunement with the student. This initial session then opened the flow of response from the student to Source for the entire day. However, during this particular attunement with Peg I noticed that she shook her head continuously. I had never seen shaking expressed before, and I sensed that she was unconsciously deflecting the movement of spirit into her form. I also sensed that the vibrational matter of her mind was disassociated from her physical body to a large extent. She had a very small frame, with almost no extra fat or muscle tissue, and her head mass seemed too large in comparison with her figure. She seemed to be holding onto a consciousness which sought separation from her physical form. That also explained her bulimic nature. In conversation with her, she repeatedly mentioned, in a bragging fashion, that she felt like she lived in her head. Judging from the looks of her, it seemed that her body agreed with her mind on this point.

While sharing the attunement with her, I sensed a lot of despair in her body. Her body seemed to be grieving its loss of her conscious connection. Later on that day, I approached her on this point. She seemed taken back, like I had revealed her secret and had brought it into the light. During our next break time, I noticed she went to her car for a cigarette smoke, and while there, spoke angrily into the air, waving her hands wildly, as if she were having an argument with herself.

She returned indoors as we moved towards our closing session. For our final hour, I decided to offer her a different kind of attunement session, a 'Representational Object' exercise (see Chapter 21). I asked her to step outside to find a small object which represented a significant spiritual essence to her at that time. She returned a short time later with a small, two-toned rock, colored white and black. Before we began, I asked her to tell me what the stone meant to her. She answered, "This stone is white and black. See here, this is where the colors meet. To me, this stone represents the power of integration. I want to bring to light my shadow self and begin to own it."

I smiled when I heard those words. It seemed that our attuned time had been time well spent. As we shared in the radiant flow together during our final hour, the woman's head remained still, and as she held onto her stone, a smile crept across her face. Entering in, Peg found new inspiration and confidence to begin to meet her challenged state without a shadow of turning. Letting spirit nurture her soul, she began to learn how to nourish herself, consciously integrating her mind with the pneumaplasmic substance of her body. Mind, heart and body connected as one through the power of our agreement with spirit.

Agreement and Creative Triangles

Again I say unto you, That if two of you shall agree on earth
as touching any thing that they shall ask, it shall be done for them
of my Father which is in heaven.

—Jesus Christ, Matthew 18:19

The healing power of spiritual agreement is sorely underestimated in our society. People agree to do activities together all the time — to build a house, to get married, to take a job. What then ensues are a myriad of interactions between themselves which are either imbued with honesty, clarity of meaning and willingness to meet together in the spirit of friendship, or not. Assumptions, hidden agendas, actions based on greed, corruption and hatred, unprocessed emotional feelings and other forms of mis-communications tend to undermine the integrity of our interactions with each other, leading to questionable outcome with sometimes disastrous consequences. Our human civilization has witnessed the passing of entire empires, great enterprises which have come and gone, enslavement and freedom of many peoples of race, creed and color, all based on the misuse of power in relation to spiritual agreement. The potential power to agree, which people carry in their hearts, is the potential promise to create or destroy individual lives and our collective society.

When people choose to share in *spiritual agreement,* those spiritually-inspired projects develop with a kind of divine grace that supercedes and governs the entire outworking, no matter if outer troubles ensue. Spiritual agreement is based on individual sensing and expression of divine wisdom and guidance. All parties involved in a spiritually agreed-upon activity value and utilize certain parameters which then serve to set a tone of integrity for all personal meditations and collective meetings and conversations.

Spiritual agreement parameters usually include two kinds of qualities, those which are personal and those which are group related. Of course, all group related activities are actually personal activities brought together, so all personal qualities find a fitting place within any whole configuration. All personal thought and behavior patterns which are based on spiritual agreement principles usually find their basis of operation in one's own internal agreement between heart and mind with spirit. A person will agree in his heart to be open and willing to do what the conscious faculties direct, when inspired by spirit. This accord finds fitting release at the vibrational level as well as in personal behavior including such expressions as: honesty, open expression of one's feelings, private processing of personal emotions and thoughts, speaking directly to each person, and trust in spiritual guidance in Self and others. Group interactions based on spiritual agreement usually follow similar criteria: open and honest expression of Self to other, trust in spirit's directing influence through Self and Other and in all collective undertaking, willingness to learn and change, respecting other peoples' boundaries, etc.

As the above criteria maintains, any outer form of creative endeavor is usually based on an invisible foundation of its agreeable parts. If you work with a contractor to build a new house, you are actually working to build a storehouse of agreement, tested and strengthened through the trials of upset and renewal. And the power housed inside the form of this house (or that is based on any agreement between two or more people) may be viewed in a 3-D fashion, not a linear line. This is because there are never just two people present in an agreement based in spirit, rather there are three entities, i.e. you, me and God, as the following diagram illustrates.

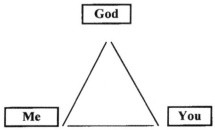

This triangular form of agreement possesses enough power to move a mountain or split an ocean. When Moses split the Red Sea, it was not by his doing, but through the action of absolute agreement between Moses, God and the Israelites that "It shall be done." Once two or more people utilize the Amen prayer to invoke Higher Source's assistance in any creative undertaking, then it is done for them. Recall the healing stories presented so far in this book. Everyone of them is based on this spiritual agreement principle. Vibrational agreement between two or more people and Source works in an absolute fashion, and is the foundation upon which all attunement healing is based.

The healing activity found in any triune relatedness was first advocated by Shears, Ackerley and Uranda in 1952, when they opened the G.P.C. (God-Patient-Chiropractor) Servers Training School on Sunrise Ranch, in Loveland, Colorado. G.P.C. agreement was first represented by the following linear, pyramid-shaped diagram:

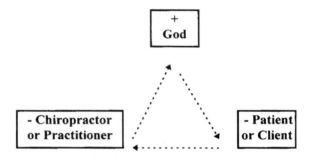

This diagram portrays the Chiropractor in an intercessory position, receiving the response from the client, and returning it to God for the client. Attunement energy was first demonstrated to work this way by its pioneers, but over the years this flow cycle has changed to reveal a freer movement of energy between all concerned. What is shared today in the G-P-C (God-Practitioner-Client) pattern of agreement is an identical response pattern which comes from the two people participating in the healing outcome (the practitioner and client). Both the client and practitioner take on negative or responsive roles in relation to the positive action of spirit, and both share responsibility in maintaining a still and receptive position in relation to Source. The Practitioner still acts as intercessor for the client, and works to clear away dissonant energy patterns in the client, but the client now gives his response directly to Source. Both parties remain open to spirit and are interested to let the new earth or new vibrational and physical pattern appear in its own natural healing cycles. That relatedness may be represented in the following diagram:

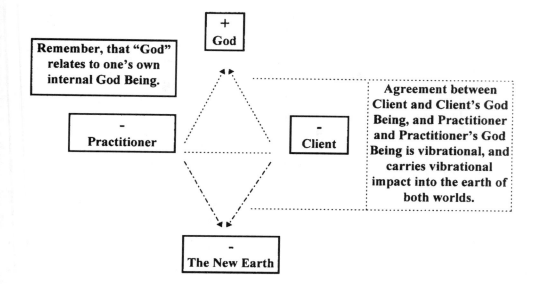

In this second diagram, notice that the client, practitioner and new earth positions have all taken on negative response demarcations (-).

Considering the powerful ramifications of this new kind of relatedness shared between clients and practitioners, let us undertake a more in-depth discussion of the points presented above. Take for example an agreement that you make with someone to begin a project together. When you begin this project, your dialogue usually accounts for a lot of your shared time and energy. The mental and emotional capacities of all parties engaged in agreement dialogue are actively employed. Attunement views this activated substance of agreement as powerful matter, responsive points which spirit utilizes to create physical form. The substance of agreement is the very energy employed in building any form. In fact, they are one and the same substance. Uranda describes the activated substance of agreement as a creative field by stating:

> *The first evidence of the fact of a creative field primarily does just that: it begins to adjust that which is harmonious to the currents involved, bringing it into the manifestation of a pattern harmonious to the points of polarity... after the initial phases have been completed, so that there is really a channel of operation and the polarities are maintained and the understanding of truth with respect to the current of divine love is cleared, it properly moves into what we may rightly call a creative sphere of activity which is bringing forth into manifestation those things that are of the divine pattern.*[1]

Uranda speaks of the divine pattern of earthly substance taking shape around the pattern of agreement which was first established. The First Law of Thermodynamics states that energy cannot be created or destroyed, it simply changes form. So too with all things in the physical realm—the same energy housed within form was the very energy used to create the form, only now it resides in a physical manifestation of the original invisible energy. Your vibrational agreement sets the tone, imbues the atmosphere, creates the spirit of the place. These not-so visible components are every bit as real and as tangible as those you can see with the naked eye. I am sure you can recall walking into a room where an argument just took place and feeling as though there was tension in the air. A lot of tension can destroy a home, or tension between personnel can destroy a business, long before either goes up for sale. The person who places a bomb had the destructive thought to cause damage long before the match was ever lit. As Candace Pert, PhD stated earlier, "Consciousness Precedes Matter."

We may understand then that the earth, or the visible aspect of any creation, bears resemblance to the invisible factors of agreement which went into making up the form, as the form is simply the outer manifestation of its internal invisible structure. Spiritual agreement may therefore be seen as a vibrational, invisible framework, lines of force through which the power of creation moves. This very creative activity is the hallmark of every attunement relationship, establishing agreement with God in the heavenly realm, so that a new, healthy earth may manifest in season.

Creative Triangle Exercises

Cognizant that vibrational lines of force serve to establish agreement between positive and negative points (Mind, Heart, God Being) or persons (God, Client, Practitioner), you are now invited to have some fun with the creative triangles present in your life by filling in the following blank diagrams. When these exercises are completed, you can repeat them on any blank piece of paper.

Creative Triangle No. 1

> *On the next page is an unmarked creative triangle. Fill in this triangle in the following manner: first, fill in the names of those persons (yourself included) who are working together on a creative project, relationship or purpose. You may also choose to fill in your own aspects of Mind and Heart.*

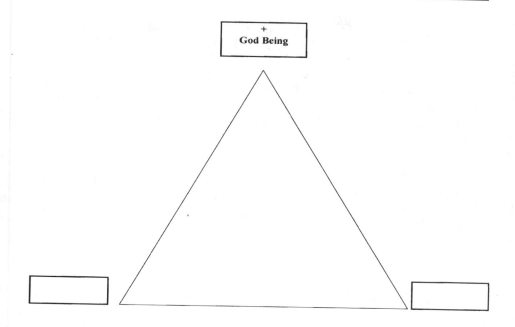

Then, within the vibrational body of the creative triangle, fill in those qualities of positive expression and attitudes of love — thankfulness, blessing, compassion, tranquility, forgiveness, etc. — that you would like to see expressed by all participants to let appear a light-filled finished form to your agreement. After filling in this triangle, try creating your own with other qualities, projects, people and places in your world.

After you are finished, consider those qualities of expression you entered and answer these questions:

- Are these positive life essences active within you now?

- How may you release these essences more fully?

- Is something blocking these essences from being released within you or another?

- Do you need to forgive anyone or anything from past experience?

- Can you think of anything else to add to this creative triangle which is not listed?

Add these elements now.

- Linger a day or two with your list and add qualities as they come to mind. Share your triangle with those people you listed and see if they can come up with additional life essences which you didn't mention.

Discuss how to empower your group with a strengthened positive agreement, discarding those qualities of expression which you mutually see are blocking the flow of spirit through your project.

- Release yourself more fully into the life process by consciously expressing the essences you listed. Utilize sanctification and/or radiant energy technique to let your release be fully complete.

Creative Triangle No. 2

In the second triangle exercise, notice that the lines of agreement from the triangle above extend below the pyramid base, demonstrating the full dimension of the vibrational field forming the new earth.

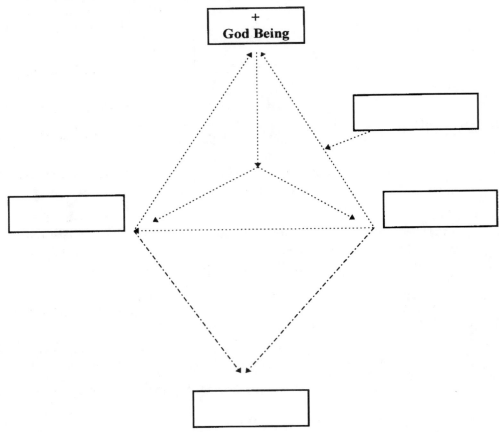

Again, fill in the names of those people who are your agreement partners (in negative, responsive positions), and also fill in the name of the New Earth project or form you are all seeking to create. You

may simply wish to fill in "Body, Mind and Heart" in the base positions if you wish to clarify those aspects of spirit through which you express yourself. If the triangle portrays a group venture, have the entire group fill in the triangle together.

List radiant life qualities which should go into the vibrational body of your project. These may include serenity, joy, humility, honor and respect. Next, inside the lower triangle, place those qualities of life you wish to experience by reason of the essences you listed above. These might include prosperity, contentment, success, creative fulfillment, and assurance. What you are doing is creating an out-picturing of the factors of truth present within your consciousness or the consciousness of the collective. Out-picturing your truths allows you to reflect, alter and add to them, distilling and expanding your conscious understanding of them. This exercise lets you view your own inner workings so that you may adjust and enhance your creative energies.

Finally, after filling in the second triangle exercise, answer the following questions:

- What has just transpired by reason of your work (together)?

- Has each participant initiated an attunement flow within themselves and between each other?

- Does anyone have further life essences or life experiences they wish to add?

- Can you think of another triangle you want to create and fill in? If so, simply create your own triangle on any blank piece of paper and fill in the same blanks which you've practiced here. When you create your own triangles, begin by considering the following but don't let these ideas limit you. The world of creative triangles awaits you!

  - Create a triangle just for yourself, to still your mind and heart and bring these capacities into alignment with spirit.

  - Create a family 'creative triangle get-together' to set a new atmosphere in the house.

  - Create a work triangle with your group project members at work in order to resonate together with specific life essences and experiences.

  - Throw an attunement party and offer these triangle exercises as private or group games. Create your own for a fun and fulfilling time.

Chapter 8 Notes

[1] Uranda, 'Stability and Agreement in a Creative Field,' an extemporaneous worship service given September 20, 1946, as quoted in *The Capstone, A Global Attunement Newsletter*, Issue 2, February, 1994.

9. Manifestation

I left naturopathic medical school when I was nearing completion of the second term of the first year. At the time of my departure, I felt exhausted and stressed out with no personal space to process my life. I also felt completely disillusioned about why I had entered the medical profession in the first place. With high hopes to learn the secrets of natural healing, my expectations were shot down within weeks of my entry into the Naturopathic Doctoral program at Bastyr University when I discovered that the core focus of the work in that first year was on the nature of disease, and not health. I knew that this was a false premise but I couldn't change the system, even though I tried. Trying to change the system was what sent me out of the ND program.[1]

When I left this school, my life moved into a void space, empty of meaning and purpose. I took odd jobs to make ends meet, not knowing where I was headed. In order to find my new path, I started attending Unity Church, and then signed up to take a Prosperity Class, hoping that this course would give me the tools I needed to get a grip on my life's purpose.

The class literally changed my life. Within the course of twelve weeks I allowed spirit to transform my consciousness from one of lack to one of prosperity. For weeks on end, I wrote and re-wrote pages which described what I wanted to be like and what I wanted to achieve in my near and far future. I re-wrote myself — who I was and who I wanted to be. Based on the universal principles of prosperity, my work with this course freed up my consciousness from one of deficiency and failure to one of humility and attunement with my inner longings.

While taking the course I got a job as a part-time telemarketer for a singles club (I wasn't married but wanted to be). One morning I answered the phone for one of the phone-in callers and within two minutes I knew that the man on the other end of the phone line was meant to be a special person in my life. I ended up marrying this man. He possessed every single quality I had been working to manifest in a partner.

Six weeks after I met my husband-to-be, I moved into a brand new house which he had designed. The house contained its own healing arts center and was situated on a peaceful 4.5 acre wooded lot on the Kitsap Peninsula. Finally free from city life, I began a loving partnership with the man of my dreams, away from crowded streets, smog and rush hour traffic.

I remember the day I moved to my new home. My husband (then boyfriend) loaded most of my things onto his truck, and drove the truck from Seattle, where I had been living, to Kitsap County, across the Narrows Bridge. I had taken my car earlier in the day and was waiting for him to arrive. When he came, he informed me that while he was driving across the bridge, a strong wind had blown the lid off one of my boxes and lots of papers had blown out, across the water, never to be seen again.

When I searched through my boxes I found the one without a lid and realized what I had lost. I then broke out into outrageous laughter. The papers which had blown away were my prosperity manifestation papers — all the work I had done to manifest my present environment. And no other papers were missing, only those. Now they were serving as fodder for water waste. This seemed like a message from Source which informed me that I no longer needed the papers to realize my dreams — I was living them now. My agreement with Source pertaining to what I wanted to achieve and who I wanted to be was just beginning. I was now at the start of living my dream, and in a specific way, beginning to fulfill the purposes for which I had come on earth.

Principles of Manifestation

You begin to spend your whole time, where you are,
in giving thanks that an abundance of the material supply
is already provided and is already flowing freely
in loving service to all mankind.

—*Uranda*

Sometimes life gives you something that you think you don't want. Sometimes you create a situation for yourself that you think you don't need. You've heard the adage, "When life hands you a lemon, make lemonade?" Well, attunement philosophy advocates that what you create is based on the quality of character you are expressing. In order to change the circumstances of your life, you need to address and change the quality of the agreement you carry between your heart, mind and spirit. When heart and mind are clear of the past, open to the present moment, and allowing the movement of spirit through them, you will then see your desired changes begin to manifest.

Remember that form follows function, that consciousness precedes matter. It is the quality of your concentration and intention during the transition between yourself now and yourself as you want to be that is the prime motive behind any manifestation you create. Also realize that it takes time for the qualitative substance behind all creative endeavors to make its appearance.

As with most endeavors, you must follow the path of re-creation by agreeing to take the specific steps which life will show you. If you skip a step because it doesn't look as attractive as you'd like, then watch out! You will probably miss out on the biggest opportunity of your life. Uranda speaks on this point by saying "Each stepping stone should be joyously welcomed as an opportunity to prove one's strength in Oneness with the Father."[2] I almost refused the part-time telemarketing job because I thought that I didn't want to work in that environment. But see how spirit opened me to accept this position: I took the job because I liked my boss. I sensed something inside of her which was attractive to work with, and which inspired me. I ended up developing a close friendship with my boss, and also developed specific sales skills which I utilize to this day in my own business. Becoming a telemarketer was an excellent practice in asserting myself without violating my own integrity. I was hired into this position, with no previous sales skills (that was a trust piece given to me by my boss), and ended up grossing the highest pay in one month of any of my telemarketing peers. If I had skipped that step because of my initial feelings (repeat with a whine: "I can't do this job — I don't have the skills!") then I never would have developed the sales backbone which I now have, nor would I have met my husband at that time. The point to manifesting things in your life is to develop a spiritual sense about what kind of opportunities life presents you, and then take those steps no matter how it feels at first. Showing a little initiative in the face of newness always meets with success.

By taking each step along your manifestation path, you will begin to see the development of a divine plan which carries divine attributes, relationships and the spirit of fulfillment. Manifesting your dream requires that you generate spiritual substance which is a new kind of morphogenetic field, a new kind of information system that is based upon your agreement with spirit and which brings to you more information about yourself than you previously had. Most people want their dream but don't want to do the internal work to let it appear. But that isn't the way life works. Life only creates things based on the *truth of being*. Become yourself in truth, align yourself with the purposes of inner God Being, and watch your dream unfold itself right before your eyes.

Manifestation Guidelines

Where there is no vision, the people perish.

—Uranda

Follow these simple guidelines to manifest your dreams and destiny.

1. Follow the *Entering In* and *Inner Healing Meditation* guidelines found in Chapters 3 and 7. Give thanks in all things and do all things realizing that the Father within is doing the work. Once your identity in God being is consistently established and you are beginning to sense the robe of radiance around you, then spirit will begin to recreate your life.

2. Express intense desire and love for that which you want to create.

3. Focus your concentration on your desire. Be specific. Write it down. Post notes all around your house, at work, at school, in the car pertaining to the exact things which you want to manifest in your life. Read them many times each day to instill their presence in your subconscious. This step is similar to what other spiritual leaders have called 'treasure mapping.' If you think you want a new car, write the specific name and model: "A new 1998 Mercury Cougar, red, with grey interior, etc." but add this piece, *"or something better."* That little ending phrase is very important! You may be limiting your dream by consciously connecting to something less than you deserve.

4. Maintain flexibility while you are in transition so that you may receive what is truly in your heart. Sometimes what you think you may want is not really so. Begin by experimenting and being open to discover what it is you truly want. If you are unsure about what you want, then post "clarification as to life purpose, employment," etc. (fill in the appropriate item).

5. As your dream begins to clarify, visualize with detail your finished goal, be it a new product, project, lifestyle, job or love life. Perfect visualization creates perfect manifestation. Write all this down too. Cut a picture of your dream out of a magazine, and post it in a conspicuous place.

6. As your process begins to find completion, you can practice becoming your goal. Identify with it. Walk around your house, neighborhood, shopping center, with a feeling that it is already present. *Become* your

finished product and know what it means to have this realized dream in your life.

7. Give thanks for your goal's appearance prior to its emergence. Thankfulness multiplies your prosperity manifold times.

8. Deny any lack which you see in your mind and heart or which comes to you via friends and family. Others will not carry your dream the way you do, and they won't see the vision that you carry. Don't expect them to. Deny any lack and replace it immediately with your own affirmation that your prosperity is now present with you. Expressing any attitude of blame, condemnation of others or self, accusation or criticism impedes your progress. Express only attitudes of joy, happiness and thankfulness that your dream is now present.

9. Your right doing will make your faith stronger. Faithful action acts upon faith like a catalyst, planting seeds of personal trust and well-being in your consciousness. Self-respect feeds self-esteem with praise.

10. When your dream appears, give thanks for it and recognize the differences you see in yourself. Usually when your dream manifests itself, you have become a different person. That is the whole purpose of this exercise — to change yourself by changing the nature of what is in your life. Take a few minutes to record how your manifestation has changed you and how the new form has filled your life with new meaning and purpose.[3]

The Paper Dot Exercise

The Paper Dot Exercise is a long-distance attunement practice whereby you may bring balance, clarification and attunement to your world. By clarifying circumstances, relationships and your own inner environment, you will change the nature of the etheric bodies associated with these things, and thereby open the way for spirit to move through them with power and light. Do the Paper Dot Exercise on a weekly basis to help your manifestation practice unfold with ease.

> *Begin by placing a dot (or any other symbol most fitting) in the center of a blank piece of paper. The paper should be white and without lines. Make the dot or symbol big enough to see and to recognize as your own. This dot represents you. Place your name underneath the representative symbol.*
>
> *Next, begin filling up the page with other dots and symbols representing those people, places and situations in your world with which*

you have emotional, spiritual and creative ties. These will be family members, neighbors, job situations, pets, personal and professional relationships, legal or medical associations, projects you are working on, future travel dates, etc. Place the symbols which represent those with whom you share the closest ties nearest to your own symbol. More distant associations should be placed further afield from where your own symbol is located. The process of filling in this page should take about ten minutes.

When you fill in this page, you will notice that those situations and relationships in your life which are not clear on a vibrational and/or emotional level will surface in your consciousness. This is an important event. Mentally record these situations and relationships for the next step in the exercise. Examples of such situations are: your upcoming dental appointment, visiting a friend or loved one in the hospital, that meeting with your boss next week which has you feeling sweaty under the collar, or the fight you had with your landlady the other day.

After filling in all the dots and/or symbols, take your piece of paper and place it on your lap. Settle yourself into a long distance attunement mode and begin to share long distance attunement with the situations and relationships which bothered you, sending a current of loving trust into each situation as it arises in your consciousness. Bring them to mind with love, calming the waters inside of yourself, and forgiving each person (yourself included). Let the current of love which you send each one open the right doors for resolution. This part of the exercise should last another 5 – 10 minutes.

Don't let your mind wander. If it does, pull it back to you and to the attunement at hand. Stay focused on each person and situation with the same care that you would want to receive. You will notice a warm feeling of peace come over you while you clarify those on your paper dot exercise paper.

You may want to keep a journal or note paper nearby because you may remember things as you work. Oftentimes when I share an attunement with my paper dot partners, I remember that I need to call someone or go somewhere pertaining to the very situation to which I am attuning. This is spirit's way of connecting you more closely with that situation. That phone call you feel you need to make to your neighbor may be the very thing to open the door for spirit's right action in the situation. During love radiation times, attunement energy will bring to mind that which you need to know, be it deep healing or mundane shopping items.

If you feel fear or dread when offering attunement to one of the people or situations on your paper, then step back from the exercise, let go, and gently try to offer something of goodness to yourself and then to them. Empower your own spiritual landscape first, and then offer this out to them. Don't move out beyond your natural limit, and don't push yourself to do anything that feels unnatural to you. This exercise is not intended to be a hardship to complete, but a joyful communion with those situations and people in your world, with whom you are naturally compelled to be with in loving attunement. If ill feelings continue to rise up in consciousness, try sharing attunement with someone else on your page with whom you feel especially attuned. Utilize that communed relationship as a contact point into the situation where you were having difficulty. And if it doesn't work the first time, then come back to this situation on another date. Love will only move into those situations where there is an opening. Let it all come naturally.

I've called this exercise 'Spiritual Chiropractic' because you will notice subtle shifts in energy moving through your life following completion of this exercise. I've often received phone calls the next day from people to whom I've sent loving energy, who verbally forgive me, or call just to say "Hi," seemingly 'out of the blue.' The Paper Dot Exercise works with amazing accuracy and always brings creative outcome. It is impossible to flunk out on this exercise. Practicing is doing. Happy Paper Dotting!

Chapter 9 Notes

[1] My description of the first year ND program at Bastyr University may be colored by the state of my consciousness at the time.

[2] Uranda, Letters to You, p. 6.

[3] Besides my own instructions, I have incorporated some ideas found in Rev. Stretton Smith's '4T Prosperity Program,' (Unity Church offers this program), and also Uranda, 'Instantaneous Manifestation,' *Third Sacred School*, (Loveland: Eden Valley Press, 1933), Chapter 6, p. 32.

THE PAPER DOT EXERCISE

(Spiritual Chiropractic)

Date: ___/___/___

Part Two

Visible Form

*The force that is at work through attunements
is not mysterious or difficult to understand.
It is not a figment of fancy, because it can definitely be felt
by those who have trained perception
and by those with a natural perception of the working
of the life force. It is not necessary that the individual
be able to feel physically the working of this force in order
for it to be effective in relation to himself.*

*The Server [practitioner] does not at any time,
under any circumstance, attempt to treat,
or heal, the servee [client].
All healing comes from God.*

—Uranda

10. The Cervical Pattern

In 1984, I attended a 'Spiritual Leadership' class at a retreat site in British Columbia, Canada. The three week class was the second of three in the 'Art of Living' series conducted by the Emissaries, and was attended by 26 students from around the world. A 24 hour immersion in attunement cosmology and leadership principles, students spent mornings in the class room and afternoons in the garden, helping with the community's harvest.

This class was intended as a training ground for future attunement practitioners and spiritual leaders, and at that time, this purpose didn't suit my life goals. I basically didn't know what I wanted to be or do. I had no ambitions aside from making my rent and expressing myself through music composition and massage therapy. My consciousness was packed with a lot of unresolved family-of-origin issues which hindered my learning during this class cycle. Many times I interrupted the instructors with self-centered questions, I was mentally self-active, and basically bucked the new vibrational pattern seeking emergence into my life. I was a troublemaker, and learned most of my lessons the hard way.

Towards the end of the class I had an 'accident.' I slipped on some water while putting away canning jars in the kitchen. My feet flew out from under me, and I hit my head hard on the floor. All around me and on top of me were slivers of shattered glass as all of the mason jars had broken into little pieces. The kitchen supervisor walked immediately to my side and put her hands in an attunement pose at the site of my cervicals (vertebrae at the base of the neck). She held the vibrational pattern in my spinal column from that point until I got up, which was about 20 minutes (as long as it took for others to remove all the glass from on top of me and around me). During this cervical pattern attunement, I felt completely encompassed by love. When I stood up, we were both astonished to see that I hadn't received a single scratch from any of the glass and there was only a small bump on my head where I had fallen. I was invited to take the rest of the afternoon off, so I showered and got into bed. An attunement practitioner arrived a short time later to share a full body attunement with me. Even though it was quite a fall, I experienced no physically-based problems as a result, probably due to the attunement energy I received immediately afterwards.

I viewed this incident as a purposeful 'wake-up call' from life. In a few days I was going to be leaving this class, and had felt as though it had been a big waste of my time. Internally, I had felt as though I had received nothing extraordinary, nor had I experienced any major changes in consciousness even though my class mates reported vast changes. This fall shook me out of my self-centered behavior. Something deep within me was released by the blow to my head, and this new presence showed itself to me in dramatic ways later on. I didn't know it then, but that fall was a turning point for me in my life, not merely during the class.

While alone in my room, I began to wonder why this had happened to me. Why had I fallen and not been hurt? What was it life was seeking to do with me? I began to reflect on my class experience up to that point, and started listening to a different part of me that I had never heard before. This voice commanded my attention because finally I was in a place all alone and open to hearing what it had to say to me. Before that, I was full up with my own verbiage and denials. It was challenging for me to stay in bed and rest during this time alone, but I laid down, intrigued with the still small voice speaking to me through the silence. I recognized this voice as a part of me that I had squelched in all of my self-activity but it now had space and time to let me know of its presence. I soon drifted off to sleep, responsive to my new-found awareness.

The rest of the class cycle unfolded much less eventfully until the final class session. During the fourth hour class, I remember feeling very anxious and frustrated with myself. Whatever *it* was that I was supposed to have gotten, I hadn't gotten it from this class. I was expected by my peers and teachers to go through a change in consciousness and I hadn't done that (so I thought at the time). All I felt was an internal pressure which I interpreted as self-recrimination. I sat wiggling in my seat and interrupted the speaker again during the final hour, and then found I had nothing to say.

Soon after my interruption, I experienced a very strange sensation, quite unlike anything I had ever experienced before. I felt as if I were leaving my body, ascending through my cervical pattern in the back of the neck. Scared to death that I was going to die right then and there and make another terrible scene in front of all the people, I clamped onto the arm rests of my chair so that this part of me which was ascending wouldn't leave my body. I completely ignored the topic being discussed in front of me, and became preoccupied with my physical experience. Needless to say, I missed the entire point of this final session, and while the other students were hugging and congratulating themselves on a job well done, I rushed to my attunement instructor and shaking, whispered in his ear, "I think I'm leaving my body." When he looked at me in disbelief, I continued, "No, really, it's happening now and I can't stop it." He took my arm and escorted me to an attunement room, and without saying anything, stood and held me in his arms for what seemed like twenty minutes while I shook. I remember that holding him there, in the stillness of the attunement room, was the quietest space I had entered during the entire class cycle.

For several weeks following that class I couldn't sleep at night. I knew 'demons at my door,' in the sense that it seemed like every evil thought that I had ever entertained stood at the foot of my bed and demanded me to pay attention to it, to love it, to worship evil. I knew that whatever was going on, I had to deal with it and not become responsive to these demons. I stayed awake at night and slept fitfully during the day. I couldn't work and don't remember how I got by financially. It seemed to me that all the evils of the world wanted to live in my consciousness. Like biblical Job, they invited me to 'curse God and die,' and I knew that if I agreed with those demons, a big part of me would die and I would be lost in the wilderness of spiritual darkness.

From what little I had learned during the class, I knew that my job during this time was to hold the vibrational pattern steady in my mind and heart, no matter what came up in my consciousness. This was a vigil, a test time for me to prove to God that I was present. I hadn't consciously participated in the class, so now was my time to prove myself. And since the purpose of spiritual leadership and world attunement included acting as intercessor for others on the planet, I sensed that I was meeting demons in my mind and heart for many other people besides myself during this time. To give myself some light relief from the intense process, I made popcorn and watched old movies while I repeated to the demons on a continual basis, "you are not true and have no place in me."

I felt that my action during this time was critical to my spiritual awakening. To help me to maintain stillness in heart and mind, I shared what was going on with several attunement servers in my area, and they all were sharing local and long distance attunement with me. We sensed that the fall I had experienced during class and the ascending process I was continuing to experience, were all part of my own spiritual awakening. In a particular way, this included receiving vibrational dissonance patterns from other people at this time. With the consciousness raising tools I had learned in class (apparently I had received more information than I thought), I was now given the opportunity to clarify some of the world's vibrational distortion patterns just by holding them in me and letting them transform through my consistent identification with Source. If there was any lesson I had learned from my class time, this was it — the doing of it, not just the theory. I didn't know if any of my classmates were experiencing the same intense experience, but it felt as if I had taken on the entire world inside of me.

These were very profound weeks for me, and I constantly extended myself through vigilant wakefulness and commitment not to give into negative power. This intercessory work meant more to me than anything else. I remember feeling as if I was being given a special opportunity to prove myself in the attunement process, and this felt like my entire life purpose during that time.

After about a month, the pattern cleared and I decided to get a better paying job in order to save some money for the final World Service Class to be offered nine months later.

Entrainment

He who becomes upset by a condition lends his capacities
to maintaining the condition which disturbs.

—*Uranda*

Entrainment is a term used by physicists to explain the energetic interlocking of two rhythms which have similar frequency rates. Leading scientific thinkers hold the view that the process of entraining biological systems through energy methods can happen through external manipulation or through internally resonant biological systems. An example of an internal entrainment rhythm is when women who live together in dormitories move into a synchronistic cycle of menstruation. An external rhythm occurs when, for example, clocks attached to the same wall and with the same pendulum length eventually come to swing with exact synchronicity.[1]

Human beings operate with an entrainment mechanism much the same as other biological systems. Recent scientific research has revealed that the thalamus portion of the brain acts as a thalamic rhythm generator or pacemaker, which produces a two part brainwave oscillation pattern. In the first part, calcium ions leak into neurotransmitters present in the thalamus every 1.5 – 2.8 seconds which trigger brainwave oscillations that spread throughout the brain and nervous system. In the second silent phase of the pattern, calcium ions build up to excess, thus stopping the oscillation. This part of the process lasts 5 – 25 seconds after the calcium ions have built up. During the silent phase of the process, brainwaves are susceptible to entrainment by external fields (earth and atmospheric energies as well as energy from healers' hands), and are said to 'free-run'.[2] This two part rhythmic brainwave pattern is said to regulate the entire activity and sensitivity of the nervous system, and also set the speed of responsiveness to stimulation by the nervous system. This responsive state can be viewed as a leading parameter in determining individual health.

Looking at the entrainment process, we may see that human beings are born with an innate ability to regulate the wave patternings generated by the brain. However, this inner directing system may be limited or stressed when presented with misalignment in consciousness and other external stresses. By applying external therapies such as Qi Gong, Therapeutic Touch, Healing Touch, Cranial-Sacral Therapy and Attunement Therapy to specific nervous system sites, these energy techniques may have a therapeutically organizing affect on the nervous system, and creatively influence the entrainment process. Attunement Therapy, when applied to the cervical and brain regions of the body, will creatively affect the thalamic generator system by bringing into balance and holding the energies associated with the longer, silent phase brainwave pattern. (More about how brain entrainment may therapeutically affect injuries and trauma can be found in *Chapter 17*.)

Viewing the process of entrainment from a larger perspective, we can see ramifications which may not be to our benefit. Examples of negative energy which impose their frequency upon us and which may alter our natural brainwave pattern through outside entrainment intervention include and may not be limited to: electric current found in high frequency wires, microwave energy and the electromagnetic energy which comes from earthquakes. Additionally, our society seems to be entraining itself to a faster-paced rhythm than is found in the natural world, and this may have negative consequences for our civilization as a whole. Author Stephan Rechtschaffen writes:

> ...*we no longer entrain to the sounds of birds, the wind in the trees, the waves on the shore. Today, instead, we move to the rhythms of computers, beepers and sirens. We complain that our computers do*

not boot up fast enough. We sit anxiously at the fax machine. We want everything to happen instantaneously.[3]

It may benefit us in today's accelerating world to attune to what is naturally present within us by sharing in energy medicine techniques which increase our inner harmony.

Balancing the Cervical Pattern

When you come to be sensibly touched,
the scales will fall from your eyes;
and by the penetrating eyes of love
you will discern that which your other eyes will never see.

—*Unknown Origin*

Full body attunement technique begins with a cervical balancing procedure which is a form of energy work that entrains the brain and central nervous system, and results in an overall relaxation effect. Cervical balancing attunement requires that the practitioner place his hands in a 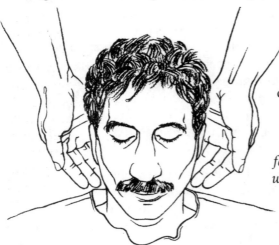 slightly cupped position, the fingers of each hand placed together, with no spaces between. This position is similar to that used during radiant energy and long distance attunement sessions. Eastern Sanskrit calls this position *anjali*, and *"refers to a worshipful gesture in which the hands are held side by side, with palms up, slightly cupped and filled with offerings."*[4] For cervical balancing, the hands are placed on either side of the client's neck, about one to two inches away from the skin, with fingers pointing down into the spine region of the back. The position and shape of the hands used during cervical balancing may symbolize for the practitioner that he is offering up the client's life force and the healing outcome of the session to Source.

An attunement practitioner will place his hands on either side of the client's neck as described below in the section entitled *The Cervical Pattern Exercise.* Give attention to the exact location of the hands in relation to the neck and ears in order to 'pick up' or sense the energy pattern in the cervical vertebrae, located at the top of the spine. Hands placed too high or too low may touch into other energy systems associated with other body parts not related to the cervical pattern, such as the temporo-mandibular joint, vagus nerve or carotid artery. The client may also wish to extend a blessing to her world by placing her hands at her sides in an anjali position, and consciously extend a blessing to the people and situations which come to mind during her attunement session.

When you balance the cervical vertebrae, you touch into and bring into harmony the energy which is moving through the entire spinal column and which finds a focus in the back of the neck. At this location, all of the cranial nerves cross and separate themselves into specific groups which then run throughout the rest of the body. By placing your hands at the base of the neck for cervical balancing, you will bring about a full body relaxation response in your client, and also initiate a meditation state if offered with silence.

Rising up to Reawaken

As you can gather from the story presented above, something happened within my cervical pattern when I didn't want to move with inner wisdom for a while. I have seen this process occur in others as well and will describe it more fully now. When someone begins to consciously move with inner wisdom (wakes up), and then changes one's response pattern to disobey, want or strive (falls to sleep again), one may feel a specific 'rising up' sensation in the back of the neck which feels like one is going to leave one's body. Inner stress may also bring on a rising up sensation, especially if one is denying one's integrity, or is not willing to listen to the voice of inner wisdom when making conscious choices. This 'rising up to reawaken' pattern is one way spirit has of saying to you, "Choose ye this day whom ye will serve." Uranda speaks on this point:

> He who begins to respond to the love center of the Triune Ray [the radiant aspect of inner Source] and then, because of the unwise desires of the outer mind, steels himself against the love force, so that he refuses to respond to it after its action has already started within himself...[brings] so-called tragedy into expression of the individual.[5]

The tragedy that Uranda speaks of here relates directly to the degree of reaction which the person expressed and the degree of response which the person experienced before reacting. In other words, if you are strongly compelled to respond to your love center, and do so for a time, and then leave this practice to react to your environment or body temple in a similarly strong way, Uranda suggests that you may draw to yourself a situation with negative consequence to re-awaken you to your love center. One such situation (with far less negative consequence than some others) is to remind you about your love centering by sending a rising up sensation in the back of the neck. If you experience this sensation after following the attunement program for a time, this may be a signal to you, from your inner guide, a reminder to you to respond to your inner love Source before doing anything else. Failure to comply to this gentle nudge may facilitate the coming of further challenges for you to face to assist you in the reawakening process.

Cervical Pattern Attunement Practice

Begin with your client lying supine (on her back) on a massage table or in a similar setting. Seat yourself at the head of your client, and place your hands in an anjali position on either side of your client's head, situated at the base of the neck. Your hands should be one – two inches from the skin and should be situated around the hollow behind the ears. Fingers of the hand (other than the thumb) should be pointing slightly down, so that the finger tips touch into the spinal energy flow. The shoulders, arms and wrists should be relaxed, and the practitioner should place his hands on the chair or massage table, to achieve a fully relaxed position. The practitioner will feel a distinct difference in his offering if his hands, arms and shoulders are held tight, i.e. the practitioner will feel a tension pattern through his hands instead of the relaxed pulse pattern which is sought.

When you first touch into your client's cervical pattern you may feel several different sensations. What to do with each of these sensations is covered in the following:

- *I feel more energy in one of my hands than the other:* This is a very common experience for attunement practitioners, even those who are quite experienced. What you are sensing here is an unbalanced energy pattern in the cervical vertebrae. All you have to do to bring this energy pattern into balance is to hold the pattern. You should not sweep, jostle or move your hands in any fashion. The hallmark technique of all attunement work is simply holding a pattern until the pattern shifts. This should take a few minutes.

- *I feel tingles, pressure or heat on one or both of my hands:* You are sensing a distortion or dissonant pattern in the nervous system. You don't need to figure out where it is localized — let spirit do that. You do not need to sweep away the heat. Again, all you need to do is hold the cervical pattern until this dissonance dissipates, which it should do after a few minutes.

- *I feel a single pulse moving through my hands:* Good! This means that your cervical balancing is complete and you may move onto the next phase of the attunement session (which is opening the endocrine glands). All attunement practitioners seek this one clear pulse sensation moving through their hands at the cervicals and at other locations on the body. Receiving a pulse signals that the area is energetically clear and balanced.

Atlas Balancing

For a related technique, try atlas balancing as a beginning point to all of your attunement work. During this procedure, you entrain the brainwave oscillations by applying attunement energy directly to the atlas of the Vertebrae (the atlas is the top-most vertebra on the spine, and holds up the head or skeletal cranium). Tom Fallon, an experienced attunement practitioner and historian explains Uranda's ideas regarding sharing attunement with the cervical pattern and the atlas:

> *The hollow behind the ears relates to the atlas. It is a centering point for the hands of the practitioner to be right on the mark. The atlas acts as a brake. When the body is sick, the life current is slowed down by the atlas and it is here that control of the energy pattern in the body may be established during the attunement. Uranda repeatedly stressed the need to hold the energy at the atlas until it was properly balanced.*[6]

To initiate an atlas balancing, again have your client lie supine on a massage table, and place your hands behind her head. Position the middle fingers of each hand softly, in the hollow back portion of each ear, with your thumbs pointing into the skull but not touching it. (When you offer atlas balancing, you gently touch your client's skin.) Atlas balancing should precede cervical balancing. The atlas of the spine may be viewed as the contact point for the cervical attunement, and may be stimulated for a just a minute prior to opening out the hands in the anjali position to proceed with the cervical balancing.

Practice these exercises once a day with yourself or another. It is best to practice with another. Attuning your own cervical pattern may force you to hold your hands and arms in a rigid position, which will block the flow of energy you feel through your hands and bring a muscle cramp into your arms. Cervical self-attunement is discouraged if you experience any of these symptoms.

Balancing the Body through the Feet

Attunement practitioners should also learn how to balance the body through the feet. Balancing the body's energies through the feet brings about a similar relaxation response in your client as that which is offered at the atlas or cervical position.

Place your hands in the anjali position, about one – two inches above the toes, so that the toes of each foot are encompassed by each of your

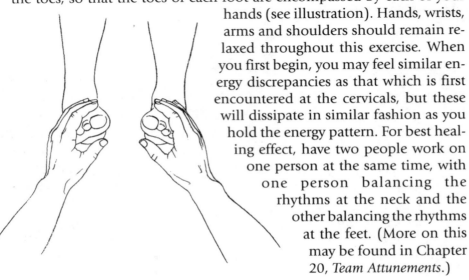

hands (see illustration). Hands, wrists, arms and shoulders should remain relaxed throughout this exercise. When you first begin, you may feel similar energy discrepancies as that which is first encountered at the cervicals, but these will dissipate in similar fashion as you hold the energy pattern. For best healing effect, have two people work on one person at the same time, with one person balancing the rhythms at the neck and the other balancing the rhythms at the feet. (More on this may be found in Chapter 20, *Team Attunements*.)

Chapter 10 Notes

1   Dr James Oschman, 'What is healing energy? Part 3: Silent Pulses,' *Journal of Bodywork and Movement Therapies*, Volume 1, No. 3, April 1997, p.184.

2   Ibid.

3   Stephan Rechtschaffen, 'Time Shifting, How to Pace Your Life to Natural Rhythms,' *Noetic Sciences Review*, Summer, 1997, no. 42, p. 18.

4   Earle Hitchner, track description for The Anjali Quartet, on *Celtic Spirit*, CD (Milwaukee: Narada Media, 1996).

5   Uranda, The Triune Ray, p. 51.

6   Personal correspondence with Tom Fallon of Cape Cod, Massachusetts, Attunement Practitioner and historian.

11. The Spiritual Path of the Endocrine Gland System

Death is a part of life, and sometimes attunement may encourage us to let go, in calm assurance of our immortality.

I once met a man who would not stop moving. He and I met in an AIDS center in a major city where I was beginning a public attunement practice. I was in the center looking over the center's literature, and was hoping to make a connection with the staff. While I read I watched the antics of this man out of the corner of my eye. He paced from one corner of the reading room to the other, swung his arms from side to side, looked aimlessly around, and laughed at himself self-consciously. He was thin and gaunt, like he hadn't eaten a good, nourishing meal in weeks. I immediately felt compassion for him, as I assumed he was a client at the center.

We struck up a conversation and he told me that he was the longest living AIDS survivor in the state — twelve years and counting. He said he had been a featured presenter on the Oprah show, and was a favorite speaker on a national radio talk show when their topic was male prostitution. We spoke for a while and I gave him my business card. A few days later he phoned me and we set up a session.

Before his arrival, I spent my usual time in prayer, preparing the healing space. I consciously prepared the atmosphere with my intention to let trust flow, establishing a connection to Higher Source and also consciously connecting my sensing of spirit to my client. I visualized that whatever needed to happen would do so. Remaining centered, I let go of the edges of the known to face the mystery of the unknown. Candles and soft music set the scene. My faith in God as my power was absolute.

He arrived a short time later, full of vim and vigor, keeping up his constant movements. While taking down his history, he mentioned that he only drank Kool-aid and didn't like the taste of water. I made a mental note to check his kidney pattern for distortion during our session. He bragged that he had never had a secondary opportunistic infection. I wondered about that. Maybe his tenacity and identity with his role as 'the longest living AIDS survivor' was his protecting armor against the unknown. Protection or not, his long standing identity with something other than his true Self was not a healthy behavior pattern. Looking on his face, I spoke the silent prayer, *Be still and know.*

We began the attunement session. As I worked with his endocrine glands, my entire body began to sweat. When I got to his adrenal glands, I felt dizzy and thought that I would pass out from the intensity of the vibrational distortion pattern which I felt there. I didn't know what to do for I had never experienced this kind of distortion before. I felt as if I were moving through uncharted territory, the mystery fully upon me, knowing only to trust in the attunement technique which I had learned, and to trust my instincts which told me to hold the pattern until it cleared. To this day, this man's kidney distortion pattern was the strongest I have ever felt in anyone.

The attunement elicited the usual parasympathetic response in my client. He fell into a meditation state with lapses into sleep and his breathing pattern deepened. He was still and relaxed, maybe for the first time in weeks. I observed peace and a restful repose. I held the pattern at the adrenals for as long as I could, about twenty-five minutes. When I stopped, the pattern had still not cleared, nor had I been able to touch into the energy patterns moving through his other anatomical systems. But our hour's time was coming to a close, and I had another client scheduled.

The man rested quietly for a short time following the attunement. It was the first time I had ever seen him conscious and still. I saw that the energy flow had clarified his etheric body enough to center him, and he seemed to be listening to his inner silence. We spoke in hushed tones for a short time and he left a little later, shaking his head with disbelief. I saw that he had connected with a still place which lay within himself but he was not used to living there. As he left I thought that he would need another attunement session soon to help him maintain this newfound stillness.

Two days later the man called me. He was in the hospital with pneumonia, a secondary opportunistic infection. Something had shifted. He had opened himself to life at another level, and was now listening to himself instead of his super-imposed psycho-babble. This experience influenced his life such that it left him open to disease. He informed me that he had let go, let go of his identity as a survivor and was now open to accepting what his illness was going to bring him. His message to the world now was about receiving and coping with his illness instead of denying his illness. The attunement session had opened a door to heal his spirit while bringing further illness to his body. Such was the course spirit had taken at this time in his life. I never heard from him again.

The Endocrine Gland System

It is only through the action of the Father within,
as radiated through the pineal gland,
that the vibratory rate of the mind aura
is intensified to a degree that allows thought,
self-consciousness and free will.

—*Uranda*

The endocrine gland system of the human body is a system of seven duct-less glands which produce and secrete hormones directly into the blood-stream where they are transported directly to target cells. Endocrine gland hormones cause changes in the metabolic activities of body cells, regu-lating growth, metabolic processes and functional activities of tissues and the vital organs. (More information on the physiology of the endocrine glands may be found in *Appendix A, The Histology of the Endocrine Gland System.*)

Together with the nervous system, the endocrine glands control the entire body through a coordinated and efficient system of interchange and operation. Endocrine secretions tend to act more slowly and have a longer lasting effect than nervous system exchanges, which have faster and shorter response cycles. Their combined importance to healthy physi-cal maintenance cannot be overstated, nor should their potential for heal-ing regeneration in life forms be underestimated. This is why full body attunement technique begins with cervical balancing and then continues immediately with opening the endocrine glands, thereby touching into and stimulating into action the two most important systems of the body. Most attunement practitioners, who are sensitive to the unique and char-acteristic patterns of each gland, can bring about in-depth positive change to the client's entire body system by touching into these vital light centers.

Some energy practitioners and scientists assert that the endocrine gland system and the chakra system are vibrationally connected, or otherwise linked together. Dr William Tiller, PhD, Professor Emeritus from Stanford University, suggests that these two systems act as 'transduced correlate pairs,' and are physically linked at a certain point inside the body.[1] Dr Tiller's theory postulates that these two systems transform physical energy to etheric body energy, and vice-versa, by reason of their interconnected links.

From an attunement perspective, the endocrine glands represent the positive force behind any transduction of energy. As a western practice, attunement views the endocrine glands to be positive in nature and the chakra system to be its negative, or responsive counterpart. The endocrine glands are known as the 'portals of light' for the body. They are of prime importance to the body because of their inherently radiant nature, being situated closer to divine being than the outer chakras. Each gland represents a specific level of spiritual or radiant expression, and each person is invited to identify with these levels of light through their thoughts, words and deeds, thereby shining the light of being through their lives.

The Seven Levels of Spiritual Expression

> *...Each moment of living is a moment of giving...*
> *Our moments add together like the digits of a sum,*
> *and the answer tells us plainly whether life or death will come.*
>
> —*Martin Exeter*

Consider the following chart. Contained on it are seven levels of spiritual expression, each having their own glandular representation, divine correspondence, human expression of a light quality and its opposite.

According to this chart, humans have the choice of expressing a positive, radiant expression in every moment of living, thereby strengthening their levels of spiritual expression and the etheric energy surrounding their glands, or expressing a light-lacking attitude. Most light-lacking attitudes produce an internal sensation of darkness or expression which lacks love in some way, and this can be tangibly felt by oneself and others. As this chart and its spiritual expression program suggests, there are actually no gray areas for human beings to express, in relation to the kind of light they may feel within and express outside of themselves. As Jesus was reported to have said, "He that is not with me is against me; and he that gathereth not with me scattereth abroad." (Matthew 12:30) There is only radiant light expression or dark expression. Personal meditation on these points and the serious ramifications for right expressive action is suggested.

THE SEVEN LEVELS OF SPIRITUAL EXPRESSION

Level	Gland	Divine Spirit or Correspondence	Human Expression	Opposite
Seventh	Pineal	Love	Love	Hate
Sixth	Pituitary	Truth	Wisdom	Lies/Ignorance
Fifth	Thyroid	Life	Radiance	Death/Tarnished
Fourth	Thymus	Purification	Assurance	Defile/Insecurity
Third	Islets of Langerhans	Blessing	Realization	Cursing/Spiritual Blind Spots
Second	Adrenals	Single Eye	Tranquillity	Stress/Dissipation
First	Gonads	New Earth	Patience	Impatience/Infertile ground for creation

You will note on the chart that love is considered the seventh level of spiritual expression. Love is the only light energy which encompasses all the others. This means that all the spiritual substances or energies contained in the other six levels are embraced in the seventh. The expression of love moves through the other levels of expression with ascending power, uplifting all the substance in its path towards its own radiant nature. Love is the transforming power present in the radiant aspect of inner being, and when expressed outwardly, has the power to transmute all things and people whom it touches. This level is associated with the pineal gland, which, according to attunement philosophy, is where the Silver Cord resides — the vibrational connecting link between the divine incarnate being and its earthly form. Uranda speaks of the seventh level of love, saying:

> *Love is the Power of the Wonderful One, and in it is the Creative Essence. Love is the Fire of Fusion whereby the outer self is uplifted into oneness with the Master within. Love cannot be engendered by the outer intellect, and he who seeks the Realms of Light through the self-activity of the intellect is bound to fail... The one Way of*

Love is Love. In doing all that is done in the Radiance of Love, the fullness of Love is experienced and the union of Love known.[2]

In likewise descendant fashion, each of the six levels of expression beneath the seventh level of love encompasses those other levels beneath them. Thus, the sixth level of wisdom encompasses the remaining five levels, and the first level, which is patience, encompasses itself alone.

The key to understanding what spiritual expression means may be found in grasping the difference between expressing the spiritual nature of each glandular correspondence (i.e. love, truth, life, purification, blessing, etc.), or merely understanding with your mind what that experience might be like. For example, if you think you know what it means to be wise, and you think you know what that experience might be like, then you are expressing yourself from the mental plane. If you *are* wise, the true *expression* of wisdom feels different to you than just thinking it so, because you are expressing yourself from the sixth level of spirit. Expressing from the sixth level of spiritual expression means that you are encompassing the other five levels through your attitudes, and you:

- can feel the vibrational energy of the radiant life force,

- have deep faith and feel assured of yourself,

- are aware of Self and the blessings your provide your world,

- are tranquil and at peace, and

- patiently steward your life processes.

The feeling of becoming one with the vibration at the spiritual expression level is a new kind of experience for most people. From our common understanding of spiritual principles, we recognize these qualities of character or see them expressed in other people, but when asked how it feels to express them ourselves, we may fumble for the right answer. We speak of Mother Teresa or Ghandi as extraordinary individuals, carrying saint-like qualities, when in fact they were only expressing themselves from the levels of spiritual expression natural to themselves and all of humanity. Simply being unaccustomed to the new vibrational territory which these levels present need not deter us from seeking resonance with them. We are all potential saints, and need only to enter in, open up and offer out that radiance which we all carry within us at these levels of being in order to reveal our own sainthood.

With reference to the first three glands (pineal, pituitary and thyroid) and their spiritual correspondences (love, truth and life), we can see a singular theme run through Jewish, Christian and attunement teachings having to do with the triune nature of God. First, the Children of Israel referred to their Ark of the Covenant as the Shekeinah, a fire that was not extinguishable. This Shekeinah flame contained three aspects: *the fire that burns, the light that shines and the cloud of glory.* According to the Jewish religion, the love, truth and life of God has been present with man since the beginning of time, and is the central nature of God's word. Similarly, Jesus expressed his own nature as the way, the truth and the life, revealing God's trinity in his teachings. Attunement philosophy also sees that each person contains within themselves this same holy trinity, love, truth and life, and that they may express themselves through these levels of spiritual expression to reveal their own light. Just as the Jewish and Christian religions know God to be a source of light which cannot be extinguished, so too may each one of us reveal our own indwelling source of divine light.

The Path of Spiritual Expression

The physical body is spiritual,
a part of the divine process of spiritual revelation,
so that what is coming down from God out of heaven
may find form in the earth.

—Uranda

You will note in the following chart that the endocrine glands are located in specific areas in the body. Three glands are located in the head region (the seat of consciousness), one is located in the chest region (close to the heart), and the last three are located in the body torso region. Although the spiritual ramifications of these placements are presented in detail later on in this chapter, it suffices to say here that the head region glands carry significantly important light qualities which reside at the upper end of the light spectrum. Through the spiritual expression of these upper level truths, we may reveal the essential nature of God (love, truth and life).

Note the following correlation between the seven levels of spiritual expression and their relating glands:

- The first three glands, the pineal, pituitary and thyroid, represent the spiritual aspects of love, truth and life which are present within each person. This trinity represents the 'heaven' aspect of a person. The heaven of you carries a more rarefied, refined and focused vibrational nature than the earth aspect; consequently the etheric nature of these glands are more subtly felt than the rest.

- The thymus gland represents the 'cross over point' from the 'heaven' into the 'earth' of the person. Located in the central cavity of each person, and close to the heart, the thymus is a powerful vibrational gateway point for purification and a fitting juncture between heavenly and earthly aspects of being.

- The islets of langerhans, adrenals and gonads represent the 'earth' aspect of a person. Respectively, they represent blessing, single mindedness and the new earth, providing proper stewardship over life cycles. For instance, patience, the level of expression associated with the gonads, is a fitting kind of attitude to express for planting and sowing seeds (which is what the gonads do).

- The energy which moves through the seven endocrine glands is similar to a figure eight energy, or lemniscate, "symbol of eternal life and dominion… harmonious interaction of the conscious and subconscious."[3] Note the following illustration of this concept:

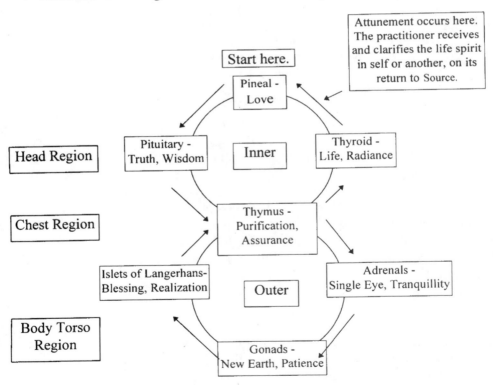

Notice how the circuitry of energy moves through this system: in its original invisible form, the truth of love moves through a process of purification as it moves into visible earth form. Having been purified, tranquil earth substance now brings forth new earth substance. New earth substance blesses outer realms with its presence, carrying the seeds of love sown within its cycle of creation. That which has been blessed ascends once again into life spirit, purified of its earthly form, before becoming one with love. Through this cycle we see the transforming power of love in expression through our lives.

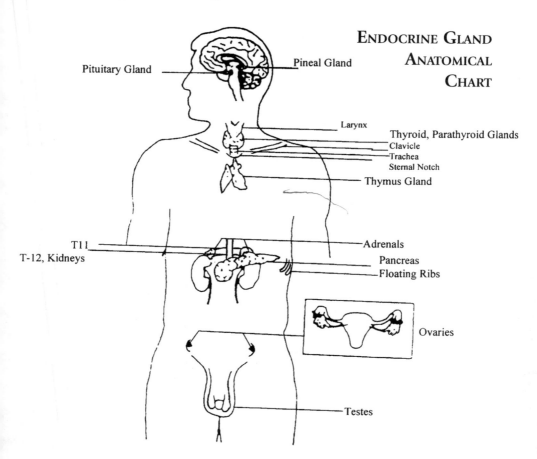

Endocrine Gland Attunement Guidelines

Now we are familiar with the spiritual cosmology associated with the endocrine glands, let me share how to attune the body to these portals of light. Follow these guidelines:

1. Remember that during this and all other attunement work, you will be using both hands at once, and will switch them back and forth, from positive to negative roles. The positive hand will be placed over the

gland being worked with, and the negative hand will be placed over its associated contact point. For this and all other anatomical dialogue, I speak of the right hand as being the positive hand to start. Remember to keep the hands about one to two inches above the body.

2. If you wish to apply more direct energy to each gland, use this technique: Bring your index and third fingers together and point them down towards each gland, keeping your fingers one to two inches above the skin. By drawing together these fingers, you will bring to focus a more powerful energy flow at the site where you are offering attunement.

3. I advise you to study the following endocrine gland diagrams, and/or keep additional gland charts close beside you as you do this work. Consult them as reference frequently. You will also want to watch your fingers as you place them over the glands, to keep them in place. (You will notice that the fingers have a tendency to move away, seemingly by themselves!) Most of the gland placements in the body are small, and very specific.

4. After you begin an endocrine gland attunement, you can use the previous gland that you just attuned as your contact point for the next gland. This means that one hand will stay with the gland you are on, and the other will move to the next gland. For example, when you move to attune the pituitary gland, you will use the pineal gland as your contact point. And when you then move to attune the thyroid gland, you will keep one hand at the pituitary, and use it as the contact point, while you move your other hand to the thyroid (throat) region. (The contact point for the pineal is the left cervical. I address this below.)

5. A word about contact points: these are very important in attunement work, and should not be taken for granted. Remember from your first exercise in radiant energy flow that the key to engaging this flow lay in balancing the electromagnetic energies circulating between your right and left hands. So too with contact points (negative points) and that which you are attuning (positive points). You need to engage the contact point before engaging the positive point, or you will not engage the flow of energy moving through the area. The contact point is the negative, receptive point to the positive, directing energy. Each contact point will begin the clarification process in the body for its corresponding anatomy by stimulating the flow of energy in the area you are attuning. Contact points begin the radiant energy flow in all attunement work.

6. Besides using the previous gland as a contact point, you may also consider using the nervous plexus located at the back of the neck as a

contact point to the pituitary and thyroid glands, and the pituitary gland for the thymus, islets of langerhans, adrenals and gonads. You may also use the thymus as contact point for the three lower glands on the body. Because each ascendant gland in the 7-tiered system contains the energy of the glands beneath it, any gland higher in the system may be used as a contact point for whatever gland you are attuning. That is, except the pineal. You should only use the cervical pattern to touch into the pineal. Experiment with whatever contact point works best for you, given the needs of your client.

7. The vibrational pattern found with each endocrine gland is subtle, intense, distinct and specific to itself. No two endocrine glands contain the same kind of etheric energy. If you have your negative hand situated correctly over the contact point to the gland you are attuning, then the positive hand should feel the gland 'pop out.' This means that when you stimulate the contact point, you are automatically stimulating the next gland in the system — contact points automatically stimulate their corresponding positive counterpart.

8. If you have a problem finding the energy pattern to a specific gland, first check to make sure your negative hand is correctly positioned over the correct contact point. It is most likely to be misplaced. If not, check the position of your positive hand and make sure it is over the positive gland which you are attuning. Then, make sure your arms and wrists are loose, and that your fingers are pointed in the right direction towards the gland. Finally, just wait a few seconds until you feel the etheric energy move, bringing with it its corresponding energy pattern. Just as it sometimes takes a few seconds to stimulate energy at the neck region, so it may take a few seconds to stimulate energy in the glands.

9. If you wish to share a shorter attunement (five – ten minutes) than the full body attunement outlined in Part II (twenty – thirty minutes), then simply (i) balance the cervical pattern, (ii) open the portals of light by balancing the endocrine glands, and then (iii) balance the cervical pattern again. You can open the body's light system and entrain the nervous system using this shorter, simpler method.

Endocrine Gland Attunement Practice

Begin endocrine gland attunement by seating yourself at the head of your client. Balance cervicals before beginning endocrine gland work. Reference the endocrine gland anatomical chart.

KEY: **RH** = *Right Hand, Positive Hand*
        LH = *Left Hand, Negative Hand*
        (Switch these if you are left handed.)

Pineal:

RH   *crown of the head*

LH   *stays at left cervical*

Pituitary:

RH   *stays on pineal. RH is now the negative hand, holding the pineal as contact point for the pituitary.*

LH   *over bridge of nose at pituitary gland. LH is now the positive hand, attuning the pituitary gland.*

Thyroid:

RH   *moves to go over Adams Apple or throat region, to thyroid gland. RH is now the positive hand, attuning the thyroid gland.*

LH   *remains over bridge of nose at pituitary gland. LH is now the negative hand, holding the pituitary as contact point for the thyroid.*

It is traditional for the practitioner to stand at this point, and position herself at the left side of the massage table. RH stays over thyroid as practitioner gets up and moves.

Thymus:

RH   *remains over Adams Apple at thyroid gland. RH is now the negative hand, holding the thyroid as contact point for the thymus.*

LH   *at the episternal notch to thymus gland. LH is now the positive hand, attuning the thymus gland.*

The hands now switch. Right hand comes to thymus and left hand moves to pancreas.

Islets of Langerhans:

RH   *at episternal notch to thymus gland. RH is now the negative hand, holding the thymus as contact point for the pancreas.*

LH   *at crook of left elbow, begin at the left lateral line and continue up to the midline of the body, covering the entire pancreas organ. LH is now the positive hand, attuning the islets of langerhans in the pancreas.*

Adrenals:

RH   *V-shaped hand (fingers opposite the thumb are drawn together and are pointed downward. The wrist is cocked and is higher than the fingers. The thumb attunes one kidney while the other fingers attune the other kidney. Kidneys are located at T11-12 (thoracic vertebrae — consult the chart or another anatomical reference for further clarification). RH is now the positive hand, attuning the adrenals.*

LH   *remains at left lateral line at isles of langerhans. LH is now the negative hand, holding the pancreas as contact point for the adrenals.*

Male Gonads:

RH   *remains V-shaped over both adrenal glands. RH is now the negative hand, holding the adrenals as contact points for the gonads.*

LH   *directly below pubic bone over scrotum. LH is now the positive hand, attuning the gonads.*

Female Gonads:

RH   *remains V-shaped over both adrenal glands. RH is now the negative hand, holding the adrenals as contact points for the gonads.*

LH   *V-shaped (fingers and hand mirror that of right hand) along and medial to hip bones over ovaries. LH is now the positive hand, attuning the female gonads.*

Holding Your Thumbs for Self-Attunement

You will note on the illustration on the next page that the pineal, pituitary and thyroid glands all have corresponding points on each thumb. By gently holding your thumbs for 5 – 10 minutes at a time, you can bring about a balance in the energy systems of your body. Arms should be rested at your sides, whether you are sitting or lying down. Make sure you don't have any white knuckles during this self-attunement exercise, for this means that you are grasping your thumbs too tightly. You need only cover these points on each thumb with gentleness and little pressure to bring about the desired relaxing effect.

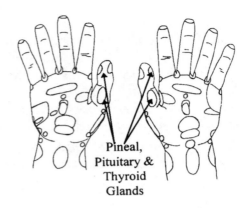

Pineal,
Pituitary &
Thyroid
Glands

SELF-ATTUNEMENT

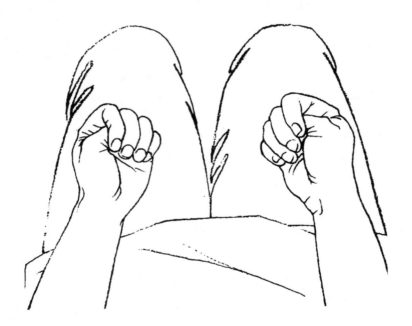

Chapter 11 Notes

[1] Dr William Tiller, PhD, 'A Symposium on Mind-Body Relationships in the Disease Process,' (Edgar Cayce Foundation, Phoenix, AZ, 1972), pp. 74–78.

[2] Uranda, <u>Seven Steps to the Temple of Light</u> (Loveland: Eden Valley Press, 1936), pp. 18–20.

[3] Eden Gray, <u>A Complete Guide to the Tarot</u> (New York: Bantam Books, 1970), p. 20.

12. Attuning the Digestive System

A woman with a long affiliation in the attunement program tells this story.

For years she had undergone repeated abdominal surgeries which were associated with a burst appendix. She had suffered a ruptured appendix when she was young, but no one had known about it then, and subsequently her body had protected itself from her leaking bowel poisons by growing massive amounts of connective tissue around the ruptured site. Her surgeries included removing parts of her small intestines as well as the connective tissue growth.

The woman's husband was a proficient attunement practitioner and shared daily attunement with her before, during and after her surgeries, allowing the healing process to move swiftly and clearly through her at all times. The woman's response to Source and attunement energy was absolute as her heart was open to the spirit of God for all things.

One day, during her rehabilitation following one of her surgeries, the woman began shaking. She shook violently from head to foot and could not stop. Her husband began sharing attunement with her but to no avail. After a little while, her condition seemed serious and it looked as if there might be unidentified reasons behind her shaking which could be related to other complications. Two more attunement practitioners were called to the scene to hold and try to clear the shaking, distortion pattern. After working for a considerable time, it became plain that all three attunement practitioners could not clear the vibrational pattern associated with the woman's shaking. They decided to call in the Attunement Master Server who lived nearby. All of the attunement practitioners present with the woman had trained under the Master Server, and it was felt that he might know best how to handle this situation.

When the Master Server walked into the room, he took one look at the shaking woman, walked slowly around the couch upon which she lay and came to a stop nearby. She then immediately stopped shaking. Nothing was said, no hands were placed over any particular site, and no other attunement server assisted him.

While telling this story, the woman confessed that she had known why she had experienced all of the surgeries (because of the burst appendix), but had not revealed this to anyone before. She said that her doctors were amazed that she was still alive, and in fact they did not know how she had managed to live through the burst appendix, let alone the surgeries. She was a walking marvel to medicine.

The key to her healing was that she was raised in an atmosphere of attunement, having had attunement shared with her since she was a little girl, and her husband shared attunement with her all the time. Her continual attunement sessions allowed for a continual stream of life force energy to inform her pneumaplasmic layer with integrative power. What then formed along these attuned lines of force was connective tissue, which provided much needed protection against the poisons being released at the danger site. Years later she grew out of her need for surgeries, and the entire vibrational pattern disappeared.

At the time the woman shared her story, she informed us that as far as she knew, the reason for the uncontrollable shaking was due to an unconscious feeling of shame and guilt that she felt about needing so many surgeries. She related that at the time she had subconsciously felt guilty for somehow failing in her spirituality. Why did she need surgery if she was a spiritually conscious person? Wasn't her alignment with Source enough to keep her from harm? The woman blamed herself for her troubles. Her guilt and shame were hidden from her consciousness, and ran rampant through her emotional system.

The Master Server knew the truth behind her shaking which was that she was a divine being with a body form, and she was under stress because her emotions were out of control. The Master Server was not distracted by her movement — he continued to see the divine being within the form, and this is what led him to offer her the healing she needed. Even though to this day, no one knows how he managed to stop her from shaking, the Master Server did see clearly at that time who it was that was empowering her to shake, and what her response was to that radiant being. He knew that her heart was in the right place — open to receive the love of God, and with this one factor in place he assisted spirit to move the negative energy out of her body. Through his shining example and her open response, she let go, relaxed and became still.

The Digestive System

The digestive system contains organs vital to the physical acceptance, breakdown, and assimilation of nourishment for the body. From a spiritual perspective, the vibrational feel of the digestive tract gives evidence of how your client is nourished. Nourishing vibrational qualities are sensed through the body as thankful resonance for all that is, and for all that comes to us. As a practitioner, you can tell a lot about how your client views himself, and how he takes care of himself, his world and others by touching into the etheric level of his digestive system. Follow these guidelines:

- When working with the digestive system, the practitioner should stay focused on allowing a greater release of spirit to occur by feeling for and holding the pattern of spirit which nurtures and nourishes. The practitioner may sense this greater release present in any part of the body, but it is most noticeable in the digestive system. A nourishing flow has a specific feel to it, like touching into a thankful setting which is ripe with creative opportunity. You may feel this deeper flow in any part of the digestive tract. Once felt, you should hold that vibrational pattern for a longer time than usual to allow the flow of spirit to release with a greater force.

- The practitioner may feel a pattern of under-nourishment, as if the body is crying out to be fed at the physical, emotional or spiritual levels. If this is the case, remember to remain sensitive as to your client's psychological state. Oftentimes, to state your objective findings outright may impose more stress on your client's ability to self-heal. You don't wish to elicit any more stress patterns in your client's capacities than are already present, and certainly you are seeking to diminish those which are there. The wisest course of action in most attunement situations is to be silent, and to wait and speak with confidence as to what is positive and healing about the session. Speak with faith to instill an open-hearted response in your client. Trust love to bring awareness in its own season.

- You may sense a major distortion pattern in the large colon. This vibrational distortion pattern is usually related to your client's high-stress diet but may also include energies related to any anal retentive behavior patterns. Extra spiritual tension usually resides in the ascending colon if there is an accompanying bacterial infection in the small intestines, or in both the descending and ascending colons if your client ingests a lot of caffeine (especially coffee).

- So that you may have a better understanding of the anatomy with which you are working, here is a short anatomy lesson on the digestive system. Study the following digestive system anatomical chart and its related face contact point chart as you follow along with this short histology lesson:

  - The stomach receives food which has already been broken down somewhat by the enzyme action present in the mouth and esophagus. The stomach then breaks down these smaller portions into microscopic substances, some of which are carried by the blood to the liver to be metabolized, but most of which is carried into the small intestines for assimilation.

  - The small intestines (which are 18 – 20 feet in length) serve to absorb nutrients previously broken down by the stomach, set them in motion into the blood stream, and then to the liver.

  - The large intestine (ascending, transverse and descending colon) serves to carry unused portions of food to the rectum, to be excreted by the body.

  - The liver is the only organ in the body with its own portal system of blood. It is thought to be the most efficient organ of the body, creating and breaking down a vast array of sugars, fatty acids, enzymes, etc., and storing substances to be utilized by the body for all its processes. The liver is immensely important to the overall harmonious functioning of the human body, and is key to its purification cycles. While in medical school, I heard the story that at one time a large corporation sought to reorganize their corporate structure, basing it on the efficiency of the liver organ. The corporation could not succeed in its quest, and found out that the liver was far too efficient a system for human beings, in their present state, to copy.

  - The gall bladder serves to excrete bile (produced by the liver and other organs) into the small intestines for nutrient assimilation purposes.

Digestive System Attunement Practice

The following lays out the sequence of contact points used when attuning the digestive system. These points should first be followed in the order presented, but later on, when you become better acquainted with this contact point system, you may change the order of your offering (this is an intuitive point).

DIGESTIVE SYSTEM ATTUNEMENT CONTACT POINTS CHART

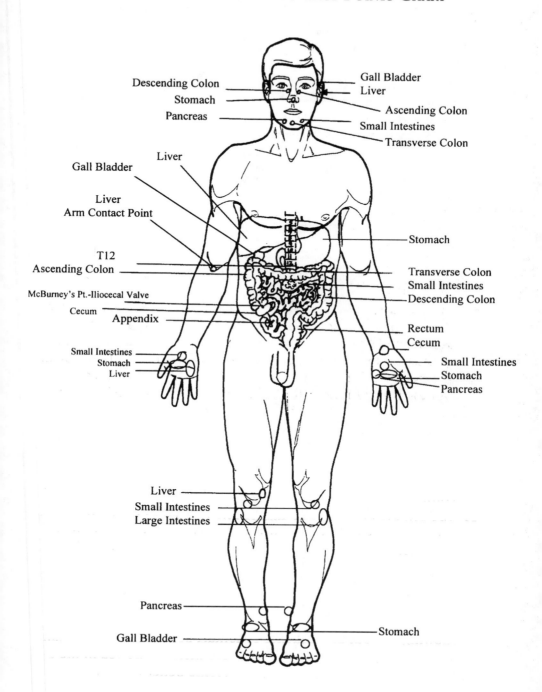

FACIAL ATTUNEMENT CONTACT POINTS CHART

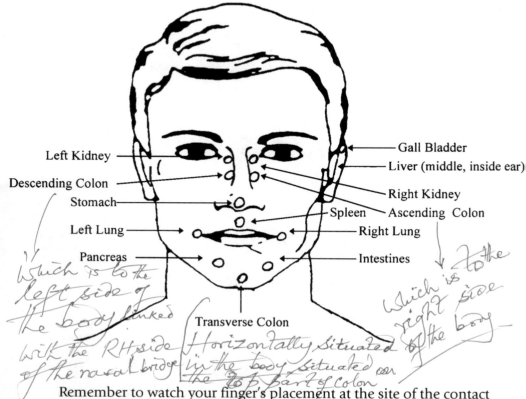

Left Kidney

Descending Colon

Stomach

Left Lung

Pancreas

Gall Bladder

Liver (middle, inside ear)

Right Kidney

Spleen   Ascending Colon

Right Lung

Intestines

Transverse Colon

Which is to the left side of the body linked with the RH side of the nasal bridge

Horizontally situated in the body situated on the top part of colon

Which is to the right side of the body

Remember to watch your finger's placement at the site of the contact points! Remember that your fingers need practice staying put on these little points. You will be referring back to the face contact point chart in later chapters.

To begin with, notice that the contact points on the face are placed on the side opposite to that of their corresponding body parts (i.e. the ascending colon contact point is located on the left side of the client's nose, and its associated organ, the ascending colon, is located on the right side of the body). The points on the face are opposite to their body correspondences because the cranial nerves cross themselves at the back of the neck. Therefore, all contact points on the face associate themselves with the opposite side of the body.

Unless otherwise indicated, the right hand will act as your negative hand and will be establishing the contact points, while the left hand will act as the positive hand and will be attuning the organs. Throughout all digestive organ attunement, the left hand should be held flat over the etheric body associated with the organ indicated, and should not be held tense or rigid. You should only use the index and/or third finger of the right hand. These two fingers should be held together, also without rigidity. This theme only varies for two other liver points and at the very start of the procedure, as follows:

Ascending Colon:

LH   *index and third fingers are out together, and focused downward to the base of the left wrist. (LH is establishing the contact point.)*

RH   *over cecum at the iliocecal valve.*

Establish the flow of energy through the digestive system by first connecting with the left wrist point. When this point is established with your left fingers, you will easily find the iliocecal valve with your right hand — it will jump out at you as you skim over the right side of your client's abdomen, searching for it. Once you have established the flow of energy through the ascending colon, quickly switch your hands so that your right hand works with the face contact points for the rest of the digestive system attunement (see chart opposite):

RH   *one finger focusing energy to ascending colon contact point on the left side of nose (left on the client).*

LH   *continue up the ascending colon from the cecum to the transverse colon.*

Transverse Colon:

RH   *one finger focusing energy downward in the center of the chin.*

LH   *begin at hepatic flexure and continue across transverse colon.*

Descending Colon:

RH   *one finger focusing energy to the descending contact point on the right side of the nose (right on the client).*

LH   *begin at splenic flexure, and continue down the descending colon to the sigmoid flexure, rectum and anus.*

Small Intestines:

RH   *one finger focuses energy downward at the small intestines contact point on the left side of the chin (left on the client).*

LH   *moves slowly across small intestine area.*

Remember that there are 18 – 20 feet of small intestines packed away in the small abdominal cavity. Make sure you vibrationally touch into the entire area!

Stomach:

RH   one or two fingers (held together) focus energy downward at the point on top of the nose.

LH   over stomach, just to the right and below the sternum.

Pancreas:

RH   index and/or second finger held together, and focusing energy downward at the pancreas contact point on the right side of the chin.

LH   just across the crook of the left elbow, extend your left hand over the pancreas, which extends across the midline, lateral to medial (refer to chart above).

Liver:

On the chart on page 139, notice that there are three contact points for the liver. Check all three points and choose to work with the one which has the strongest flow of energy.

RH   index and/or third finger held together, pointing into the body of the client's left ear.

LH   palm laid flat, move over the entire etheric body surface of the liver area, including your client's right side. For other liver contact points, switch hands:

RH   palm laid flat over liver area.

LH   fingers together, focusing the energy flow in the crook of the right elbow, and/or

LH   fingers pointing together, and extending to the right knee contact point (refer to chart on page 139).

Gallbladder:

RH   one finger focusing energy downward at the top point on your client's left ear (refer to chart on page 139).

LH   follow an imaginary line down (caudal) from your client's lateral right side of the neck, down to the gall bladder (with your right hand on the contact point, on top of your client's ear, the gallbladder energy should 'jump out' at you).

13. Attuning the Circulatory, Excretory and Respiratory Systems

A woman under doctor's care, who suffered from a wide variety of illnesses, came to see me to share attunement. She suffered from lupus, pernicious anemia, chronic fatigue syndrome, insomnia, severe migraines, sjogran's syndrome, and a suppressed immune system. The woman lived in close proximity to her two sons, one of whom was a drug addict and the other who was mentally deranged. When she first started seeing me to share attunement, she seemed to be in a crisis state because her sons' presence in her life terrified and confused her and left her feeling helpless by their erratic and tyrannical behavior. She told me that she felt the reason she was ill was due to "years of traumatic stress." She also reported a lifetime of bad relationships with all the men in her life, including her father, husbands and these two sons.

Besides attunement services, this woman had chosen alternative therapies to treat her illnesses. She was receiving acupuncture, chiropractic and reflexology treatments, and recently had started taking prescribed homeopathic remedies.

The woman was quite beautiful. Looking at her, I never would have guessed that anything was wrong. She wore a bright smile which showed no force of habit, was polite and pleasant company. She didn't complain about her illnesses, and in fact acted as if they were simply her life's work at the time. When I mentioned to her these findings she stated that she felt it would be rude for her to appear any other way. With that statement, I began to see that her smiles to the outside world was her way of hiding how she truly felt. I began to sense her screaming on the inside. There seemed to be a dark chasm between what she felt inwardly and how she felt she needed to present herself outwardly. I decided to probe more deeply to see where her body-mind connection was misaligned.

After a few more sessions, I began to see a pattern of consciousness emerge which mirrored her physical disabilities. She explained to me through letter and conversation that she equated her internal world with her physical world. She believed that her physical illnesses dwelt inside herself, and she believed that no healthier or other kind of conscious state could reside there simultaneously. I educated her on the principles of spiritual orientation, as taught by the attunement program, that she was a divine being and was not the sum of her capacities. As our conversations continued week by week, she slowly woke up to the fact that she was hiding her true feelings from the world, and that she had a habit pattern of squelching them in order to show the world a face of health and reliability. Her husband had abused and then divorced her, and now her sons abused her privacy with threatening and dangerous activity. She didn't like what was happening to her, but felt out of control and didn't know how to stop what was going on around her. She said she felt obligated to lie to everyone about how she really felt, for this was how she was raised and this was how she always acted with men. Instead of telling her burdens to others, she could always be counted upon to shoulder the weight of their troubles. The woman was a true codependent.

I knew that by counseling and sharing attunement with her, the healing energy she received would bring her into a greater understanding of herself and her world, and free her of this lifelong habit pattern. Something more radiant was beginning to break through the surface of her consciousness and this light was compelling her to change. Through the course of our time together, she began to trust the provision of love which was there for her as well as for her sons. Slowly, she began to let them go. The heaviness I sensed in her thymus area (gateway to purification) eased up tremendously as she purified her life, and, feeling assured that doing so was right, let it go. She began to realize that just as she was whole unto herself, her sons were whole unto themselves and apart from her. As a woman who had lived her life up to this time with codependent behavior, she needed to see that there is a distinct separation between Self and Other, and that life moved autonomously through each.

By the time of her last session with me, she was feeling happier, had more 'up' energy, was sleeping better, and her headaches had disappeared. Her naturopathic treatments were going well and she was on a prescribed healing program. Her sons were both apart from her, one incarcerated and the other institutionalized. She had processed their separation from her adequately enough that she was now beginning to concentrate on those things which brought her personal fulfillment and happiness, such as her career and hobbies.

I also noticed that she had begun to show irritation, despair and anger towards me. I noticed worry lines around a face which once shone smooth and clear. She spoke of beginning to be aware of her negative communication with others. The anger which she had suppressed for so many years was beginning to come out, and this release brought about a balance in her expression as well as a balance in her physical life. I viewed her burgeoning anger as a useful sign that her inner strength and will were beginning to assert themselves. With her transition out of a codependent survival mentality, her life current and expression were showing signs of greater trust and assurance to express herself just as she was, without covering up her feelings. Her stronger will to express the truth of her life was a necessary component to her healing, enabling her to meet the challenges of her life with integrity.

During the weeks that I shared attunement with her, I did not suggest that she align with God Being within and express attitudes of thankfulness as her prime attunement objective. I knew that she needed to let a different part of her expression come forward during this time and that the deeper thanksgiving would begin to surface in time. I saw that her consciousness was waking up to other kinds of strengthening patterns which she needed to actively express. I focused my counseling and attunement skill on simply offering her hands-on one-on-one sessions, with self-empowerment skills as the basis for our dialogue. As we moved together through her crisis time, we began to see that her crisis cycle had actually turned out to be a cycle of personal awakening and growth.

The Circulatory, Excretory and Respiratory Systems

What is right with you is the point.
What is wrong with you is besides the point!

—Bill Bahan, DC

As we continue with full body attunement technique, we come next to the other major organ systems of the body including the circulatory (arterial and venous systems), excretory (kidneys), and respiratory (lungs) systems. These vital organ systems complete the main portion of full body attunement training.

Remember during all attunement session work that you should not be focused on what is wrong with your client, nor on fixing ill tissues. Remain focused on what is right with your client, and where you sense the spirit of life moving. Ignore the disease. Focus only on what is healthy. Let the healing current of life take care of that which is living, and trust its movement to heal.

Circulatory System Attunement Practice

Let your heart rest. All is well. Trust life to govern all things.
—Martin Exeter

For where your treasure is, there will your heart be also.
—Jesus Christ, Matthew 6:21

The heart is a great pump and valve, which forces blood to move through large arterial blood vessels that carry nutrients and oxygenated air to the tissues. The force of pressure exerted by the heart is also felt and used by the lymph and venal portal systems. The venal system returns 'used blood' to the lungs which re-oxygenate and revivify it. The venal force of blood helps to return waste products to the lymph system to be excreted and phagocytosed (destroyed).

The heart and its accompanying system represents that which circulates in our lives. People with heart disease, degenerative heart failure and those who suffer heart attacks usually suffer from more than just clogged arteries. That which becomes closed off in the arterial system is simply a physical out-picturing of what has manifested itself at the vibrational level of emotion. Uranda writes about the heart, "Remember well that thy heart is the focal center of thy outer mind, and the bloodstream of thy body is the channel of the active flow of thy outer mind."[1] From Uranda's words we may gather that much of what we each think, say and do in the world around us, and all which passes through our own consciousness, carries a strong vibrational consequence into the circulatory system. From an attunement perspective, the heart is the contact point for the movement of spirit into our lives.

Recall from your reading in *Chapter 8* that the capacities of mind and heart need to be open to express attitudes which are consistent with and comparable to the nature of spirit. When spirit begins to move through your capacities, you sense its movement through your heart, not your mind. Spiritual expression is not a mental exercise, but a multi-leveled sensation which incorporates conscious recognition, physical sensation and emotional feeling.

Because the heart is the contact point for spirit as it moves into your outer or external world, it is important to train the heart capacity to have deep feelings for what is right, i.e., for what is sensed to be appropriate and correct in the vast scheme of things. Through your heart realm you learn to discern that which 'feels' right to you. Because the heart is your mighty contact into your world, it is wise to teach this capacity to express often qualities of thankfulness, joy and forgiveness. In this way, you may be assured that your positive expressions will have a creative impact on you and all which your spirit touches.

When you share attunement with the heart capacity in others, you will feel most of your client's subconscious emotional stresses as a vibrational distortion pattern in the heart. If your client is expressing attitudes of resentment, blame or criticism, or if your client has a history of heart disease, you will feel large tingles and a vivid blockage of the flow of spirit at this site. Maintaining an attitude of resentment and other negatively-based attitudes is like stepping on a hose which has behind it a huge head of water waiting to pour out. Resentment causes illness because it stops the flow of life which is longing to come through personal expression at the heart level.

Since the heart is the throne of the emotional realm and the contact point to the movement of spirit, you may assist your clients to open more readily to spiritual outpouring by supporting their expression of attitudes which generate a giving nature. When people with heart problems learn that their giving nature may be the key to their own healing, then they may begin to view their giving nature as their true wealth. "Life is for giving!" said Bill Bahan, DC, one of the founders of the attunement program.

We can learn about giving by looking at other societies. One Native American Indian tribe is a prime example. For the Northern Blackfoot Indians, the richest man of their tribe is the one who gives away all that he owns. By giving all that he has to the poor, children, widows and the destitute of the tribe, their richest man "demonstrates how capable, intelligent, strong, hard-working, generous *and therefore how wealthy he is*, since wealth in this society is determined by the possession of these character attributes." Among the Blackfoot, the poorest person was considered to be the one with the most possessions.[2] The lessons contained in this book are designed to strengthen attitudes of forgiveness, compassion, honesty, joy and thankfulness, which you may then pass onto others. By opening the heart capacity to the movement of spiritual flow, you will let spirit express through you out into your world.

Besides sharing in the traditional heart attunement technique offered below, remember to follow these guidelines when you share attunement with the circulatory system:

Circulatory Attunement Practice Guidelines

- To begin your session, you may want to stimulate the solar plexus contact points located on your client's feet. This will set in motion a more subtle and quieter flow of healing energy for the entire cardiovascular area in the chest region. (You will find the solar plexus contact points for the feet located in *Chapter 19.*)

- For all contact point work with the heart, stand to the left of your client. While working in the circulatory system, both hands act as positive and negative poles, as they switch with different contact points. Again, have your left hand lay flat against the etheric body associated with the heart. The index and third fingers of the right hand should again be gently situated together, with their energy pointing downward into the contact points listed.

- Similar to the liver, the heart and circulatory system has more than one contact point. There are four contact points for the heart. Remember to check all four points when attuning this system. Find the strongest flow of energy and stay with that contact point.

- If you happen to be present at the scene of a car accident or any other injury where there is severe bleeding, you can hold the heart pattern at the carotid or femoral artery points (depending on where the wound bleeding is most severe) while other attendees apply good first aid technique.

Heart:

LH   *palm laid flat over the etheric body associated with the heart (left hand acts as the positive hand here).*

RH   *(Four contact points, refer to chart opposite for placement.)*

1. index and third fingers are gently pressed together and point downward, halfway between left elbow and left shoulder.

2. index and third fingers are gently pressed together and point downward, at the angle of the left side of the jaw at the carotid sinus (left arterial side is best).

3. index and third fingers are gently pressed together and point downward below the lobe of the right ear at the site of the vagus nerve. (The vagus nerve (not shown on chart) runs parallel to the carotid artery, and is an inhibitory contact point, inhibiting the flow of blood down the body. This is a very good point to use during emergency work or to calm down a client.)

CIRCULATORY SYSTEM ATTUNEMENT CONTACT POINTS CHART

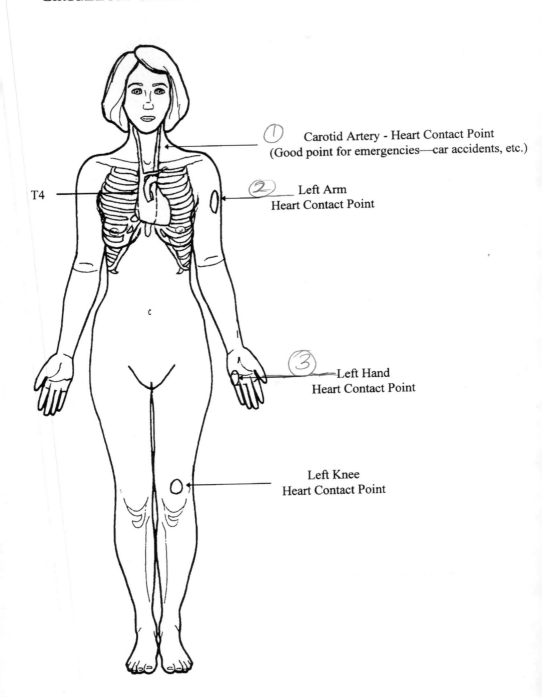

① Carotid Artery - Heart Contact Point
(Good point for emergencies—car accidents, etc.)

② Left Arm
Heart Contact Point

T4

③ Left Hand
Heart Contact Point

Left Knee
Heart Contact Point

Switch your positive and negative hands for this final contact point:

RH   4. *palm down, across the etheric body associated with the heart.*

LH   *fingers placed gently together, extend the energy from your hand towards the contact point on the left knee (see chart).*

The inferior vena cava and superior vena cava and other major arterial and venous structures are other points with which you may wish to work. Hold one positive hand over the structure while the other negative hand's fingers (gently held together) connect the attunement flow at the contact points mentioned above. Check each point for the strongest flow and stay there, holding, clarifying and balancing the vibrational pattern.

Excretory System Attunement Practice

Let the unreal state pass away in you and around you.
Weep not for the passing but rejoice in the coming.
Nothing that is real or true can ever be lost.
Only false values and distorted states shall vanish from the earth.
Do not look back nor mourn their passing.

—Martin Exeter

From a physical standpoint, the excretory system represents that which needs to pass away from the body. When helping to regulate the excretory system, you will note the Vasopressin hormone regulation factor (mentioned in the *Histology Notes* in Appendix A). This hormone regulating factor comes to focus in the posterior pituitary gland, which then regulates water reabsorption and blood volume in the body through normal hormone release. For all kidney and excretory attunement, you may use the pituitary gland as a major contact point, as this gland governs much of the activity of the kidney through its hormone regulation. Utilize the pituitary gland, particularly with clients who present with water retention, urinary tract infection or incontinence.

For these points, refer to the face contact point chart on page 140. Remember these points are on the opposite side of the face to their physical counterparts!

Right Kidney:

RH   *index finger points down at the left bridge of the nose (see chart for placement).*

LH   *hand is gently held flat over the etheric body associated with the right kidney.*

EXCRETORY SYSTEM ATTUNEMENT CONTACT POINTS CHART

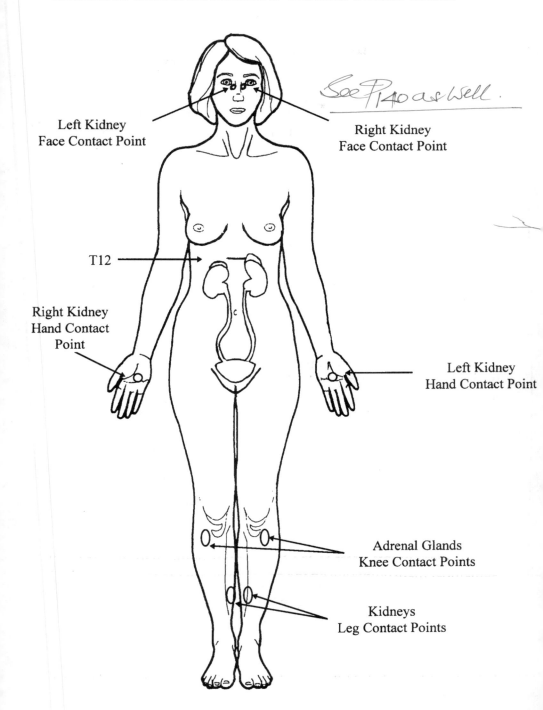

Left Kidney
Face Contact Point

Right Kidney
Face Contact Point

See P 140 as well.

T12

Right Kidney
Hand Contact
Point

Left Kidney
Hand Contact Point

Adrenal Glands
Knee Contact Points

Kidneys
Leg Contact Points

Left Kidney:

RH   index finger points down at the right bridge of the nose (see chart for placement).

LH   hand is gently held flat over the etheric body associated with the left kidney.

Or, use the pituitary gland (facial) or its corresponding point on the feet as additional contact points for all kidney attunement.

Respiratory System Attunement Practice

> *He who learns to harmonize with love, so that*
> *he uses it constructively, finds that the greatest*
> *and most potent force in the earth*
> *is flowing through him.*
>
> —*Uranda*

The respiratory system represents the mechanisms of 'letting go and letting come' into our lives. Breathing in pure oxygenated air, and breathing out carbon dioxide and 'used up' air after it has circulated in the body, this system provides a consistent balancing process of giving and receiving and assists in the restoration of new and damaged tissue. The act of breathing is basic to humans, and represents the spirit of God Being filling in and filling out our lives. Guru Ram Das, meditation and Kundalini Yoga teacher, invokes the power of breath and healing through this portion of his inhalation and exhalation prayer:

> *Inhale and hold your breath for the peace of the world, for the health of all, to make everybody happy, so that those who are lonely may have their partner and God may find mercy on everybody, on each individual, say this prayer on this breath, and* please *exhale. This is the charity of the breath.*[3] *then*

For those who present with challenges of the lungs, you will note distortion patterns primarily at the pulmonary artery insertion points, the bronchial branching plexus (more so on the right side, since there are three bronchial branches, as opposed to only two on the left), and at the base of the lungs. The right lung will normally house a more distinct distortion pattern than the left, unless there is an underlying problem with the left, specific to that area. Watch for vibrational sludge patterns at base of both lungs due to poor deep breathing habits, lack of aerobic exercise and/or too much stress.

RESPIRATORY SYSTEM ATTUNEMENT CONTACT POINTS CHART

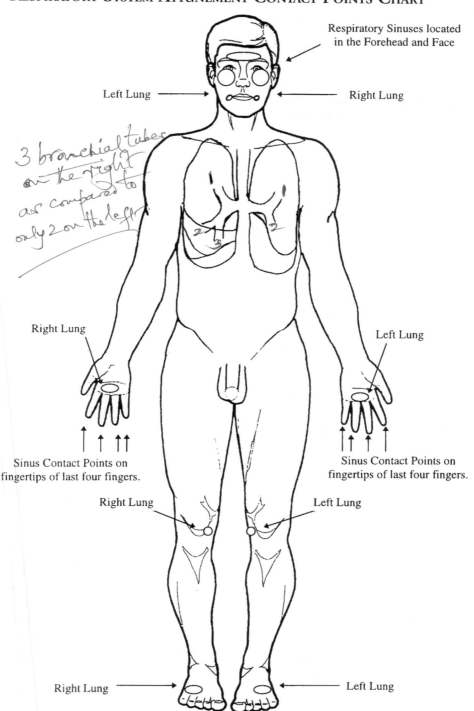

Respiratory Sinuses located in the Forehead and Face

Left Lung

Right Lung

3 bronchial tubes on the right as compared to only 2 on the left

Right Lung

Left Lung

Sinus Contact Points on fingertips of last four fingers.

Sinus Contact Points on fingertips of last four fingers.

Right Lung

Left Lung

Right Lung

Left Lung

Refer to the face contact point chart presented on page 140. And again, remember these points are on the opposite side of the face to their physical counterparts.

Right Lung:

RH   *index finger points energy downward at the left edge of the lips (client's left).*

LH   *palm lays flat against the etheric body associated with the right lung, and moves across the entire right lung area, from the apex at shoulder to below the lung at the lung's cavity lining.*

Left Lung:

RH   *index finger points energy downward at the right edge of the lips.*

LH   *same as right lung direction.*

Chapter 13 Notes

[1] Uranda, <u>The Triune Ray</u>, p. 63.

[2] Julie Glover, 'Is Serving Others Self-Serving' excerpt found in *Noetic Sciences Review*, Summer, 1997, No. 42, p. 6.

[3] Guru Ram Das Ashram, <u>Kundalini Yoga</u> (Los Angeles: Arcline Publications, 1988), p. 22.

14. Attuning the Immune System

I gave my first public attunement in 1987 to a woman who had responded to an article I had written in a local northwest paper about Emissary and attunement meetings. Her life story and its association with attunement practice is one of the most fascinating stories of any of my clients.

Having been bitten by a monkey while in Africa at age 8½ my client, whom I will call Aura, developed Simian AIDS. Since medical science did not then know about AIDS (she was bitten in 1962), Aura was misdiagnosed with other kinds of disorders, none of which were her true illness. Among her diagnoses was mental illness, and she was placed for a time inside a mental institution, and even given electric shock treatments to curb her mental distress.

In 1987, when I began to see her, she was living alone and secluded from the outside world. Aura had developed into a highly sensitive woman. In fact, by the time I began to work with her, she knew that she was born a 'sensitive,' someone highly attuned to life force who was able to receive and respond to psychic impressions. What I did not know at the time, was that in 1986 Aura had entered the terminal stage of her disease, and soon afterwards she had in full consciousness embraced death. Aura wrote the following about this time in her life: "Divine intervention took place involving the consciousness of numerous individuals. In the course of one month, she [Aura] experienced three core 'near death events' and was healed." Being healed meant that her near death experience somehow changed her positive HIV status to negative. This change was confirmed by blood tests.

After her allopathic medical experiences, Aura decided to live a completely natural life, and began receiving Chiropractic adjustments twice a week (home visits), ate only wholesome and natural foods, took nutritional immune-enhancing supplements, drank pure water, and filtered the air inside her house. She rarely stepped foot outside of her house. Her friends and family helped her by shopping and running errands for her. At her doorstep were signs informing each newcomer to take off their shoes and immediately wash their hands.

I began sharing attunements with Aura on a weekly basis. I recall during one session that enormous electric shocks entered my hands when I began sharing an attunement with her cervical vertebrae. When I informed Aura of this, she told me to place a large black cone between my feet, which grounded the electricity. The shocks were coming from her nervous system, and were leftover impulses from the electro-shock therapy still present in her nervous system. I placed the black cone between my legs, felt the electric shocks decrease considerably, and continued with the attunement.

On another visit, I entered her house just after she had experienced a wind draft which had blown down her chimney and had sent a torrent of ash into the air of her house. She was in a desperate situation, in a lot of pain and finding it difficult to breath. I worked for a time with her respiratory and circulatory systems, establishing a balance and clarifying the distortion patterns found there.

I shared attunements with Aura for many months, and later I moved away to complete my university education. I left Aura in the capable hands of another attunement practitioner who continued to visit her for two years following.

Sometime later I returned to that city to attend a large public Emissary event. Seated behind me was my attunement practitioner friend, and a woman. When I turned to speak to my friend, I was surprised to see Aura, and even had to be reintroduced to her, since I didn't recognize her at all. She looked radically different — she had gained what looked to be about 30 pounds, and had vibrationally filled-out at all levels of her being. She informed me that her life was going well and she was able to go out in public now. Her natural lifestyle, combined with weekly attunements, had clarified her life pattern to the point that she was beginning to experience life in a more normal fashion.

In 1996, I re-established my connection with Aura in order to follow up on her progress. It was at this time that she informed me of the near-death experiences and her movement from AIDS positive to AIDS negative status. Aura informed me that she had been working as a Sensitive, offering spiritual intuitive counseling with other people and had developed a clientele. She also mentioned that she offered attunements to her clients, and wrote me later of her attunement experience:

"When I share an attunement, I feel strong rushes of energy currents gather and channel themselves cohesively, for deep healing and strength. My brain feels bathed in nourishing energy as does my spine. I feel a peace and integration within me as that which 'I AM' is brought into synthesis. All that sits within to express and acknowledge comes quickly into expression as it releases, often with very deep emotions. My awareness of my own process energetically and multi-dimensionally becomes tangible and alive. My kinesthetic experience is magnified and I am filled with a warm glow, knowing my own inner light and love that I am. I am left feeling purified inside, like I have been bathed by a glistening waterfall.

I now begin most every healing session that I offer others with attunement. Attunement sets the tone in my work with others for alignment, stillness and receptivity."[1]

Aura also spoke of her recent trip to England where she had participated in medical research experimentation, and had left her blood and blood products with scientists there, as they were keenly interested to understand the origin of AIDS and find its cure.

I have shared long distance attunement off and on with Aura, for many years. At this time (February, 1998), she has informed me that she is in her final stage of life and is moving towards closing her time on earth.

Lymph and Immune Systems Attunement Practice

You will not grow if you sit in a beautiful flower garden,
but you will grow if you are sick, if you are in pain,
if you experience losses, and if you do not put your head in the sand,
but take the pain and learn to accept it, not as a curse or a punishment
but as a gift to you with a very, very specific purpose.

—Elisabeth Kubler-Ross

At the physical level, the lymph and immune systems serve to purify and protect the body from foreign invaders. A key proponent in proper immune function is the thymus gland, which is the seat of purification, from an attunement perspective. The thymus gland is located only a few inches below the thyroid, and is situated behind the sternum of the chest. Before puberty, the thymus gland produces t-cells, helper t-cells and killer t-cells which are the major players in the immune system's fight against infection and disease. Once produced in the thymus, t-cells then migrate to specific regions of the body, namely to various lymph nodes and the spleen, where they take up residence and fight-off harmful viral infections. Another form of bacteria fighters are b-cells, which are produced in bone and also circulate throughout the body. T-cells act like the protective guard, warding off illnesses by encircling the enemy, and then like a machine gun, killing with antigen. Waste product produced by this invasion is phagocytosed (eaten) by lymphocytes, which are also present throughout the blood stream and in lymph nodes, and which are designed as microscopic garbage disposals.

Follow these immune system guidelines when attuning your client:

- You will probably want to offer immune system attunement to your client if she complains that she has unprocessed memories or negative emotional patterns. When you work with specific lymph nodes, you will probably find associated dissonant energy patterns there. Holding these patterns between your hands (positive and negative poles) will help to dissolve and release the dissonance into a more calm energy flow.

- The immune system seeks to rid the body of unwanted bacterial invasion, but can only work up to speed if people work with the healing process in such a way to support its operation by their mode of living. Becoming burned out, working too long and hard, and not taking enough rest breaks and vacations may lead to your immune system becoming over-loaded with distortion. Dr Stuart White, Chiropractor, comments on the rest which human beings need to offer themselves to assure a healthy immune system: "The immune system thrives on sleep, rest, relaxation, and most powerfully love and passion, while stress, worry and anxiety interrupt immune activity."[2] If your client complains or presents with burn-out due to work exhaustion, family disputes or crisis, you may also want to teach her how to share daily *Sanctification* or how to hold her thumbs as a relaxing self-attunement technique.

- Actively awaken the lymph to a more peaceful flow by providing a gentle and patient focus of attention to your attunement work. With all lymph and immune system attunement sharing, it is very important for you, the practitioner, to be consciously tranquil. This calm flow of energy imparted to your work may inspire a similar flow in your client's consciousness.

It may seem as if very little happens during an immune system attunement, yet oftentimes after you are finished, you and your client may feel completely refreshed, exuding relaxation such that you both recognize that you have entered into a more light-filled and gentle state.

Remember that your release of all expressions of ambition, especially to see specific results, may deepen your combined experience of purification even further.

- In humorous moments I like to view the immune system as a protective hedge like the CIA, complete with walkie-talkies, laser guns and viral-proof vests. Maybe you and your client can visualize a successful defense against a bacterial enemy attack sequence during your immune system attunement session. What other specific visualizations can your client come up with to enhance her own faith and belief that her immune system is working better for her? Talk through several scenarios before selecting the one best suited for her present situation. Medical visualization techniques often utilize powerful carnivores such as sharks, scavengers like vultures, and boundary-keepers such as armadillos. Consult your favorite zoo or medicine cards to find the perfect animal for your visualization needs.

- Offer immune/lymph attunement to your clients who suffer from such illnesses as lupus, breast implant syndrome (make sure the breast implants are removed for full attunement effect), fibromyalgia, chronic fatigue syndrome, cancer and post-cancer, the flu, and all other acute or chronic illnesses.

- Your client may also enjoy working on the *Paper Dot Exercise* (Chapter 9), using her immune system as the central focus.

Immune System Attunement Practice

Immune system attunement should follow cervical, endocrine gland, and all anatomical organ attunement. In this way, you have already stimulated the vibrational pattern to the immune system by working with the whole body, specifically at the thymus gland. To stimulate further clarification, use the thymus gland as the main contact point for all immune system attunement. You may also consider using the pineal, pituitary and thyroid glands for full love, truth, and radiant contact into the attunement process.

Standing to the left of your client, you will use the endocrine glands as the contact points into the immune system. Begin by placing your left hand (negative pole) over the thymus gland (index and middle fingers should be together, with energy pointing downward to the gland), using it as your first contact point. Then, place your right hand (positive pole) over the many lymph sites in the body, one at a time, moving your hand in small circular movements along the same flow channels as the lymph

LYMPH SYSTEM ATTUNEMENT ANATOMICAL CHART

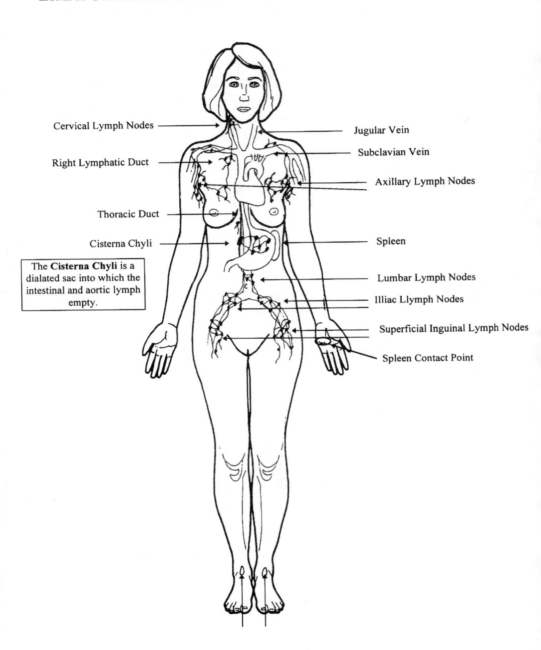

Cervical Lymph Nodes

Right Lymphatic Duct

Thoracic Duct

Cisterna Chyli

The **Cisterna Chyli** is a
dialated sac into which the
intestinal and aortic lymph
empty.

Jugular Vein

Subclavian Vein

Axillary Lymph Nodes

Spleen

Lumbar Lymph Nodes

Illiac Llymph Nodes

Superficial Inguinal Lymph Nodes

Spleen Contact Point

move. As you attune the lymph system, follow lymph flow which is specified below for best technical performance. Consult the chart opposite for lymph site locations:

Lymph Flow Guidelines

- The lymph from the upper limb drains into the **Axillary Lymph Nodes**.
- The lymph from the head and neck drains into the **Cervical Lymph Nodes.**
- The **Thoracic Duct** collects all lymph from the entire body except that which flows to the **Right Lymphatic Duct.**
- The **Right Lymphatic Duct** collects lymph from the right upper portion of the body, including the right arm, and hand and the right side of the head, down past the liver.
- The **Superficial Inguinal Lymph Nodes** drain the gluteal region, external genitals, anterior and lateral abdominal walls, part of the uterus and the inferior part of the anal canal.

Spleen Attunement Practice

This vitally important though small organ helps to regulate the blood system by forcing all blood vessels through tiny cysterna housed within it. These cysterna act as a 'police barrier' for the circulatory system, testing each red blood cell for its critical holding capability so that healthy cells may return to the blood stream to accommodate oxygen, carbon dioxide and vital nutrients.

Refer to the Lymph System Anatomical Chart to find where the spleen is located. Standing to the left of your client, attune the spleen by following this technique:

Spleen:

RH   *index and middle fingers, gently placed together, pointed downward over the small groove above the upper lip.*

LH   *fingers together, pointing inward over left side of the body where the spleen is located, in the left mid-thoracic area, just below the left ribcage.*

Focus on Lymph Tissue and the Breast

Remember these focus notes when you work with breast tissue, especially if your client has had breast cancer, or presents with breast cancer. Moving your positive hand (your negative hand is at the thymus or other endocrine gland) in small circular motions along the etheric body associated with the breast tissue, recognize these points:

1. Breast lymph drains cutaneous or superficial, and deep lymph areas.

2. Cancer of the breast spreads frequently through venous channels traveling to the lungs, liver and bones. For bones, cancer spreads through intercostal veins which communicate with the vertebral venous plexus.

3. When cancer prognosis is based on lymphatic drainage, the breast is divided into 4 equal quadrants. The best prognosis is with cancer found in the upper outer quadrant, and the worst prognosis is with cancer found in the lower inner quadrant (which is the closest location to the peritoneal cavity.)[3]

Refer to the Lymph Anatomical Chart on page 160 for specific lymph area locations. Your immune/lymph system attunement session should last about 20 minutes.

Chapter 14 Notes

[1] Personal correspondence with Aura, July 19, 1996.

[2] Stuart White, DC, 'Immune-Lymph System Awareness,' *The Capstone*, February, 1994, Issue 2, p. 3.

[3] For both the Lymphatic System and Breast Focus Notes, this information is taken from my medical school anatomy lecture notes.

15. Holding Patterns — Attuning the Brain and Spinal Cord

A woman with a previous spinal cord injury came to see me on a number of occasions to share attunement. She had been involved in a car accident years before which had damaged her spinal nervous system, and she had undergone several spinal cord surgeries to repair the damage. Yet, she was still suffering from a nervous disorder which left her physically weak, unable to lift or carry objects and psychologically unsure of herself.

She had recently been accepted into a massage therapy training program, and even though she knew that the program made rigorous physical demands, she was determined to prove to herself and others that she was a healer. She had faith that her own healing would come about gradually, as she learned how to heal others. Like so many other wounded therapists I knew, I could see that this woman possessed the same inner wisdom and faith in the healing process of life which is common to many in the healing arts profession.

The woman shared a few attunements with me over several weeks, and after each session she indicated to me that she felt better, was more relaxed and in touch with her inner power. I sensed however, that there was something else which needed to shift within her, in order to release a deeper holding pattern which I sensed was residing in her spine. After one of our sessions, I asked her about her relationship with her husband. She commented in an non-specific way that he was supportive of her healing arts interests, and that he was a devout Christian. I suggested that for her next session we include him in the attunement process, and that he could assist me in attuning her by sharing attunement through certain contact points on her feet which I would show him how to do. The woman liked this suggestion and we agreed that her husband would attend the next session.

The following week they both arrived, and after a few minutes of technical explanation regarding the feet and where and how to hold his hands, we began the session. As we were beginning he asked me, "Does attunement work with prayer?" I said, "Yes it does," and explained the use of non-directed prayer. I suggested to him that if he desired to pray during the session, the prayer should be focused in a non-result orientation, and that he seek Higher Power's will, not his own will, to be done during our time together. The husband liked this idea, and bowed his head in prayer as we began.

The husband's fervent attitude fascinated me, and so I watched him pray as I worked my way through the attunement process. When it came time for me to work on the woman's spine, I noticed that her husband looked close to tears. In the next moment, I could feel that he had repented in his heart. I could feel his emotional release through my own work on her spine. Immediately I felt her pattern beneath my fingertips shift from one of tension to one of relaxation. I realized then that the woman's husband had repented in his heart from his attitude of demand which he had apparently been expressing to his wife. The woman had responded to her husband's demanding attitude by allowing it to 'land' in her back, at the site of her previous injury. Through humility and prayer though, the husband now began to let go of his need to control his wife. Since the wife had been moving with the spirit of attunement for the previous weeks, this pattern easily shifted, and was freed-up within her spine.

Following the session, I presented my findings to them both. They both cried and nodded their heads in agreement. With loving hands and hearts, I left them in the session room, each holding the other in their arms, and caring for each other for the first time in many days.

Holding Patterns

> *No one can reveal God, but all can have the sacred privilege*
> *of **Letting God Reveal Himself**...Let every change prove itself...*
> ***Let it work out**...Let the light of His presence*
> *release the radiance of reality through your temple being.*
>
> —*Uranda*

On a mental level, we sometimes seek to control the outcome of our relationships and endeavors. When we let our mind rule us, we put the mind in the driver's seat, which we have previously seen is not its correct placement. The mind's correct place is as an open vehicle to the movement of spirit, and its role is to act as a servant of the *One Who Dwells*. The spiritual flow of love emanating from within is the inspiring and directing influence in all human outcome. The *One Who Dwells* is the governing Source for all things, and when yielded to by the human mind and heart, is perfectly capable of handling any situation with spiritual direction and divine intelligence.

Eric Leskowitz, MD, writes of the brain's true role as being a "filter or receiver, not the generator or transmitter of thoughts."[1] Thoughts are not created by the brain, but by a source and power much larger than those physical constructs. We have all held in mind thoughts which were self-generated (generated by the mind and not the spirit). This is an act which is out of alignment with divine spirit, and which then acts as a holding pattern, confining spirit and keeping personal self-willed purposes locked outside of spirit's flowing channel. Self-willed purposes hold people and situations in place without allowing spirit to touch and influence them.

A mental holding pattern which locks out spirit always carries negative consequences for ourselves and other human beings. These holding patterns are set in motion through one person identifying with the outer mind only, and thus identifying with all the memories, wounds, unprocessed emotions and outer world advertising that is present within its scope of perception. In other words, holding patterns are set in motion by the unresponsive energy from someone identified with their mental processes. Without divine spirit flowing through the mental capacities, the individual and group consciousness is open to such evils as illness, disease, sorrow and catastrophe. Greed and selfishness are prime self-acting holding patterns. They seek to lock out the flow of spiritual intelligence which seeks divine providence for all.

From a dynamic energy systems approach, scientists now know that the role of the human mind is to work together with the heart as one unit, and to synchronize, organize and integrate coordinated cellular function, potentially interacting between people in a similar way.[2] Entraining the capacities of heart and mind to the flow of radiant energy which emanates from within, we may allow spirit to touch all of our endeavors and relationships with divine grace and guidance. Just as the story above suggests, when we let go of our personal wanting, we free spirit to move within ourselves and to move out to others without our intervention. Identifying with spirit allows this letting go process to move with much more ease.

Brain/Cerebral Cortex Attunement (Fissure of Rolando — Central Sulcus)

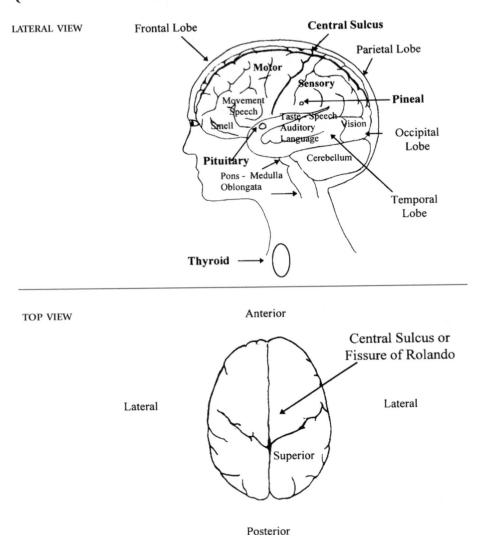

LATERAL VIEW   Frontal Lobe   **Central Sulcus**

Parietal Lobe

Motor

Sensory

Movement
Speech

Pineal

Taste   Speech

Smell   Auditory   Vision

Language

Occipital
Lobe

Pituitary   Cerebellum

Pons - Medulla
Oblongata

Temporal
Lobe

Thyroid ⟶

TOP VIEW   Anterior

Central Sulcus or
Fissure of Rolando

Lateral   Lateral

Superior

Posterior

Attuning the Brain at the Fissure of Rolando or Central Sulcus

We have an opportunity to entrain and attune the brain to its natural rhythms by focusing our attention at the Central Sulcus or Fissure of Rolando. This is a cross-shaped cranial suture located at the top of the head.

The Central Sulcus is the meeting place for all of the vibrational contact points of the body. By attuning the energy of the body at the Central Sulcus, we may touch into the energies associated with a person's memory, personal associations, motor and sensory projections.

The Central Sulcus divides the brain into four distinct regions or lobes. Each lobe houses its own set of vibrational contact points which directly influence a specific area of human function. Refer to the chart opposite as you consider the following contact point reference guidelines:

- *Frontal Lobe:* human intellect, sexual function and intimacy, tendencies towards aggression, reasoning, abstract thinking, language, motor movement and speech.

- *Parietal Lobe:* symbols and ideas, language, sensory taste and speech.

- *Occipital Lobe:* vision, awareness, and discrimination.

- *Temporal Lobe:* auditory function, language, sympathetic and emotional substrates.

- *Pons:* connects cerebral hemispheres.

- *Medulla Oblongata:* Cardiovascular and respiratory centers of autonomic nervous system. Note also that Uranda specified that the medulla oblongata was the resting depository for the vibrations associated with the ascending atoms of the body. There these vibrations would wait for 3 days before they ascended into the invisible realm of being.[3]

- *Motor and Sensory Canal of Central Sulcus:* (i) Superior — pain, touch, temperature, pressure, position, foot, leg, thigh, abdomen, back; and (ii) Lateral — shoulder, arm, fingers, head, mouth, face, position.[4,5]

Technique:

Begin by placing your hands together, in a prayerful pose, having your hands touch at the thumbs. Your hands should be facing palm side out and your other fingers should be laterally extended. Even though this positioning requires your hands to occupy a position unnatural to them both, you need not over-flex or over-extend either of them to gain the proper positioning.

Next, as you reference the Brain Top View chart on the opposite page, place your hands, in the aforementioned formation, one – two inches above your client's head region, and slowly bring them down along the central axis of the head until you feel or perceive an energy flow emanating from that area. That energy flow, stimulated by your fingers, is the site of the Central Sulcus. Hold your hands in this placement for a few minutes, keeping your wrists, arms and shoulders as relaxed as possible. Silently hold and balance the energies you feel until you sense a single pulse running through your hands. Keep the contact point chart next to you for easy reference. Your hands should pick up little tingles at first, but these should turn into a gentle warmth radiance, which also is a signal that the vibrational pattern is attuned.

Since you usually work with the Central Sulcus towards the end of a full body attunement session, the points within the Central Sulcus should easily 'come out' into your hands, because you have already established an energy flow throughout the entire body.

Spinal Cord Attunement Practice

The spinal column is the main contact point system to reach all of the anatomical systems of the body through the nervous system. Study the public domain chart, opposite, which was presented in one of the original *Gray's Anatomy* reference books. Notice how the nervous system, which is surrounded and protected by the spinal vertebrae, is associated with each anatomical organ system separately through specific nervous plexi. This chart allows you to easily see which part of the spinal column innervates which specific anatomical organ system. In this way, you may attune your client's anatomy by applying attunement energy at specific sites along the spinal column.

Spinal Cord Balancing Technique:

To begin, ask your client to lay on her side. Make sure your client is comfortably situated, with pillows placed on her sides if necessary to ensure that she won't slip off the massage table.

Next, place each hand at the opposite ends of your client's parasympathetic nervous system, i.e. your right hand should be placed inside the cervical vertebrae area, (between cervical vertebrae 1 – 7) before you reach a slight rise in the spinal column (this is cervical vertebra 7). Your left hand should be placed at the sacral nerve plexus area which is located within the sacrum and coccyx area (refer to the chart opposite for specific location). Remember, with attunement work, you don't touch the body. Instead you touch into the etheric energy field one – two inches above the physical form. Reference the above chart for these placements. Your shoulders, arms, wrists and hands should be as relaxed as possible. By beginning with the parasympathetic nervous system, you will initiate a flow of deep relaxing energy into your client's body. Balance the energies until you feel a single pulse run through your hands. You may also feel less tingling in your hands and a range of warmth spread between your

SPINE AND NERVE CHART

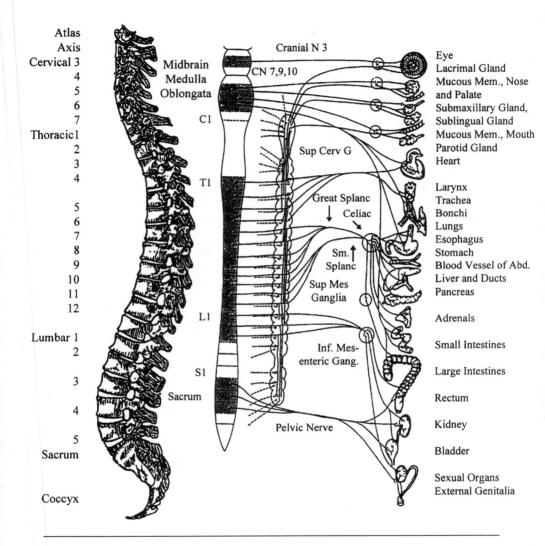

hands. These other signs will signal to you that the parasympathetic system has been attuned.

Spinal Cord Ascension Technique:

Uranda called the sacral plexus the 'storage battery' of the body, where unascended vibrational substance was housed before it moved upward, along the spine towards the medulla oblongata.[6] You may assist your client in her ascension process by moving the vibrational pattern felt along the spine upward towards the brain stem. When applied completely, this ascension technique is quite meticulous and lasts 15-20 minutes.

1. *Hold your right hand at the position of the medulla oblongata, which is at the base of the neck. Bring your left hand upward to meet it, moving slowly from the sacrum to the neck. The left hand should be placed palm down along the spine, or you may choose to bring the fingers together to focus the energy as one unit.*

   Along the way, stop and hold the energies you feel at specific areas along the spine. Coincide these stopping points with the spinal chart shown on the previous page, to find out where the possible distortion patterns exist, and their pertinent organ systems. By sharing attunement with each nervous plexus along the spine, you will move the vibrational body of the spinal column upward towards the medulla oblongata. This ascension technique, quoted by some as the 'Miller Technique' should follow the balancing technique described above for optimum therapeutic effect. The Miller Technique was developed in the early 1950's by Eddie and Gladys Miller, who were two of Uranda's personal attunement practitioners. Apparently Uranda's first Miller technique attunement was offered to him on the Millers' kitchen table![7]

2. *While stopping off at specific areas, keep in mind your client's presenting problems. For example, thoracic vertebrae 4 corresponds to the aorta and superior vena cava, which may have significance to your client if she presents with a heart problem. The lumbar vertebrae 1 – 5 correspond to the lower anatomical nervous functions affecting bowel, reproductive and lower leg anatomy (and may relate to sciatic problems).*

3. *With their agreement, you may utilize your client's spine to share a non-local attunement with someone else who needs to share radiant energy into a specific organ region. Simply focus your attention on the area of the spine which is associated with your long distance client's trouble spot. Approach the client in front of you as a contact point into the other client who is situated further away.*

4. *Complete your spinal work by again bringing into balance the spine at the parasympathetic sites at the base of the neck and the base of the sacrum. Quietly end this portion of your session with a silent prayer that the clarified energy now moving through your client's body will be sent where it is needed, along the nervous pathways to those organ systems with which they correspond. A full spinal attunement should last a good 15 – 30 minutes, depending on what you find needing to be brought into attunement.*

Attunement through the Eyes

Each one will see that which he is actually looking for.

—Uranda

You will recall from *Chapter 7* that response is the second phase in the attunement process. Response comes from within your own capacities of mind and heart and is given to the radiance of your inner Source. You can help to clarify the responsive flow in your client by sharing attunement with her through her eyes. Sharing attunement through the eyes was first developed within the Emissary attunement program in the early 1950's. Martin Exeter (then Cecil) said that sharing attunement through the eyes would open responsive flow to Source by clarifying their spiritual perception:

> *Distortion patterns in the individual capacity of spiritual perception prevent the individual from seeing things as they are, therefore it is evident that whether in relationship to the body, the physical eyes, or whether in relationship to the capacity of spiritual perception in the individual, there is a need for clearing, a need for changes to work out so that there may be clear vision.*[8]

He also commented that during eye attunements, others "can receive radiation through their eyes to all parts of their being."[9] As Uranda wrote years before that, "...according to your Vision or Perception, so will you go. You move toward that which you are looking upon."[10] Sharing attunement through the eyes will help clarify what your client sees and how she thereby discerns her world, spiritually or otherwise.

Sharing attunement through the eyes is also another way to attune the pineal gland, as the pineal is fed through the electromagnetic spectrum in the light force (see *Appendix A* — Histology of the Endocrine Gland System for further information on this point). The attunement energy you offer to the pineal gland through the eyes will, in turn, directly nourish the pituitary gland. This is because the pituitary sits in close proximity to the pineal, and receives neurological signals from the pineal to send out its own hormone stimulus to the other glands in the body. Therefore, sharing attunement through the eyes helps to accomplish all of the following: attunes the pineal, attunes the pituitary by way of the pineal, attunes the other endocrine glands by way of the pituitary gland, and attunes your client's spiritual perceptions by clarifying how she sees her world.

Eye Attunement Technique:

After attuning the spinal column, have your client lie on her back once again. Place both of your palms over her eyes and focus the flow of energy through your palm chakras into her eyes. You may also choose to apply specific radiation to the eyes by drawing together the fingers of each hand and pointing the energy downward into each eye. If you attune each eye one at a time, utilize the pituitary gland, pineal, left or right cervical pattern placement or occipital lobe as possible contact points. Your client may keep her eyes open or closed during this time.

Of course, if your client presents with eye irritations, cataracts or other kinds of eye troubles, sharing attunement with the eyes will speed-up the healing process at that location. Also, offer attunement through the eyes prior to, during and after all of your clients' eye surgeries.

Attunement energy may also reverse some known eye impairments. For example, I once knew a girl who was born with one blind eye. Her father, an experienced attunement practitioner, began sharing attunement directly through her eyes when she was a teenager, and she slowly began to see light through her blind eye! Of course, the young girl had been attuned to the flow of attunement energy for many years, which might have accounted for this light reaction at that time in her life.

We may also recall the New Testament account of the Master's healing of the blind man. "I once was blind, but now I see," said the blind man of his healing at the hand of Jesus. In this example, we may recall that Jesus covered this man's eyes with a specific kind of mud which he mixed with his own saliva. We may meditate on the spiritual significance of the man's statement as well as the fact that the man was healed of his blindness due to the attunement which the Master shared with him through his eyes.

Chapter 15 Notes

[1] Eric Leskowitz, MD, 'Metaphors in the Teaching of Holistic Medicine,' *Alternative Therapies*, July 1997, Volume 3, No. 4, p. 111.

[2] Linda G. Russek and Gary E. Schwartz, 'Energy Cardiology: A Dynamical Energy Systems Approach for Integrating Conventional and Alternative Medicine,' *ADVANCES: The Journal of Mind-Body Health*, Fall, 1996, Volume 12, No. 4, p. 4.

[3] Personal correspondence with Tom Fallon.

[4] Keith L. Moore, Clinical Anatomy, third edition (Baltimore: Williams & Wilkins, 1992), p. 693.

[5] The Emissaries, Anatomical Diagrams (Loveland: Eden Valley Press, 1984), p. 6.

[6] Personal correspondence with Tom Fallon.

[7] Ibid.

[8] Martin Cecil, 'Almsgiving' an extemporaneous worship service given at 100 Mile House, B.C., Canada, August 9. 1953.

[9] Ibid., p. 14.

[10] Uranda, Letters to You, p. 23.

16. Attuning the Skeletal System

A man who has shared attunement all of his life tells this story of how he was helped to heal his broken leg when he was young.

Out riding his horse one day, his attitude was a bit off-kilter, which affected his horse, so he lost control. Suddenly, his horse stopped short in front of a tree and sent the boy flying with his foot still caught in the stirrup.

The boy lost consciousness for a time but when he came to, he was shocked to find that he was unable to move his left leg. Some friends arrived and carried him to the house of the Attunement Master Server who lived a short distance away. The Master Server shared attunement with the boy and gave him a special drink made up of liquid and calcium supplements.

Friends then drove the boy to the hospital. X-rays confirmed that he had a broken leg, only now there was so much swelling at the site of the injury that the doctor couldn't put on a cast. The doctor sent the boy and his friends home with strict instructions to ice the leg to bring down the swelling, and then bring him back later so that he could set the bone and place a cast on the leg.

For the next couple of days, the boy's family iced his leg while the Attunement Master Server continued to share attunements with him. The boy slowly began to feel better with the warm current of energy that the Master Server sent through his body with each attunement. He began to relax and felt more at ease with his injury, thankful for the attunements which helped ease his progress.

After a few days, the boy returned to the hospital to receive his cast. The journey to the hospital was bumpy and this hurt his leg, but the

Attunement Master Server accompanied him this time to the hospital. Again he felt the warm energy from the attunement he received, and he didn't mind the pain that much.

When it came time to re-set his leg, the doctor couldn't believe what he saw. The bone had set itself, and the anesthesiologist was not needed for the surgery. New X-rays confirmed a perfect set, and the boy didn't have to undergo surgery. The cast then went on easily.

Though the doctor was amazed at the outcome ("I've never seen anything like it!"), the Master Server was not surprised, nor was the boy. They both knew that the healing power of spirit, when allowed to magnify, did a fine healing job all by itself.[1]

Skeletal System Attunement Practice

Working with the skeletal system establishes a clear connection into the structural integrity of the body. You may naturally realign the skeletal system without applying forced manipulation by stimulating into place the natural lines of force present in its etheric body counterpart. By holding the energy pattern found in wrists, ankles, joints and long bones, it is possible to realign the skeletal system. Follow these several methods outlined below.

1. The first method utilizes the wrists and ankle joints of the body, and was developed by Uranda in 1951. A simple and effective technique, you cup the fingers of each hand around each of your client's wrists or ankles, keeping your fingers about one inch above the skin. Point your thumbs into the hollow portions of the bones (the hollow portion is the indentation found in the center back portion of the wrist or ankle). Wait until you begin to feel an energy flow, and balance this energy pattern just as your would balance the cervical pattern at the neck. Uranda pointed out that this was an excellent energy balancing technique when the practitioner couldn't attune the neck area due to the client being bed-ridden. He discovered that the wrist and ankle joints carried an extension of the energy pattern found at the cervicals, and could be used just as effectively as balancing the body at the neck.[2]

2. The second method is called the *Long Bone Technique*, and by was created by Paul Price, a Canadian Attunement Practitioner. This non-touch attunement approach seems to set in motion a healing resonance from within the skeletal system. This benefits the client who suffers from such discomforts as those found in low back pain, sciatica, and hip and knee joint difficulties.

THE HUMAN SKELETON — LONG BONES ANATOMICAL CHART

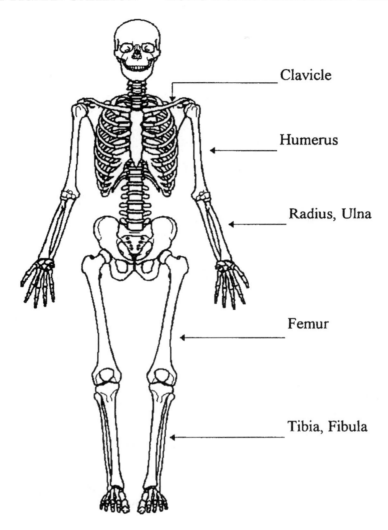

Clavicle

Humerus

Radius, Ulna

Femur

Tibia, Fibula

Begin by working with the shoulders, radiating into each long bone of the arm through the shoulder joint until there is a balance. Keeping the left hand at one of the shoulder joints, I move the right hand to the opposite hip joint, forming a diagonal across the trunk of the body; I stay until there is balance. I use the same procedure, working with other diagonals (shoulder and hip joints) until the current balances. I then move both hands to the hip joint and balance again... When you are working across the trunk of the body, you will likely find that it takes longer to find a balance because of the many organs, etc., that are located there...

The same procedure approach as above is used as I move down the body. You put one hand on the hip, the other on the knee forming a diagonal. Repeat using the other diagonal and move both hands to the knees, always looking for a balance of the current. I usually keep the left hand above the right (i.e., left at the hip, right at the knee, etc.). Again work with the diagonals using the knee and ankle joints, ending with both hands at the ankle joints. To close, I return to the cervical pattern and will usually find a stronger flow and keener sense of balance than at the initiation of the attunement.[3]

To stimulate new blood cell formation and attune the other physiological functions of long bones, place your hands longitudinally over the long bones of the body, one hand on each side of the body. Set up the energy field and allow a balance to come into those areas. You may also place one hand at a time over each long bone and use the pituitary gland as your contact point for this attunement (the pituitary gland sends out hormone stimulators which act on long bones through a negative-feedback loop process).

Attunement and Massage Sessions

People hold conscious and emotional pattern imprints in their soft tissue. Having worked in the field of massage for many years, I am always fascinated by its magical process, and how it frees-up emotional distresses, stress and anxiety after only a few minutes of concentrated effort. I remember offering massage to one client in particular, a woman who consistently held in her anger, and subsequently needed me to rub it away from the small of her back. It was as if each time she expressed her anger, her upper back began to hurt with parallel anguish. My deep effleurage, petrissage and tapotement strokes would loosen up the emotional memory traces which she held within her soft tissue, but it did not dissolve these imprints completely. Massage only seemed to loosen and move this energy around, transforming it from being stuck to being fluid. In order to transform the energy into positive matter, and to instill a sense of closure to the session, the practitioner needs to apply a proven energy medicine technique, such as attunement. I suggest the following to end your massage sessions:

1. Share an attunement with your client at the cervical pattern to close your massage session (your client should be in a supine position, lying on her back). Balancing the cervicals at the close of any session will strengthen the flow of energy through your client's back and bring about a sense of closure, while increasing your client's feeling of ease and well-being.

2. Try sharing a full-body attunement with your client following completion of a full-body massage session. Most of my massage clients appreciate staying for an additional half-hour to receive a full attunement, as it brings about a deep sense of peacefulness. Or, if your session runs short, fill-up your remaining time by attuning the cervicals and the endocrine gland system to open your client to her portals of light before she leaves.

3. If your sessions ends with your client resting on her stomach, you can instill her with an additional level of peace and stillness by ending your session with an attunement spinal balance. Standing to the left of your client, place your hands above the parasympathetic points on her spine (the cervicals and sacral areas). Spread out the fingers of your right hand at the atlas point, extending your thumb and pinky fingers across the atlas, into the hollows of your client's ears. The other three fingers of your right hand should be together, and pointing upward at the position of the atlas. Your left hand should rest above your client's sacral-iliac line. Simply hold this energy pattern — do not touch your client with a rocking or gentle shaking motion, as some practitioners choose to do. By holding this pattern of energy, you will 'still the waters' of the massage treatment, and bring about a sense of serenity and peace for you both.

Chapter 16 Notes

[1] Abridged version of 'The Humbling,' from <u>The Boy, A Coming of Age</u>, (Loveland: Foundation House Publications, Inc., 1991, pp. 172–176.

[2] Private correspondence with Tom Fallon.

[3] Paul Price, 'The Long Bone Attunement Technique,' *The Capstone*, (New York: Center for Health, Healing and Attunement), January, 1993, p. 2.

17. Wound Healing

"Okay, hon. So, we're going to dinner now and then a movie, right?"

"Yes we are!" he answered, and we were on our way. My husband and I had just finished shopping, and we were looking forward to eating at our favorite local restaurant. We had decided to take this time off mid-week to relax and enjoy each other's company. As both our work schedules had recently become quite intense, we relished being able to take this spontaneous time alone together.

While we were stopped at the left turn lane, I turned to him from the passenger seat to talk about the movie we were going to see. Somewhere in the back of my mind I registered the sound of a car skidding itself to a stop. When it slammed into us, it took me by complete surprise, hurtful with unexpected shock. This certainly wasn't supposed to happen to us! My head hit hard against the back seat head rest, I was thrust up violently into my front seat shoulder belt and felt a rippling shock wave move down my spine. For a few seconds afterward, I was speechless and then intuitively knew that something had happened to my neck and back and that I shouldn't move either one for the time being. My husband was alright and got out of the car immediately to assess the damage. I held my head between my hands to keep it from moving, and began sharing self-attunement with my cervical pattern.

The man who was stopped in his car in front of us heard and saw the crash and came over to see how he could help. So, while others attended to the technicalities of the crash and called 911 for help with my possible injuries, I sat alone in the front seat of my car, holding my head and keeping my fingers on the pulse I felt in the hollow behind my ears.

While I sat there in silence, watching the scene unfold around me, I assessed the situation. I knew that something had happened to my back, and that I would probably need medical attention. That meant all of our effort to make space in our lives for a relaxing evening was shot. Instead, a new space began to open up inside me. I realized that this whole experience, in which I was a major participant, had set in motion an entirely new series of events, of what I knew not. I had no idea what lay ahead of me and could only hope for the best. At least the damage to the car was minimal or none, the driver who hit us did so at not more than ten miles per hour, I was conscious and could move all of my limbs, and even though I needed medical attention, the injury was probably minimal to moderate at worst. My husband was handling all the details about the car and we were fully covered on insurance, so I didn't have to be concerned about anything. I began to feel very thankful for these factors, and open, responsive, and trusting of the process and the people involved in it with me. And, I also realized that for the first time in many weeks I was in a position of needing to be completely still, which was a much needed blessing. Everybody else was doing the work, and this thought made me grin. That was a new space, indeed, and so I began to relax into the flow of help which was enveloping me.

The lady who had hit us came over to the car window, and talking into her cellular phone, told me that she was talking to 911, and wanted to know how I was. I said, "All I know is that I feel like I shouldn't move my neck." She conveyed this to 911 and within minutes I heard the ambulance driving toward us. I was so impressed with their quick response time! Very soon there was a team of paramedics surrounding me, making an initial examination. Mike, the one who was feeling for broken bones said, "Well, it looks like you might have a whiplash but just to make sure, we'd like to put you in a stationary position, strap you down with a neck brace and take you over to the hospital to get you x-rayed." I sensed that this was the right course of action (even though I didn't think anything was broken), so they proceeded to get the neck brace on, strap me down to a hard wooden board and carry me to the ambulance. Gratitude became my abiding sense. I kept repeating to the men surrounding and helping me, "I am so thankful that it's not raining!" (It had been raining earlier in the afternoon). And I thanked them for assisting me with such efficient timing.

I was also quite thankful that I was fully conscious and not in a lot of pain (at least not yet). The entire episode fascinated me with its streamlined detail and care. I was whisked-off to the nearby hospital, and after a short drive, arrived with hardly a jolt. While in the ambulance, I began to hold my thumbs because that was the only attunement technique available for me to do (my arms were strapped down to the board). During the drive to the hospital, I could feel the balanced flow of energy pulse through my entire body. I commented to Mike and his team how impressed I was with their efficient procedure, and how thankful I was for it. Mike acknowledged my compliment and called the hospital from the car to let them know that we were coming. The left side of my back began to hurt while we were driving in the ambulance and I mentioned this only once to Mike to share that information with him. When we arrived, another team of professionals met us at the front door of the emergency entrance. I was stable, stationary, in good hands and thankful to be so as they wheeled me into the ER.

After being taken into an examination room, a team of nurses proceeded to ask me questions, take and record my vital signs and remove my clothes for x-rays. I told them how thankful I was to be fully covered by insurance. And then I remembered something and laughed out loud as I told them, "You know, I'm not supposed to be here. I'm the massage therapist. I just got through seeing a Personal Injury Protection client for a cycle of massages. Now I get to see how the patient feels!" They grinned their response and we talked about what a learning experience this would be for me. I then told them how impressed I was with their efficiency, personableness and expertise. I couldn't believe everything was happening so quickly and effortlessly. My husband hadn't arrived yet (one of the nurses said he was filling out the Sheriff's report), but they said that they would keep an eye out for him in the hallway. The atmosphere around us was light and cheerful. They placed a warmed blanket over me and then left when the doctor entered the room to ask me some questions and do some tests.

Soon after the physician left, Pete, the X-ray technician, came in to wheel me into the X-ray room. Again, I was met with smiling faces, strong hands, expert awareness about the possibilities surrounding my care, and happy small talk. I thanked them for taking my X-rays and taking such good care of me. They smiled and told me how happy they were to be working as a team together. Pete wheeled me back into the examination room where my husband was waiting for me. I told him how thankful I was to see him, and we held hands and talked about going to dinner (we were both very hungry). Soon, the doctor came in to tell me the good news, that I had no broken or cracked bones, and would only suffer a possible whiplash from the accident. He took off my neck brace and straps, and tested my neck's range of motion. I was very stiff and beginning to feel pretty sore in my upper back area, but all in all, I felt that I was very lucky to have come through this ordeal with only a minor injury. With my anti-inflammatory prescription in hand, we left the hospital and went to dinner.

We returned home that night very late, too late to call my long distance attunement practitioner. So, the first thing I did the next morning was to call him and tell him what had happened to me. As we were already set to share a long distance attunement that morning, he immediately began sharing long distance attunement with me and continued to do so for weeks following.

Looking back at this experience, I was amazed at the new space which emerged in my life due to the fact that I was immobilized and other people had to do everything for me. I was freed up to just be and not have to think about any of the details. I just lay in the hospital rooms and stared up at the ceiling. Life gave me no alternative but to be still, and Boy! did it feel great! Thankful for the new space, I didn't try to buck the process, but felt relieved, at ease and thankful to have the best hands in the world supporting me. My injury experience was one of relaxation, not of stressing out about the future. "Be still and know, that I am God" took on new meaning for me, for when I looked out from this still point and looked around me, I could see the face of God on every face of those helping me. I realized that as I continued to express a sense of gratitude, that this attuned attitude increased the flow of healing energy moving through me, which in turn helped to maintain my conscious focus on the healing process. The definition of 'First Aid' also took on new meaning. First aid really meant just that — giving aid to someone else first, before oneself. This injury experience reminded me that we were indeed each other's keeper.

The Nature of Wounds

Wounds are like tears placed in the fabric of your being. Whether you injure yourself, go through surgery, or suffer from trauma and/or shock, when something enters your body to break its coherency apart, you then break apart the dense weave of etheric body substance which surrounds and interpenetrates your physical form. Because this invisible sheath contains parts of yourself that you can't see, such as your emotions and mental processes, when you put a tear into your etheric field, you automatically signal an accompanying memory trace inside your emotional and mental bodies which register their association with that particular injury. These somatic memories usually find hidden cause to root themselves within you with destructive force, sometimes disrupting your life after the injury.

Dr Judith Lewis Herman, MD, comments on the nature of trauma by suggesting that the underlying cause of all post-traumatic stress disorders is a feeling of powerlessness which the victim experiences at the time of the incident. "At the moment of trauma, the victim is rendered helpless by overwhelming force…" thereby causing the victim to feel out of control, lose connection with surrounding structures and their meaning, feel disconnected from the present moment, and lose judgmental powers. Herman cites three main symptoms of trauma-related disorders: hyperarousal of the sympathetic nervous system which causes a persistent expectation of danger; continual intrusion of the memory of the event into consciousness; and constriction of any kind of reasonable response to the event at the time it occurred, with accompanying suppression of bodily activity.[1] All of these reactions may play themselves out in exaggerated and unplanned ways, stifling a person's creative powers with surprising distraction.

Sharing energetic light work with an injured victim or hospitalized patient at the scene of the wound infliction has been known to defuse and dissolve the conscious and subconscious memory traces before they have a chance to root themselves within the etheric body framework. Dr James Oschman explains that energy work which is offered at the time of an accident or surgery, or shortly thereafter, tends to discourage the memory trace from ever taking place. He writes, "Trauma is set in place virtually instantaneously, in the fraction of a second before our self-awareness can notice it. Remarkably, its resolution can be as quick and almost as unnoticed."

Oschman writes about the work of William Redpath, an energy healer who discovered how to release blocked energy systems. Redpath discovered that it wasn't through movement therapies that people heal themselves from trauma-related illnesses and stresses, but through stillness techniques which establish an entrainment energy promoted by the thalamus. It wasn't movement that initiated what he called a serious action (healing action) from the nervous system, but an immobility, that entrained energy pattern which the brain looks for to foster health and well-being.[2]

Sharing attunement with yourself and your surround at the time of an accident or invasive surgery may unblock the flow of constricted energy which tends to lock itself around your trauma. Having an attunement practitioner present to assist you through this clearing process is best, but if you do not have someone around you to share attunement, then it is best that you offer attunement to yourself so that your energy pattern will maintain its balance and composure. Tom Johnston shares this story of how he held onto his negative emotions surrounding his whiplash incident, and how these later settled into his body for years following:

...physical injuries have emotional consequences. When my car was hit from behind, I felt betrayed. I felt angry toward the person who hit me. I felt overwhelmed by all the details and obligations I had to handle... I stored all these emotions in my body... Never was the injured part of me cradled or given permission to feel and release the emotional hurt, anger and abandonment I stored in my tissues at the moment of injury.[3]

Instead of allowing yourself to feel anger, resentment, depressed, anxious, distraught, or guilty (if you happen to be the person who harmed someone else), follow these simple guidelines, as described in the story above, for a healthier response pattern to injury and surgery:

1. Offer attunement to yourself or another only after proper first aid is administered. Attunement should never replace standard emergency procedures.

2. Share attunement with yourself or another, or have someone attune you immediately following any accident. If you are going into surgery, have an attunement practitioner work with your energy pattern before, during and after the surgery, and continue receiving attunement (local or long distance) until your wound is healed.

3. During your conscious moments immediately following the accident or surgery, give thanks for all things. Tell the people who assist you how thankful you are for their help. Compliments open the door for a positive flow of energy to come back to you and surround all concerned with healing grace.

4. Try to be still as much as possible. Let other people take care of you. Let go of trying to control the outcome. Just let life continue without any added strain.

5. Talk about your feelings, the pain you feel and your concerns with an open mind and heart. In a recent medical study, it was found that patients who spoke openly about their experience tended to reveal a "greater optimism and faith in the mind and body's ability to heal. Participants began to understand the power of honestly identifying and expressing their thoughts and emotions, which in turn provided greater personal power to confront any major event in life."[4]

6. Let yourself rest. Know that your poor concentration following an accident or surgery is your body's way of telling you to rest and recuperate.

7. If you begin receiving attunement for an injury or surgery site long after your body has healed, please note that the energy pattern will not be the same and will not be as intense as if the injury received

attunement immediately. Chris Jorgensen, an accomplished attunement practitioner writes, "If you don't begin to work with an injury such as a burn until hours or days later, the pattern has set, and as a result, the re-creation process is longer. This is because the pattern has been largely crystallized as being real in the person's consciousness and subconscious mind."[5] Because the pattern has set in, dislodging the physical substrates from the invisible flow may take longer and require more diligent attention from the practitioner.

Injury Treatment Attunement Guidelines

Follow these guidelines when you share attunement with injured sites: all wounds, injuries and accidents should be worked with in detail, slowly clearing away the distortion pattern, taking short breaks and coming back to the area to clear away more distortion. Oftentimes, as with a leg break, burn or operation, the energy pattern feels quite intense when you first begin and gradually dissipates into calmness as hours go by. (Please see *Chapters 19* and *20* for story matter relating to this point).

- When you begin to attune someone who has suffered an injury, attention should go first to the cervical and endocrine gland patterns, and then to the site of the injury. Utilize some of the glands as contact points if you are aware of any held negative feelings present in your client. For example, if your client expresses resentment about having been in the accident, utilize the purifying flow of energy coming from the thymus gland as a contact point to the injured site.

- The following describes how the flow of a distortion pattern dissipates: As you work to clear away distortion at the injured site, stay focused on the area until you feel a lull in the intensity of the pattern. Usually, if you step away for a short break when this lull is reached and then come back into the pattern again after a little while, you will feel a large increase of distortion rush into your hands, but this pattern will decrease in strength quicker than before. If you work with this increasing-then-quickly-decreasing pattern until it mostly subsides (this may take hours, depending on the nature of the injury), then you may stop for the day and return the next day to the pattern. When you return again, the pattern should feel much more relaxed than the day before, which should tell you that much of the distortion has dissipated and the healing process is well on its way. This pattern works the same whether you are on-site for an injury or sharing long distance attunement.

- Send radiant energy to the wound by shaping the fingers of your positive hand to fit the wound site. If the wound is small, place your index and middle fingers together gently, and focus the energy moving from your fingertips to the site. If the wound is large, use the flat surface of your palm, sending energy to the site through the palm chakra. In both instances, bend your wrist slightly to fit how your hand needs to be situated to the injury site, but do not force your wrist to bend in any uncomfortable position. Always use good judgment when shaping your hands to an injury because you will probably be there for a while!

- If you share (give and receive) attunement regularly, and follow the sanctification, entering in and other practice approaches found in this and other positively-based spiritual faith systems, you will find that your receiving attunement during an accident will feel natural to you, as well as increase the rapidity of your wound- healing. Because your emotions and thoughts are already well attuned to your radiant inner guidance system, you will probably move swiftly through the process (as my story demonstrated), have less damage to your person, and have no ill effects or secondary problems following the incident. Maintaining a healthy attunement program in your life is part of maintaining a good, balanced preventive medical program!

- It is best to have your family members learn attunement technique so that anyone may assist the other in times of emergency.

Pre-Surgery Self-Attunement

If you wish to attune yourself before surgery, it is important to invite your consciousness and the cells directly involved in the forthcoming surgery to let go. Encourage the letting go process by sending supportive messages to your body. Inform your body that a healthier pattern and lifestyle is forthcoming, and to trust the healing process. Tell your body that this upcoming surgery is needed, and that it is the best thing for you at the time. Notify the cells which are going to be 'sacrificed to the knife' that they are going to die, and thank them for the life-giving service which they have provided to you so far. Support your body's letting go process by affirming the positive points about the surgery, i.e. that the surgery will allow something better to be born for the whole body, and that the surgery will occur without any mishap. Invite the cells of your body to join you in consciously preparing for the unknown by maintaining faith in Higher Power to heal all wounds.

If you don't have an attunement practitioner to share attunement with you prior to surgery, you can attune your cells to let go by simply placing your hand within the etheric body directly over the site to be operated. Stimulate the energy pattern over the site and invite it to change as you sense its rhythmic energy pattern. Inform the cells within the energy pattern that they need to leave (be simple, yet strong about this invitation) because their leaving will allow something new and better for the body to be born. Focus the energy by bringing your fingers together at the site, and directing the flow of energy to the site, or use the flat portion of one palm, and hold it gently against the etheric body of the site with healing energy. You don't need to use a contact point to perform this pre-surgery attunement. Attuning your site before a surgery, you may be amazed at the easy healing outcome which emerges.

To share a story about pre-surgery self-attunement, I performed this exercise prior to my gum surgery which I experienced in 1997. Because of the position of one of my wisdom teeth, the tooth next to this wisdom tooth did not grow into its place with enough bone, and subsequently an empty cavity grew around it. The area required surgery so that it could be filled with bone replacement. For two days before my surgery, I warned my mouth that there was going to be an invasive treatment performed in that area and to let go of its known energy pattern. I invited the space to move forward with me in consciousness, and to let come something new and healthier for my body. Then, for thirty minutes before my gum surgery, I sat in my car, outside the periodontist's office, and attuned the site of the surgery, telling it through my conscious thought process and energy from my hand that everything was going to be okay, that the doctor was very good, that I knew this was the best thing for my body at this time, and that the surgery would go smoothly. After following all the required healing procedures suggested by the doctor, my dentist informed me six months later that my 4 millimeter gum reading (it had been a 9 millimeter reading) was one of the healthiest sites she had ever seen following a surgery, and that my mouth was completely healed.

Beyond Woundology

For if ye forgive men their trespasses,
your heavenly Father will also forgive you:
But if ye forgive not men their trespasses,
neither will your Father forgive your trespasses.

—*Jesus Christ, Matthew 6:14–15*

Caroline Myss, PhD, speaks about 'woundology,' the phenomenon in our culture that wounded people like to associate with other wounded people.

She calls this kind of relationship having 'Wound Mates,' and says: "A whole tribal culture has been created around woundology, in which we exchange an unconscious agreement in the negative, to support our shadows and not our health." Her woundology discourse goes on to say that we've also developed a large support system in our society wherein we give each other credit for talking about our wounds. Counseling circles, focus groups, rap sessions and group therapies are like "taking a boat across the river and forgetting to get off on the other side."[6] All this talk and emotional cycling may be keeping us from taking the individual steps which we need to, in order to completely free ourselves from the power that our wounds have over us. And that is to *forgive the person or event who wounded you, feel yourself be transformed in the process, and allow whoever it was who wounded you to be transformed in the process as well.* Treating the cause by letting all be healed, you lose the symptoms.

Someone who has forgiven their trespasser can shine the light on the process. Take the contemporary example which appeared on TV recently: an American girl went to South Africa to help in the post-apartheid process and was murdered in the township where she was helping. Her family visited South Africa, met the families of the perpetrators and the perpetrators themselves, and there was a reconciliation which affected many more people than the individuals immediately concerned. In this and other examples of forgiveness, the act of forgiving transformed the forgiver, while also transforming the forgiven. When one person is forgiven, a whole world receives forgiveness. When the Son of Man (who was Jesus Christ) forgave his tormentors, forgiveness began to flow out into humanity with a ripple effect which has continued unceasingly for millennia. The forgiven themselves were transformed, and the seed was planted to grow into our own time where we await its fruition. Ghandi and his people learned that the act of non-violence had the power to change the course of an entire nation. Turning the other cheek and forgiving one's trespasser can bring about creative transformations in ourselves and in others which has long lasting effect.

Uranda suggests that giving and receiving forgiveness is possible because God has already forgiven us for all of our sins before we even contemplate thinking or doing them:

> *Your Father has already forgiven you, in actual fact. God, by whatever name called, however conceived, God has, from the foundation of the world, in relationship to every human being, He has forgiven every ill thing that man has ever done, that you have ever done, or anyone else has ever done… but you must receive his forgiveness. It is not a question as to whether God has forgiven you; it is a question*

as to whether you have received the forgiveness that God has already given.[7]

The challenge which we face is to individually receive the forgiveness which God has given us, and extend this same forgiving nature to each other, thereby completing the cycle which God has initiated. If we don't receive the forgiveness or extend it to others, we stop the flow of love energy coming our way which is there to move us forward with our lives.

What we may not know or be able to accept is that when we receive forgiveness (when we complete the cycle), a new energy pattern enters our life which then changes our future. No longer are the ill seeds, which were planted by reason of the trespass, going to grow and be harvested. Forgiveness changes the vibrational pattern associated with life patterns. Forgiveness brings with it a healing nature as well as a shift in behavior. Oftentimes, when one's life pattern is healed, is forgiven, then healing of the body follows suit.

Loving God and receiving divine forgiveness may be the key which we may use to unlock our wounded relationships. The energy it takes for me to receive God's forgiveness is simply a turning upwards in my mind and heart to accept it. When I extend this same upward motion to another, I empower them to move forward with their life, free of their trespassed moments. The power of forgiveness *is* the power of love. When I forgive someone who trespassed against me, I begin to actually love that person, and that's a lot more powerful an expression than just thanking them for the lesson.

After all, who is it we should be thanking? When we begin to place the credit for our emotional healing on each other or even on the learning process, we lose sight of where the true credit needs to go in order for us to move forward in life's ascending process. The power to express forgiveness and to express love comes from Source. When I return this love to Source, then the power of forgiveness begins to flow through me to my trespassers with transforming speed, awakening Self, and initiating the same process in others. In my experience, thanking God first, last and always is the very upward movement I need to impel my world forward with healing latitude.

Speaking in the temple at Jerusalem, Jesus told his listeners, "(And) thou shalt love the Lord thy God with all thy heart, and with all thy soul, and with all thy mind; and with all thy strength: this is the first commandment. And the second is like, namely this, Thou shalt love thy neighbor as thyself. There is none other commandment greater than these" (Mark 12:30–31). Who would we know ourselves to be if we actually did this in every moment? Loving Source with all reduces the impact of our wounds to an easier style of managing their losses while at the same time opening up our consciousness to fulfill the second great commandment, "Love thy neighbor as thyself." When we love Source, we lose nothing, and instead, we gain more love of Self and Other in the process. I love my neighbor as I love myself as I love Source. In that trilogy, my wounds are released.

Chapter 17 Notes

[1] Judith Lewis Herman, MD, <u>Trauma and Recovery</u>, (Basic Books, a division of HarperCollins, 1992), pp. 33–35.

[2] Dr James Oschman, 'Therapeutic Entrainment,' Energy Review Part 3b, *Journal of Bodywork and Movement Therapies*, April, 1997, p. 192.

[3] Tom Johnston, 'Massage and Emotion Release,' *Massage*, Issue No. 34, Nov/Dec, 1991, p. 68.

[4] Rodgers D., Beltz G., Oven M., 'Psychospiritual therapy as adjunctive treatment for cancer,' *Alternative Therapies*, July, 1997, Volume 3, No. 4, p. 99.

[5] Chris Jorgensen, <u>Attunement: Love Made Visible</u>, (Kansas City: Self-published, 1996), p. VII–180.

[6] Caroline Myss, 'The Courage to be Healthy,' *Noetic Sciences Review*, Spring, 1997, p. 26.

[7] Uranda, 'Forgiveness,' an extemporaneous worship service offered on Sunrise Ranch (Loveland, CO: Eden Valley Press, 1953), p. 3.

Part Three

The Creative Field

*What is healing but the removal of a
chaotic condition, the removal of a discord?
What is healing but the bringing of peace into the tissues,
into the mind, into the heart?...
Blessed Ones, if there is to be healing it must be
more than healing of one human being;
it must be healing of the world of human beings,
so that they may be brought into harmonious arrangement
according to the Divine Design,
in blessing to all who would receive.*

—Uranda

18. The Life Process

Dr Michael J. Moore, a Chiropractor practicing in Redding, California tells this story about the birth of his daughter, Alisha:

"One evening, about a week before my wife, Donna was due to give birth, she started having some mild 'cramps' which occurred sporadically, every five, fifteen and thirty minutes without any set pattern. She felt an intensity of energy, but nothing serious enough to convince us that she was in labor. At about 2:30 in the morning we decided to share an attunement. As I moved through the technique, stimulating all the contact points in order, she remarked that she felt the intensity of the contractions increase with the attunement. By the time I finished, about thirty minutes later, the contractions were strong, five minutes apart. This was enough to convince us that she was in labor."

"We called the midwife to tell her to hurry over for the birth, but once the atmosphere had been created to welcome our new child into the world, labor progressed quickly. Our daughter was born within two hours of the attunement, during the quiet early morning hours of the first day of spring. She arrived without help from our midwife, and without complications. It was a beautiful experience of allowing life's natural balance and harmony to be restored in the body, freeing the miracle of life to unfold."

Conception and Birth

> *The greatest influence on a child*
> *is the unlived life of the parent.*
>
> —Carl Jung

The patterns of agreement and relationship we keep outside the womb mirror those agreement patterns we first feel inside the womb. That welcoming pattern of energy which is provided before the child enters the world may be clearly identified and maintained with attunement. Over the years, within the Emissary Ministry, attunement practitioners have always played an active role in providing such a loving atmosphere before, during and after the birth process, and have been on hand to share attunement with family members for all major life events and transitions.

During the conception, gestation and birth process, attunement practitioners will share weekly attunements with the mother, father-to-be and the developing fetus, and will teach the couple how to do this for themselves, counsel them for attitudinal release of negative emotions, keep track of their progress, and be on hand to hold the energy pattern during and after the birth cycle. By providing a local or non-local atmosphere of agreement, tranquility and thankfulness while gently clarifying the energy pattern associated with the birth cycle, attunement practitioners have traditionally been viewed as a necessary team member for all home or hospital deliveries. Standing back, out of the way of medical and family personnel, the attunement practitioner will hold and balance the energy pattern occurring during birth while other trained personnel take care of the unfolding event occurring at the physical level.

If possible, the attunement practitioner should be made aware of the full medical histories of both parents, including a detailed description of the diseases or illnesses present in all family members (through grandparent level) brought about through genetic transference, both recessive and dominant. Also, the practitioner should be made aware of any history of taking steroid hormones, birth control methods, sexual abuse and any drugs currently being taken by both partners. Sharing this information with your attunement practitioner will allow light to flow through the etheric level of being, informing the gestating baby with creative force. Forewarned knowledge of drug use, domestic violence, etc. will alert the practitioner to send radiant love energy along specific conscious lines of force during session time, which will help to creatively shape the course love may take during gestation. In this way, the formation of the child and its surrounding relationships will unfold with clear intention and purpose. Parents should also be made aware to ingest only wholesome foods during the gestation process, and to surround themselves and the child with love, beauty and harmonious interactions.

Even though attunement therapy may not clarify some genetic disorders prior to the birth of the baby, attunement will provide a clear channel for spirit to move untrammeled, healing whatever functional illnesses arise during the pregnancy. Chris Jorgensen comments on his personal experience of sharing attunement with many pregnant women over the years:

> *The first twelve to fourteen weeks are vital in providing attunement radiation. I have come to the awareness that a being arrives within this time frame. Whereas previously only physical factors were at work developing pneumaplasmic substance, another spirit-being is now in the picture.*[1]

Chris suggests that mothers-to-be share attunements one to two times a week during the first trimester, three to four attunements a week during the second trimester, and daily during the last month. He suggests also that the practitioner can begin to share attunement directly with the developing fetus later on in the gestation cycle when the torso and head are apparent.

Over the years, Emissary couples have reported positive findings in their children from attunement sharing during pregnancy and the birth process. Because the attunement process enhances the flow of life energy, many people have noticed that 'attunement babies' have emerged with the following characteristics: they are healthy, usually weigh more, have no or fewer complications with delivery, can pick up their heads at birth, know their fathers at sight, and have a unique or keen sense of themselves and their own identities which allows them to connect more easily with others and the life process.

It has been the general experience that Emissary children who were conceived and bathed in the attunement spirit during gestation, and who have continued to share attunements through childhood, adolescence and adulthood do carry an authentic sense of themselves, are well-adjusted to the changing nature of life, take few fear or self-esteem problems into adult life, and receive support from family and friends as to their own evaluation of their future worth and activities. Their self-esteem was not slighted because sharing attunement on a weekly basis in their home life fostered radiant consciousness and behavior. For the family unit, aligning with spirit on an individual and collective basis opens a space for nurturing personal talents. It encourages attitudes of trust and open-hearted goodwill towards each other while cultivating personal integrity and honesty to meet life challenges. A qualitative subjective research project which may reflect these findings is currently in process.

Attunement sharing promotes a caring attitude in those who share in the practice, and this has been shown to elicit better health patterns later on in life. In a *Harvard Mastery of Stress Study* recently completed, it was shown that parental caring for children has a beneficial health effect later on in life. The study showed that of the subjects who rated their parents as low parental care-givers, 87% were diagnosed with diseases in midlife, while only 25% of the subjects who rated their parents as high parental care-givers had midlife diseases.[2] It may be advantageous to all family members to teach positive, caring and life affirming attitudes by providing an example, thereby training the next generation to positively affect their own life cycle.

Children and Foot Attunements

Children are especially receptive to adults sharing foot rubs or foot attunements with them, especially at bedtime. Since foot attunements elicit a more subtle energy flow, you can soothe children to sleep by gently rubbing and attuning their feet, softly talking over their day, and calming their fears before bed. Sharing bedtime foot attunements sends children off to sleep with a mild current of spirit, reassuring them that all is well. (Consult *Chapter 19* for more information on sharing foot attunements, and to find the foot contact point charts.)

Attunement and Pets

I once received a call from a woman who wanted me to share an attunement with her dog. A few years before, her dog had been involved in a car accident which had severed the nerves leading from the dog's brain to his left front paw. This break left the paw useless to the animal and he hopped around on three legs. I went to visit this woman and her dog and was met with a voracious, big and bouncy sheep dog who bounded around on three paws, excited as ever to meet a new stranger. If he had a nerve severed, and was supposed to be in grief because of it, you couldn't tell.

I listened to the woman's story and then settled down to share an attunement with the animal. I sent attuned energy to his body and the paw. Both felt perfectly fine to me, i.e., I found no dissonant energies. When I finished the session the woman approached me, wondering if I had healed her animal. I informed her that there was nothing 'wrong' with her dog in the etheric sense, and that the dissonant pattern, if any existed, lay inside of her. She felt sorrow for her beloved pet when the dog felt none, and in fact, was perfectly happy to be bouncing around and lapping his tongue all over everybody, totally engrossed in his own happiness. The dog's pattern of love was radiant and didn't need to be fixed. I offered to share an attunement with the woman, but she declined, and so I left.

This story points out an important distinction between our domesticated pets and ourselves. Pets (dogs and cats, primarily) are responsive creatures with their own radiant natures. Because we have responsibility over their lives, their response to life comes to us primarily, but this responsive nature is not an invitation for us to lay upon them our own conscious thoughts about what we'd like to see them do or be. Actually, when we instigate our own wanting within the lives of our animals, we only complicate our own energy pattern because this thought process resides inside ourselves and not them. It is wise to love our beloved four legged pets and cherish their presence in our worlds with the same innocence, happiness and light that their presence bestows on us.

Young Adulthood

> *Work like you don't need the money.*
> *Love like you've never been hurt.*
> *And dance like nobody is watching.*
>
> —*Karol Lee McLeod*

Attunement philosophy may find a fitting ground for cultivation within the consciousness of today's young adults. By advocating inner peace and attunement with Source as a solid way to approach life challenges, Generation Xers may find solace and strength to face their mad-paced world by going to the holy place inside themselves. Matt Frazer, a 23 year old member of Generation X, and senior at Loyola University Chicago believes that his generation will find the strength and integrity they need to meet the challenges they face by going inward, increasing personal awareness and repositioning their value system to match what they see inside themselves. He says, "I suggest a 'look inward' as a start to our goal because I am confident that self-reflection will reveal the human commonalties inherent in all of our natures and ultimately call for their cultivation."[3] Frazer then goes onto suggest that the other part of his vision includes creating the type of community which acts as a container to receive and support the outward and inward journeys of others.

Other young adults also see the need for their age group to come from a stable place in consciousness in order to successfully meet the challenges they face. Stacey Ann Wolf, a Generation X member who lives in New York writes, "The more we anchor our individual power and mature into our unique place on this planet, we will realize the legacy we were born into."[4] Attunement service may provide these confident young adults with the inner sanctuary space they seek. By entering into the Holy Place, opening up to Source and offering out their own inner wisdom, young adults may connect with others with their own inner truths.

The Four Forces of the Creative Process

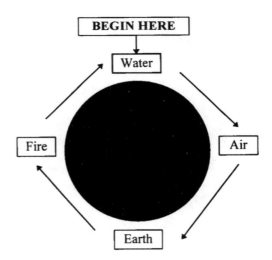

According to attunement philosophy, life has four creative forces which move in order to bring about new creation. These forces are similar to the 'elements' which ancient Greek and medieval philosophers considered to be constituents of the material world and the human psyche. Each element has a particular quality, with its own spiritual essence, of which we may be consciously aware, and with which we may consciously choose to identify. Individual life-forces are dominant at different phases of our life and undertakings. By identifying with each as it shows itself, we may increase our conscious connection to the creative flow of life as it moves into our projects, activities, and relationships, and feel less tension in the process. We feel less tension because we are identifying with the very nature of life, and we are allowing life to create through us, naturally and with control.

In the diagram opposite, the circle represents a creative cycle surrounded by four distinct forces, each focusing its own aspect of creative power for completion of the cycle. Each force works in sequence to establish and generate a particular part of creation. The following table lists these four forces in order, and offers several different symbolic ways of looking at their unique nature:

THE FOUR FORCES			
Water	Stillness	Relaxation	Intent
Air	Connection	Trust	Activation
Earth	Action	Letting	Resonance
Fire	Fulfillment	Knowing	Fusion

This table outlines the specific progression of activity which occurs, in sequence, during the process of creating form. According to attunement philosophy, all new projects and activities, both in our earthly world and in our surrounding cosmos, move along these lines of creative force in this natural order. Follow along below for each step's description:

1. Water — Stillness, Relaxation, Intent. At the start of any project, the consciousness which surrounds its formation has little physical substance from which to work. For instance, according to the biblical account of the first day of creation: *"In the beginning God created the heaven and the earth, and the earth was without form and void, and darkness was upon the face of the deep"* (Genesis 1:1–2). This is a very apt description of the Water phase in the creative process. First there was the heaven, the realm of invisible essence established before the earthly plane appeared. There was stillness, a relaxed approach and a creative intention to form solid substance sometime in the future.

2. Air — Connection, Trust, Activation. Continuing with our biblical discourse, *"and the spirit of God moved upon the face of the waters."* Now there is movement, activation, a connection with the invisible essences present in the heavenly realm. Things start to move, to vibrate, especially with the creative command, *Let there be light.* Now we have a stimulated creative field, pulsing with light force and frequency, touching into the vibrational essences of space. Things begin to connect, energy substance collides with other energies, exploding into a celestial dance of matter interacting other matter.

3. Earth — Action, Letting, Resonance. Now things are really hopping. The creative explosion causes further evolution at the biological and physical levels of being. We begin to see earthly substance appear, resonating with its heavenly and earthly aspects.

4. Fire — Fulfillment, Knowing, Fusion. The substance which now has an earthly form is capable of housing the divine spark, of carrying forward the work of creative action on its own initiative and by its own power. The power of love, the supreme radiant force, streams through the earthly form, imbuing it and its surrounding cosmic neighborhood with light.

This simplified storyline of our world's creative process may also be seen empowering any other life form which houses the divine spark. It is important to recognize that the creative process is a universally established procedure which does not change, at least not for human beings. Life moves according to universal, unchanging law. As we saw with the table presented in *Chapter 3*, indwelling Source, which is what we are in spirit, does not change or move (even though we may choose to turn away from it). Like its Source, the nature of life is stable and unchanging. One may trust completely that these forces of life will proceed in their designated pathway forever.

Understanding Stress

> *When we hold steady and function correctly,*
> *opposition permits us to take hold of the pattern.*
>
> —Uranda

In our increasingly fast-paced lifestyles, we deal with stress everyday. We feel stress because something outside of us is not happening according to our desires. Actually, if we take a step further back, we see that stress and its associated illnesses first begin to appear because our outer capacities are not attuned, open and receptive to inner divinity. This was what they were created to be and do, to be servants to the Master within. Being out of alignment, it is very easy for the capacities of mind and heart to want something which spirit would naturally give them anyway, but which now they feel they must produce for themselves — money, fame, power, relationships, health.

Just this, the normal pursuit of prosperous and fulfilling lives, causes stress in the modern age. We work, have families, encounter relationships with new people and situations, etc. Because of the day and age we live in, we juggle our responsibilities as best we can, trying to fit too much into too little time: children, work, play, home chores, and travel. We drive during peak traffic hours only to return home for a few minutes, rush dinner through a microwave, and dash off again to an evening class. In our race to achieve the 'better life,' or to self-improve, we tend to side-step proper maintenance of our bodies, often depleting our primary energy resources. Stress is created because the mind and heart want something for themselves without first yielding to love. By yielding to love, relaxation comes easily, without strain. By moving against love's purpose for one's life, one begins to feel stressed by all the hardship one has to face.

Uranda talks about the rise of the energy and computer age he saw coming before his death, and how identification with these stresses may cause increased illnesses:

> ...we are living in a world of speed and great change. Where there is this increased tempo and we are required to undergo constant adjustment to the conditions of life, there develops tension, which is a primary factor in the increase of heart problems and many others — underlying conditions of emotional and mental distortions.[5]

We can't live in a vacuum, away from any kind of stress, for indeed, life is change and change necessarily carries with it a certain amount of stress. There is a natural stress cycle which inherently plays a part in any creative cycle, and if we attune our understanding to it, we may thereby diminish the harmful effects of having too much stress in our lives. The following chart outlines the progression of a naturally occurring stress cycle, pinpointed by the steps of the creative process mentioned above. If we follow the guidelines presented after the chart, we may understand and attune ourselves to the nature of life's creative process:

THE CREATIVE PROCESS

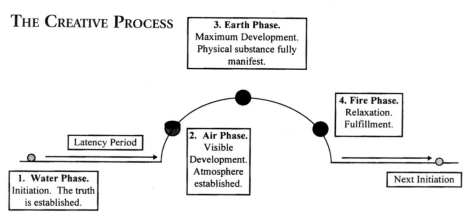

3. Earth Phase.
Maximum Development.
Physical substance fully manifest.

4. Fire Phase.
Relaxation.
Fulfillment.

Latency Period

2. Air Phase.
Visible Development.
Atmosphere established.

1. Water Phase.
Initiation. The truth is established.

Next Initiation

Creative Process Guidelines

1. Following the point of initiation, there is always a latency period which occurs before any noticeable development may be seen. Be patient, the form will come.

2. Following latency, visible development begins and develops slowly. Don't rush the process.

3. The point of maximum development naturally leads into relaxation. (Don't beat a dead horse.)

4. Relaxation precedes the next point of initiation. As intensity naturally eases, don't interpret this as something 'wrong' and thereby miss seeing the next initiation.

The progress of this creative cycle applies to all areas of living and all creative cycles at work in our lives. By choosing to integrate the nature of the creative process with our conscious understanding, we may more effectively function in harmony with life. This lessens our stress load and closes the gap of misunderstanding, which may lead us to a more relaxed and fulfilling lifestyle. Uranda states:

> We can work under tension as long as we are in control, a pattern greater and stronger than any of the tensions in the unreal world. It will not hurt anyone who is willing to yield to the spirit of God, but it will crumble ill conditions. It will cause the walls of Jericho to fall down.[6]

Uranda had a keen eye how to establish a balance when there were stressful or disorientating factors present in any situation. He said that it was necessary for tension to be present in all human endeavors, because without creative force, nothing would get done. But the way humans choose to work with that tension determined the nature of its creative, or uncreative outcome. In one of his *Creative Life Papers* he proposes a strategy based on the elements of the above diagram, emphasizing that the principles of balance and rhythm should be applied in any creative endeavor, and if one's expression of balance outweighs the stress factors, then one maintains oneself in a position of control and is able to positively influence the stress factors with a balanced energy flow:

> If you are functioning on the basis of control, dominion, the reality of the Kingdom of Heaven that is at hand, and you function *in* the pattern of tension and relaxation, then you maintain the control; you are balanced in it. And the tension can mount and mount, and it does not hurt you... So, we are not seeking to escape from tension.

We are simply learning how to function rhythmically in relation to tension and relaxation.[7]

Functioning from a controlled and balanced position, one could be *in the world but not of it,* as Jesus Christ suggested.

Charting Your Own Stress Indicators

Now let's take the opportunity to establish a balance in your own world by completing the following exercise. Below you will find an empty Creative Process Chart which is similar to the chart presented above. Fill in the blanks with the points where you believe yourself (and others) to be in relation to your present creative process. This should be a fun exercise, but be mindful that it is also intended to give you a beginning place to meditate upon your own identification or attunement with the creative forces of life moving through you. The purpose of this exercise is to inform you of the nature of your own creative processes, so that you may better equip your mind and heart with useful information as to where you are in the process of life. Through this identification process, you may find yourself in a better position to know when to relax and when to push with the crested flow of fulfillment.

Charting Your Own Stress Indicators Exercise

Your name: _____ Date: ___/___/___

Name of creative project/activity: _____

Names of others involved: _____

Instructions: *Consult the previous pages to remind yourself of each phase's specific quality before you begin. Then, fill in the boxes with the life characteristics that you see are present in your creative cycle, i.e. in the '1. Water Phase box,' fill in the water essences which made up that part of the cycle for you, and do the same for the other boxes if you've reached them. If you haven't reached some of the boxes then fill in those creative essences which you're aware of as needing to find expression at this point in time. Share this exercise with others and answer the following questions:*

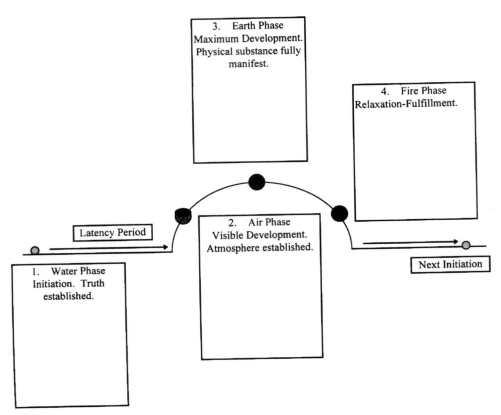

Questions:

1. Do you see a pattern of connected movement between each box of creative essences?

2. Can you feel an easy flow of energy move between your designated essences? Where is there blockage, if any?

3. Where have you been and where are you headed?

4. Are there things you can do or say or other expressions you can offer to support the outworking of this process which you haven't seen before?

5. If you feel an intensity surrounding the crest cycle of fulfillment, are there things you can do now to creatively support your presence at that time? With your calendar in hand, perhaps you can schedule yourself an attunement or massage at the crest point to help you ease the tension out of your body.

6. Plan a rest break or small vacation during the latency periods when you won't be starting anything new until the next creative impulse reveals itself.

Chapter 18 Notes

[1] Chris Jorgensen, <u>Attunement: Love Made Visible</u>, p. IX–210.

[2] Linda G. Russek, PhD and Gary E. Schwartz, PhD, 'Perceptions of Parental Caring Predict Health Status in Midlife: A 35-Year Follow-up of the Harvard Mastery of Stress Study,' *Psychosomatic Medicine*, Volume 59, 1997, p. 144.

[3] Matthew Frazer, 'The Outlook for 'Generation X' May Depend on its Ability to Look Inward,' *Connections*, February, 1998, Issue No. 3, p. 16.

[4] Stacey Ann Wolf, 'Letters,' <u>Ibid</u>., p. 6.

[5] Uranda, as quoted in Grace Van Duzen, <u>The Vibrational Ark</u>, p. 221.

[6] Uranda, 'The Creative Life #8,' Extemporaneous Worship Service, (Loveland: Eden Valley Press), January 27, 1954, p. 9.

[7] <u>Ibid</u>., p. 7.

19. Terminal Illness

The following true story comes from Bill Comer, an attunement and healing arts practitioner who lives in Montana. Bill wrote to tell me of the time when he was called to his father's death bed. His father Al was apparently dying of prostate cancer, and had only a day or so to live. When Bill heard the news, he flew immediately from Seattle to Montana to be with his father during his final moments. That was in October 1993.

When Bill arrived at the hospital, he stood in his father's hospital room looking down upon him and was shocked at what he saw. Al lay asleep, drugged with pain medication, his skin ashen. Bill had never seen his father so ill in all his life. Now, he lay before him sliding toward death. Bill let his grief turn to tears for several minutes, and when those subsided, switched roles from son to practitioner and shared an attunement with his father.

The vibrational pattern in Al's adrenal glands was so weak that Bill could barely detect any activity. The solar plexus area felt like a cold void while the thymus gland felt fiery hot. Bill perceived from this dichotomy of sensation that Al's body was virtually out of energy, but was trying to mount a response to the invasion of the cancer cells. Emotionally, he saw his father giving up and letting go of his life. Bill strained within himself to keep his intent clear of manipulation to allow healing energy to come through to his father. His conscious thoughts were active, giving his father permission to leave. Sometime after midnight, while holding Al's life force pattern in his mind, Bill drifted off to sleep.

The next morning Al and Bill were awakened by the attending nurses. Though very weak and groggy, Al was able to recognize Bill, and understood that he was there by his side. After the nurses retreated, Bill shared another attunement with Al. Al's doctor came by to check on him and informed Bill that Al would succumb to death within 24 – 48 hours. Even with this stern sentence, Bill continued sharing attunements with Al throughout the day and evening. He left the hospital that night to get a good sleep.

When Bill returned the next day, Al's vibrational pattern began showing signs of a shift. His adrenal glands remained very weak and his thymus fiery hot, but Bill began to detect activity over the solar plexus area — a pulse, a stirring, and not so cold. Bill worked with this area and with Al's response pattern to the attunements throughout the evening of the second day.

On the third morning, Bill returned to his father's side, and was pleasantly surprised to see Al propped up in bed, looking somewhat brighter and able to converse with him. Bill informed his father that he had been sharing attunements with him repeatedly for two days. Al knew what attunement was, and needed no explanation as to what Bill had been doing. He knew of the healing force and peaceful experience which attunement usually elicited. The doctor checked in on Al twice that day and maintained that Al would likely pass away any hour. Bill was unmoved by this prognosis, and stayed by Al's side well into the night, conversing with him whenever he awoke, and sharing attunements while he dozed. Later on that day Bill left the hospital to rest, having perceived that Al's status had changed for the better in spite of the physician's grim forecast. He wondered if his perception of his father's apparent healing was real, or if it were just the hope of a grieving son. Bill didn't actually know if his father was getting better, but maintained his assurance in the working of spirit to do whatever was creatively needful in this situation, no matter what happened.

On the fourth day, Bill arrived back at the hospital and found Al sitting up in bed and looking brighter still. Bill was then convinced that Al was not going to die for some time. That day the doctor told Bill that it was not unusual for someone in Al's condition to take a turn for the better a few days before finally succumbing to his disease. The doctor also commented that by all medical signs, Al should not have been feeling as well as he apparently was feeling.

Al continued to defy his prognosis for the next two weeks, and even exhibited enough strength to walk short distances. He was soon well enough to be transferred to a long-term care facility. The doctor eventually gave up predicting when Al would die. Bill continued sharing attunement sessions with him twice a day.

After another week Bill returned to Seattle to re-gather his life there. Before leaving though, Bill arranged with Al to share long distance attunements at given times, though he knew it was unlikely that Al would be able to remember them on a daily basis. Later on, Bill returned to Montana to visit his father over Christmas, and found Al to be in good spirits. Apparently Bill's absence had not caused his father's recovery to lose ground. Bill discovered that in fact, when pain medications hadn't interfered, Al was able to remember the long distance attunement appointments most of the time! This meant that Al had been consciously alert to receive the healing energy at his appointed hour. That Christmas, Bill and Al had a wonderful time together, laughing and telling stories.

In February, 1994, Bill decided to move to Montana and concluded his affairs in Seattle in order to provide full time care for his father, and to share with him whatever time remained. After he arrived, Bill shared attunements with his father on a daily basis while they arranged for Hospice home care. Al wanted to leave the nursing home and return to his beloved mountain village to live out the rest of his days.

By the last week of April, 1994, Bill had everything all arranged for Al's return home. However, on the morning of April 28th, Al informed his son that he knew he would not be going home. Al knew it was time to die. The next day he went into a coma and on May 5th he crossed over to the other world.

The extra time Bill and Al shared together proved to be a blessing for them both in that they were able to put Al's affairs in order and complete his time on earth with integrity. Integrity was one of those true qualities of character which Al had exhibited all of his life. Their extra time spent together also allowed father and son to share deeper insights into their lives together than they otherwise could have done.

Later on that year, as a continued blessing and a representation of the outpouring of spirit given through attunement, Bill married the Director of Nursing of the nursing home where Al had been cared for during his last months. Together, Bill and Joanne Comer established a private healing arts practice in Montana. They have since had the privilege of providing attunement and health care for other terminally-ill patients.[1]

The Greater Release Pattern

Contained within Bill's story are many lessons for all of us about life renewal. Bill learned about the power of his own inner faith in the face of challenge. His commitment to see a loved one's dying process through to the end proved to be a compelling force within his own life, and allowed new growth of relationship to blossom between himself and his father, and his new wife also. Knowledgeable of energy medicine and attunement technique, Bill and Joanne then moved ahead to share their unified vision with others. As we have all seen in our lives, the power of spiritual expression, when fostered and nurtured with personal care and commitment, will take on a seeming life of its own and inform our personal worlds with newness and beauty.

Closeness to a loved one who passes away brings other personal rewards, if the consciousness of one or both parties is awake to the potentials. Richard S. Gunther, entrepreneur and public servant, speaks about his awakened spirit following the passing of his beloved granddaughter, "I feel my heart has been opened to the pain of others, and I have a broader, more piercing compassion for the hurting world in which we live…"[2] By touching into our deepest pain we may grow in love with empathy for others.

Chris Jorgensen, attunement practitioner and Reiki Master suggests that death is actually a time of greater release for all people closely associated with the dying person. He says, "When working with the terminally ill… a tremendous opportunity exists to bring blessing and influence, not only to the dying person but to family and friends."[3] You may recall from Part II that when you share an attunement, the primary energy pattern you are looking for is the greater release pattern. Through that increased harmonization, life is enabled to move forward with enlightenment. A greater release pattern feels like a big sigh has entered the life of the person with whom you are sharing attunement. Its magnitude is quite distinguishable during an attunement session and during the birth and death processes.

During a greater release, personal matters shift into a clearer frame and this shifting process may require your listening ear with family members who may need to openly process their feelings with regards to the passing of their loved one. I've often found that during a family healing or greater release pattern, sharing attunement with other members of the family allows for an overall relaxation response to flow into the household, permitting an easier release of emotions. Staying quiet with the family for a day or two following the passing also helps to loosen the connective substance which the family feels for their departed one, and frees up the morphogenetic field surrounding the person who is gone. To further facilitate the passing of a loved one with easiest flow of attuned energy, follow the guidelines presented next.

Death Transition Attunement Guidelines

- Try to share two attunements per day with the person who is passing. Morning time is best, as their energy flow may be most active at this time. If you share attunement in the evening, make sure your own rhythm is slowed down to a more soothing and assuring flow.

- Make sure your work with the head region sets a strong tone of control. This stable tone will allow the transition to occur clearly. Chris Jorgensen makes the following observations on the final moments of transition:

  > When the cycle comes very near the end, a definite period of transition occurs when things begin to shift. You will sense that things are complete. This is the stage where the spirit-being begins to come forth from the human form. It may last as little as a few hours, or it may begin a day or two before departure. A person will usually begin to leave his or her body from the extremities (arms and legs).[4]

Foot and Hand Attunement Practice

Foot and hand attunements work well for the dying client. They are soft, gentle, unintrusive and help to bring about a balance to the energies moving without disrupting the conscious processes of the client. You may also wish to touch the person who is passing by gently rubbing their hands and feet. Oftentimes, people who are in the process of dying do not receive enough physical touch. On the other hand, normal non-touch attunement to the needs of your client may assure him that all is well during this process, and bring an added dimension of comfort and support. Those who may benefit most from normal non-touch attunements include clients who are touch deprived, touch sensitive or for whom deep touch is contra-indicated (AIDS or rheumatoid arthritis clients). Geriatric and terminally ill clients also benefit from foot and hand attunements since their rest patterns are most likely to be intermittent and/or more frequent, and since their vibrational pattern is such that intensifying it with head and body torso attunement energy may induce discomfort. Children especially love foot attunements, as the gentle flow of spirit often lulls them into a quiet and tranquil sleep. Hand attunements are easy to share, e.g., in a car, seated next to a partner or friend, or lying next to your sweetheart.

I can recall sharing an attunement with a practitioner after having spent hours in bed writhing with stomach cramps. The practitioner began the attunement by balancing my cervical pattern. Immediately, I told him that this energy flow had intensified my nausea. He then switched to the feet, and completed the entire attunement from there. Five minutes after he left, I threw up. His foot attunement served its purpose by bringing my body energies into balance, which then allowed me to finish the job in no time at all, and to my great relief!

You will note on the foot and hand anatomical charts presented opposite that the anatomy of the body is reflected on the feet and hands with placement similar to that which you find on the body itself. Those organs and systems found at the top of the body and in the head region are found situated on the top portion of the feet and hands, and on the lower portion are the lower organs of the body. Organs found on the right or left side of the body are found on the right or left foot or hand. For example, the heart is placed on the foot and hand similarly to where you find it on the body — in the upper mid-portion of the left foot and hand, and the liver contact points are found on the right foot and hand, which are on the same side of the body as the liver organ.

You will also notice that the energy you sense in the feet and hands is of a more delicate kind than you find through the organ systems in the torso region. Contact points on the feet and hands are smaller, usually feel fainter, and are sensed in a much more subtler fashion than your work with the body. The energy you touch into through these extremities comes from the neurological end points present in the feet. These end points are a part of the nervous system and are similar to reflexology points.

If you are sharing a full body attunement with someone and cannot bring about a balance to the particular organ or energy pathway you are working with, you can always move to the feet or hands. Then access the energy of whatever system you are working on in order to achieve a balance to the area. Usually, after moving to the feet for a few minutes and then returning to the torso, I find that the area is opened up considerably and the full body attunement may continue to its completion.

I sometimes choose to begin a full-body attunement session by first checking certain balancing factors in the feet or hands. These balancing factors include the cervical pattern (tops of toes for feet and wrist points for hands), solar plexus or heart area (contact points are present on both hands and feet), and the endocrine glands. After spending a little time to bring about a subtle balance in them, I then move up to the head region to begin the full attunement. For me, this way of beginning an attunement opens the pathway for energy flow in certain people needing special care, i.e. those with complex emotional or physical problems, geriatric, or surgery clients.

Foot Attunement Technique

1. *Begin sharing foot attunement by balancing the energies found in both feet (see Chapter 10 and foot attunement illustration there). As in balancing the cervical pattern, perceive the energy patterns emanating from each foot and hold their patterns between your hands, allowing them to balance out. With the fingers of your hands together, and your hands placed loosely, one to two inches above the feet, feel for a single pulse pattern before finishing this part of the attunement.*

FOOT ENDOCRINE GLAND CONTACT POINTS CHART

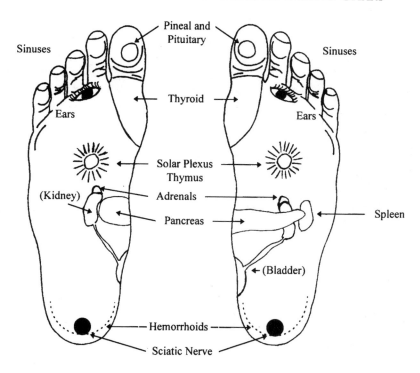

2. *Continue next with the endocrine gland contact points on the feet, sharing attunement with them in the same order as you would on the body, but your hands will be different. Draw together your index and middle fingers of each hand and focus a stream of energy directly at the contact points described below. Notice that the pineal and pituitary glands are situated together, in the meaty portion of both big toes, and that the thyroid contact point is located at the base of each big toe. Beam a single radiant current into these two areas to begin the endocrine gland attunement. To share attunement*

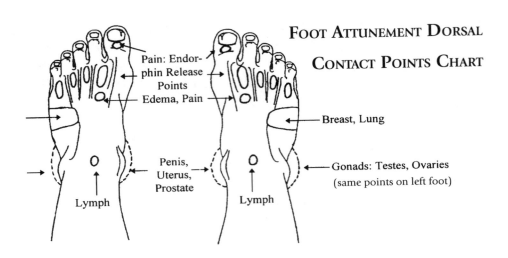

FOOT ATTUNEMENT DORSAL CONTACT POINTS CHART

Pain: Endorphin Release Points

Edema, Pain

Breast, Lung

Penis, Uterus, Prostate

Gonads: Testes, Ovaries
(same points on left foot)

Lymph

Lymph

with the thymus gland, access the solar plexus area. The pancreas is found mostly on the client's left foot, with a residual portion on the right. The adrenals may be difficult to find initially, but with diligent effort, you will be able to pinpoint your focused energy right on them. The gonad contact points (both male and female) are located on the medial and lateral portions of the shins. To access lateral points, place your hands alongside each shin, on their outside, and encompass these points with your anjali hand positions (just like you do with the cervical pattern). When working with the points inside the ankles, you may wish to cross your hands to access this energy pattern for easier practitioner comfort.

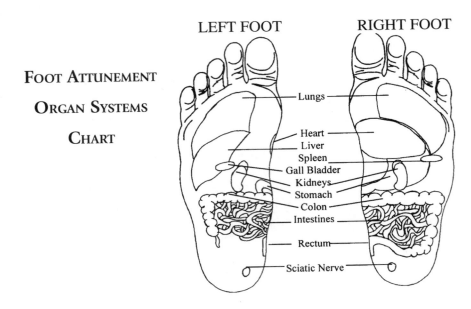

FOOT ATTUNEMENT ORGAN SYSTEMS CHART

LEFT FOOT

RIGHT FOOT

Lungs

Heart
Liver
Spleen
Gall Bladder
Kidneys
Stomach
Colon
Intestines

Rectum

Sciatic Nerve

3. *After sharing attunement with each of the endocrine gland points, continue with the rest of the body, beginning with the digestive system (ascending, transverse and descending colon, small intestine, stomach, liver, pancreas and gall bladder), respiratory, circulatory, immune, excretory, etc., and finish by again balancing the feet as you did to begin the session (see No. 1 of this section). The entire session should last 15–20 minutes, and is most relaxing for client and practitioner alike.*

HAND ATTUNEMENT CONTACT POINTS CHART

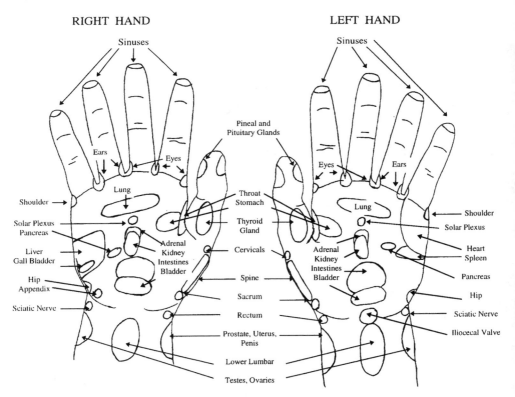

RIGHT HAND   LEFT HAND

Hand Attunement Technique

You may share attunement through the hands using much the same method as sharing attunement through the feet. Begin by first balancing the body's energies at the wrist points (see *Chapter 16*), and then move on to the endocrine and other organ systems by stimulating their life force through the contact points found on the hands. End your hand attunement session by again balancing the energies of the body through the wrists. Remember to suggest to your client that she hold her thumbs for self-attunement at any time following the session.

Chapter 19 Notes

[1] Edited private correspondence of William A. Comer, BSc, HTP.

[2] Richard S. Gunther, 'Tales of Transformation,' *Connections*, Issue No. 3, February, 1998, p. 19.

[3] Chris Jorgensen, <u>Attunement: Love Made Visible</u>, p. IX–215.

[4] <u>Ibid.</u>, p. IX–216.

20. Team Attunements

The day after my husband proposed marriage to me, his father suffered a mild heart attack. Although his father had no prior knowledge of the proposal, we still ponder the synchronicity of these two events, and recognize that our new team spirit may have had a profound creative effect on his healing process.

The day after our engagement we found out about Dad's condition. Since Dick, my husband-to-be, was somewhat shaken, I drove us to the hospital and did not begin my long distance attunement with Dad until after we arrived. When we found his hospital room, we went in to visit him, one at a time. While I waited my turn, I 'camped' in the waiting room outside the ICU, and began sharing long distance attunement with him. In my hands, I found his pattern erratic around the edges and somewhat hot. I worked to steady the rhythms of his energy flow which I sensed were over-worked and unbalanced. I held this pattern for several hours while my family stayed with him, and after returning home, I shared another long distance session with him for about one hour.

The next day we went back to the hospital to be near him while his doctor performed a delicate angioplastic surgery (inflating a small balloon inside his clogged heart arteries). Before the surgery, Dick and I were able to share a team attunement session with Dad which lasted about 40 minutes. Dick first shared Reiki energy with Dad while I held a long distance attunement pattern between my hands. Then, he took his place at his dad's feet, and we shared a team attunement. I provided Dad with a positive point of radiant energy at his head and torso region, sharing a full body attunement with him and giving specialized attention to his cardiovascular system, while Dick shared attunement with him through his feet, following my lead with the various gland and organ systems. Within five minutes of our starting the team attunement, Dad fell asleep.

Following our team attunement, the hospital staff arrived to bring Dad to the surgery unit, so we all moved to the waiting room. I again began sharing long distance attunement with him, and felt a continuation of an erratic energy flow moving through the circumference of my hands. The surgery lasted for a few hours and I held Dad's spiritual pattern during that time. Afterwards, the doctor informed us that everything had gone very well, but that he needed to perform the same surgery the next day to open up a few more arteries which he didn't have time to do that day. So, following our good-byes to the patient, we left to get a good night's rest. I continued my work with Dad with another long distance evening attunement session.

For our second day together, we returned to the hospital waiting room. Our circle included Mom (Dick's mom), Dick, myself and Lisa, Dick's sister. Within this happy family circle, we talked quietly, joked and read a few of the hospital magazines. At one time we began talking about how the surgery was going and there was an immediate unanimous agreement amongst ourselves that everything was going well, with no complications. We just knew this, matter-of-factly. I continued to share attunement for two or three hours while we were all together.

The atmosphere where we were sitting was filled with tranquillity, assurance and trust, but outside this space I began to notice a shift occur in the ambiance. Within the circle that encompassed us in the waiting room, all was well, but outside our field I noticed confusion, noisy disruption and annoying behavior. From other groupings of people we heard loud cursing and criticisms of how the hospital was mistreating the patients, complaints of being pissed-off, children running around unattended, and an appearance of general chaos.

I noticed a distinct difference between the energy field surrounding the healing outcome of our loved one, and that of other people. Consciousness from others did not seem to be attuned to setting in motion the right outcome for the patient they were there to see. Their thought and emotional ties seemed so far removed from a healing intent that their space was filled with negative vibrations, including accusation, blame and criticism. I wondered how this was affecting the wellbeing of the sick person with whom they were connected.

Our attuned consciousness to right outcome, the healing energy of our team attunement and my continued long distance attunement sessions had definite clear and positive effects on Dad's wellbeing long after he left the hospital. With no complications to the surgery, Dad was soon released from the hospital, and immediately began a weight loss and exercise program. Within weeks, he lost about 25 pounds, began exercising three times a week, changed his diet and began feeling much better. I've continued to share long distance attunement with him and our family members from time to time, and always enjoy touching into our shared agreement in right outcome.

Hospital Settings and Surgery

Going to the hospital to be with an ailing loved one can raise a lot of emotional disruption in someone's life. Oftentimes schedules need to be rearranged, visitors don't eat or sleep with regularity, monetary problems may arise and other family complications surface. It seems that when someone is hospitalized, the entire energy field of the family involved becomes chaotic, and this may raise issues relating to how the family copes with the loss of time, money and power of the one hospitalized. Usually, other family-of-origin issues surface amid the stress and need to be addressed once again, often exacerbating the tensions felt.

When someone comes to the hospital to undergo surgery, they move as it were into a new home where everything that is given to that person is offered with precision, on schedule, documented, hygienically clean and sanitized. (This is often not the way normal families operate!) It is like moving into a foreign land, where practically all the patient's power is taken away from them and given over to an apparently proficient and technically trained grouping of strangers.

Though appearing methodologically efficient, most hospital staff personnel are not trained in pastoral or energy medicine practices which provide and support right outcome through etheric body offerings for all involved. Some hospitals are beginning to offer energy practice as part of their research team offerings during surgery, and in some instances, you may find nurses and other staff personnel within a hospital setting who are trained in and actively practice techniques such as Therapeutic Touch. Offering these types of practices to the patients in particular but also to the patients' families, friends and the surrounding hospital staff may open many doors of relationship and purposeful action which might otherwise be missed.

Some medical studies now show that offering specific forms of energy medicine to surgery patients prior to and during the time of surgery may provide greater comfort and relief of some common post-operative adverse effects. These findings show that not only does the patient heal more readily and without problems, but the entire medical setting seems to work more coherently and smoothly. Julie Motz, MPH, MFA, who has conducted numerous 'energy chelation' sessions (monitoring energy patterns through the head, feet and body parts) with patients prior to and during surgery, reports these findings:

> *None of the 6 LVAD [left ventricular assist devices] patients on whom I worked in surgery had any rejection on their first biopsies, and all had lower than normal postoperative heart rates. Six months after surgery, all consistently had rejection rates that were lower than normal... The 3 coronary bypass patients on whom I worked had very little postoperative leg pain or weakness. None of the 11 cardiac patients on whom I worked had any postoperative depression, which affects an average of one third of all cardiac surgery patients and is the primary indicator of mortality.*[1]

Motz informs us that operating rooms may instill fear, hostile emotions, and other draining and negative energies for the patients and others present during surgery. Not only the patient's emotional state but the emotional imprint in the live transplant organ may need attention. Motz recalls that during operations, "transplant organs come into the operating room in a variety of emotional states, and these affect the way the heart behaves in the recipient's body."[2] While she served as an energy practitioner during surgeries, Motz worked to transform those energy patterns from negative to positive ones. Motz also notes that patients respond to anesthesia in a variety of ways during surgery, oftentimes taking an emotional journey which re-stimulates old traumas, negative childhood memories and bitter experiences while in the womb.[3]

Energy medicine practitioners who have worked consistently in hospital settings report that when patients are given anesthesia, drastic changes unfold which could be safeguarded through attuned energy offered to them before, during and after surgery. Chris Jorgensen, shares his findings:

> *Anesthesia dissipates or dissolves what I would refer to as the mental range of pneumaplasm. You may find that a person is mentally foggy or 'spaced' for a period of time following surgery. Be aware of it, enfold it in the attunement current, and look for ways to assist the person to regenerate his or her pneumaplasm at that level.*
>
> *When in the follow-up stage, attunement every day is essential... Within a few days after surgery some form of uneasiness usually appears; often it looks like depression. This is a sign that the physical body is coming to terms with the imposition of the surgery. The uneasiness may not be depression but rather a grouchiness, irritability, or unreasonableness... Once the person is home, two attunements a day for a period of time helps to lessen the intensity of this adjustment to the physical trauma.*[4]

Sometimes people complain of the questionable quality of care which they received in a hospital setting. What may be overlooked (oftentimes while opinions fly back and forth between angry individuals) is that the quality of one's *own* offering is a critical component in any hospital encounter, whether one is acting in the role of a family member, hospital staff, patient or visiting friend. It is so much easier to point the finger of blame at someone other than oneself, but it pays to remember that whenever we point a finger at someone, we've got four more fingers pointing back at ourself. When we each begin to see that as we enter a hospital setting, we are actually taking part in a much larger group endeavor than we may personally realize, and that our individual attitudes play a large role in determining the outcome of patient care, then maybe we can begin to offer reassurance and peaceful calm within our group, even though circumstances may stretch our capacities. We can care for each other, even if its only through a word, a smile, a nod, a shake of a hand. Uranda brings to mind a crucial point relating to team coordination in attitude and spirit:

> *To the degree that you bring a spirit or attitude of dissension, fault finding, complaining, gossip, condemnation, and such-like expressions of the baseless fancies of the outer-mind, into the Group,* **whether you give such things audible expression or not,** *you thereby prevent your own harmonization, and tend to prevent the perfect function of the Group.*[5]

What we don't see may hurt us and others. The conscious quality of spiritual expression which you offer into any hospital group setting may in itself uplift the vibrational nature of an encounter, bringing with it a more serene and tranquil offering of assurance to all with whom you are associated.

Team Attunements

> *You truly serve your brother man in love*
> *because in your love for your Lord you let your Lord*
> *release His love through you into the earth.*

> —*Uranda*

When two people come into agreement to share attunement with a third person, the power of love offered is intensified at least tenfold. Team attunement offers an expansively rich and healing atmosphere into which the client or patient may come to receive healing touch which is felt throughout the body, stimulated at the head, torso and foot regions simultaneously. Sharing in a team attunement is always a much more powerful way to share an attunement, as the client or patient is enfolded in a complete circle of radiant life force, being energized at both ends of the body at the same time.

During my Attunement Therapy Training Intensives, I always teach attunement in teams of two or three, utilizing a learn-as-you-do approach. All partners clustered together switch positions before the learning session is completed, so that all involved may receive and give attunement from the feet, hand and torso positions. In this way, the power of team attunement is exemplified within one's personal life experience, and the students walk away from the training weekend having shared in something larger than themselves, and often in dramatic ways.

Team attunements are wonderful ways to learn hands-on attunement since each practitioner can assess if the other is 'on' the corresponding anatomical part or contact point with which they are already working. Because all students are working with the same organ or gland pattern, people can easily assess who is on and who is off. This peer interaction is often self-guided, and serves to enhance the self-learning process.

Team Attunement Guidelines

Choose two other people with whom you'd like to share and/or practice a team attunement and follow these guidelines:

- The primary attunement practitioner is the one positioned at the head of the client to begin. She will work with the face contact points, and their corresponding body parts, as described in previous chapters.

- The primary practitioner works in agreement with the secondary practitioner who is located at the client's feet. It is usual for these two individuals to work together as the attunement proceeds, exchanging nods, or agreement glances with each other when it is time to move onto the next organ system. Usually, the primary practitioner takes first lead, moving to each organ system with the secondary practitioner following suit. In this way, a team attunement is like an energy dance between friends — one leads and the other follows, but both are moving to the same place.

- The secondary attunement practitioner shares attunement through the feet of the client, and moves to those areas on the feet which correspond to the areas which the primary is working. Thus, if the primary practitioner senses it is time to move from the heart realm to the lungs, the secondary practitioner will move to the lungs in synchronistic fashion.

- After completing one attunement session, the primary, secondary and client roles should switch, so that all practitioners involved will receive and give attunement from all positions, increasing their knowledge with attuned flow.

- Team attunement exercise time is often accompanied by a deep sensing of personal relaxation and letting go. But even if the flow of energy deepens, remember to stay focused during your team attunement time, or else you will probably lose track of the contact points.

Chapter 20 Notes

[1] Julie Motz, MPH, MFA, segment in 'Voices' Column, *Alternative Therapies*, May, 1997, Vol. 3, No. 3, p. 21.

[2] Ibid.

[3] Ibid.

[4] Chris Jorgensen, Attunement, Love Made Visible, pp. IX–213–214.

[5] Uranda, Letters to You, pp. 22–23.

21. Representational Objects

I attended my final Emissary educational class in 1985. This class experience was entitled *World Service Class* and brought to focus attunement technique and philosophy from a world perspective. With about 22 other students and four faculty members, we considered how to center ourselves amidst the accelerating pace of the world, and how to share attunement from within a collective grouping, offering healing energy to other people, places, and situations in crisis.

During one particular attunement session, the students and faculty divided themselves up into pairs, and while seated in chairs, shared representational object exercises with each other. This representational object exercise was a specialized form of attunement sharing wherein the person receiving the healing energy held a small object that represented a pattern in consciousness to which the person wanted to send love energy. The other person in the pairing offered attuned healing energy to the one holding the object. Both were instructed to stay consciously connected to the attuned flow of energy as it entered and clarified the dissonant life pattern represented in the object. This dissonant pattern could be anything to do with personal health, professional goals, relationships, or even larger patterns, such as the crisis in the Russian government (which was going on at the time). All world situations were welcome.

I brought with me a letter I had received from my music director. This communication had bothered me for some time because I felt I had been misrepresented by her, and I wanted our relationship to be clear of any negative repercussions. Not by coincidence, my partner in this session brought in a large snare drum which he told me represented 'noise pollution.' I immediately saw the connection between our two objects — one was intended to be used to clear emotional distortions between people involved with making music, and the other was to be used to dissolve dissonant sound energies, also created by people. Both areas focused on the dissolution of disagreeable energy patterns relating to sound and music. We smiled, knowing that the seeming coincidence of our pairing was not by chance, but obviously had a larger purpose to it. For this exercise, we decided to switch each other's objects, so he took a hold of my letter while I shared an attunement with him (in this way, he was working to dissolve my emotional disturbance while I was attuning him).

I will always remember this session because it was one of the most intensely wondrous attunement sessions I have ever experienced. While I stood behind my partner, attuning his endocrine glands, my head became filled with the most glorious orchestral music I had ever heard. The lyric violin strings seemed to reach the heights of heaven, while beneath rang brass, harp and winds. The music seemed to come from nowhere and everywhere at once, returning to that very core place which was within my being but seemed all present everywhere. I felt as if I had been transported into a cosmic radio station where the music you sensed had magical healing effects upon you, where you felt that everything in life was perfect, things magically appeared and disappeared at will and all things fitted together with perfect ease and delight. For those few minutes, my life was filled with amazing harmony. My partner was attuning my world and I was attuning his, but in reality our energy fields were blending with the energy field of my music director (who was a phenomenal composer and organist), with full agreement to let love have its perfect way.

Minutes after that session I was aware that the bad feelings I had held towards my music director had disappeared. I realized that I had fabricated that particular scenario without just cause, and that there had actually been nothing wrong. Where did my demands for justice go? What had happened to my arrogance? They simply vanished, disappeared, as if they had never been present to begin with. They had been transformed forever from ego-based energy to love-based energy.

When I finished sharing the attunement with my partner, we switched positions, and I sat down, holding onto my partner's snare drum in my lap. I held the drum and felt its foundational power. I recalled that within any musical score, the drum provided a staying power, a deeper, richer tone which sounded out the rhythms of the music with consistency and precision. Inherent stabilizing qualities of the drum were tempo, rhythm, communication, and dynamics, all released with sound. I thought of Native American Indian drum music, how Indians used the drum to send messages to their community, and how it signaled the drawing together of the tribe's power.

I sent these thoughts about the foundational power contained in the drum into my imagined perception of noise pollution — that chaotic jumble of car horns tooting, traffic noises, loud boom box music and sidewalk chaos. I sent a gentle, rhythmic pulsation with measured meter into those visualized situations. For those moments while I was sharing attunement, the world of chaos met the world of order. When we finished, I felt immensely satisfied with our work together, like a selected portion of the earth had been touched and harmonized with a staying power and had melted under the larger integrating force of love.

Representational Objects

> *What you do in miniature sets up the vibration*
> *that reaches out to that which is not yet visible.*
>
> *—Uranda*

If we could only see the vibrational results of our actions, how far afield they settle, and how they influence the lives of so many other people on the face of the earth, I am sure that we would think and behave differently. I believe that if we could see these situations, at the moment of their impacts, then we would choose to be and do something else.

We utilize representational objects every day — in the words we speak, the stories and fairytales we read, the image-creating music we hear, the ritual and ceremony we practice, the hero archetypes we try to emulate and the good luck charms we grip in times of stress. We use them in our exchange of money for goods and services, in our artistic creativeness and visualizations of future events, and even in watching television or movies. The exchange of money represents an exchange of personal character and love energy. Words are symbols which represent tangible objects. Hero worship and emulation represent our secret inner longing to regain our original garden state. When we see or do something which represents another thing, we put into daily action the power of an archetypal presence. Set in motion is a powerful vibrational flow of belief about one thing which represents something else.

The creative power which is inherently present in representational objects contains within it great potential to touch us and our worlds in ways which bring about healing and creative change. However, instead of focusing attention and care on their presence and how we use them, we tend to take them for granted. The presence of representational objects in the American culture has become second nature to us — we buy our children Superman toys, read to them bedtime stories about winged horses flying through the air, fire imaginary laser guns at objects while playing at the video arcade, surf the Internet searching for unknown lands and adventure. What we may be missing in our search for power and beauty outside of ourselves is our own inherently powerful and creative nature which lies dormant within us, relegated to the dimension of the archetype. Harnessing this energy which lies within us and channeling its flow through our lives may open these interior conscious and subconscious archetypal patternings and release their creative power into our worlds.

Using representational objects to share attunement is like holding onto a homing device — you hold in your hand a symbol of something you'd like to change with love, and focus your awareness of love's flow into the symbolic area which your object represents. Love energy will find its way there through your consciousness, opening, revealing, encompassing, changing, transforming, without interruption or dissipation.

We can begin to use everyday objects as attuned contact points into our worlds, empowering them with love's force. Simple acts of our everyday world may begin to take on new significance, as we turn them into a spiritual ritual. Writing a check to pay a bill may become an opportunity to send radiant flow of energy into our financial picture instead of a mere drudgery. Watching the news and seeing pictures of war, poverty and violence may become a means of worship, as you connect with Source in your heart and send love energy through these representational pictures to those faraway places. Hugging a friend may become a more vivid conscious act of extending your love into your circle of friends.

From a larger attunement perspective, people and places are in fact contact points into the larger world, for wherever there are open hearts and minds, *"there am I in the midst of them."* Consciously connecting to people and places *through other people and places* may set in motion the flow of radiant energy out into the world. I can recall spending years with other Emissaries, consciously attuned to one man who lived in Russia before the fall of communism. He had offered himself to spirit, and spirit had answered, sending him to Moscow to participate in the 'Getting to Yes' program which was part of the Harvard Negotiation Team. During those years of hearing about the ramifications of his presence in Russia, we who shared attunement with him recognized that spirit was at work through his open heart, opening the doors of consciousness to the presence of spiritual expression. In time, communism ended in Russia and the man returned to the states.

There is now scientific evidence to show that people who share the same energy pattern begin to synchronize with each other's brain wave and cardiac activity. In 1994 and 1996, Russek and Schwartz discovered that when two people sat in front of each other with eyes closed and did not touch, then the electrocardiograms and electgroencephalograms "of both individuals (were) recorded, and the rhythms (were) analyzed for the presence of *between-person cardiac-brain synchronization.* Such synchronization (was) present..."[1] If two people can sit quietly together, not trying to attune to other people and places and still entrain themselves to a unified and creative energy pattern, imagine what we can accomplish if we consciously attune ourselves with the life force and extend this vital energy to other people in the process! Stephan Rechtschaffen, physician and personal growth workshop facilitator shares this vision: "One way to shift what's going on in our world is not to try to rush to do more, but to allow ourselves to go deeper into that moment of being present. Perhaps we then become the entrainment rhythms that start to create more peace in our world, and out of that comes healing."[2]

Using a representational object during attunement takes you outside space-time. You can use a symbolic messenger to send your love energy to another happening which took place in the past, present or which may take place in the future. You can work to dissolve any conscious or subconscious emotional or psychological barriers by using a representational object to symbolize such presence in your life, and then send love to it. You can solve a problem, clear future roadblocks, resolve past differences and/or refocus present projects and plans simply by holding that symbol of choice in your hand and focusing on it with love during the attunement. World events have been known to take on new direction when a grouping of attunement practitioners and interested people in different places form a radiant gathering and utilize representational objects and other people to send love energy to needed situations and places in the world (see next chapter). You can work to inspire new changes in your world by following these next set of guidelines.

Representational Object Practice Guidelines

1. Begin your representational object attunement by choosing a handheld object that represents for you something to which you would like to send love energy. Choose something simple like a postcard from a person with whom you wish to connect, or perhaps a postcard which has a picture of a place where you want to send your love energy. Pendants, car keys, CDs, books, memorabilia — the opportunities for choosing the right contact points are endless. Just be mindful that the symbol you choose carries a specific remembrance pattern to you of the thing, place or person with whom you want to make a connection.

2. It is best if you share a representational object exercise with another person, but it is not necessary. If you have a partner, let your partner hold your object while you share the attunement with him, or vice-versa.

3. Before starting the session, confide in each other what your objects mean. You both should have a good idea of the situation surrounding each object before you begin.

4. Each person should share a complete full body attunement with the other. Your partner (who is holding your object) will be attuning, or sending radiant love energy through your object, into the place, circumstance or person you defined. Your attention will be simply to attune the person in front of you. Then you switch — you hold your partner's object and your partner attunes you.

5. If you are alone and wish to share a representational object exercise, simply establish a long distance or radiant creative field between your hands, and then extend a loving flow to the place, person or situation you wish, keeping in mind what your object symbolizes. Keep your object either on your lap or in close enough proximity that you can see it clearly.

6. You may choose to share a representational object attunement with someone in the hospital or with someone who is far away, using long distance technique. Simply establish an agreed upon time and share radiant energy with them across the miles, having them hold their representational object in their lap or in their hands.

7. After the attunement, you may wish to swap stories about your different experiences. You each will have two different stories. Don't be surprised if your stories are similar, or even very different. Either way, hearing the other person's story may enlighten you as to the greater healing effect of the attunement.

8. Remember that using a representational object to share your attunement is probably one of the most expansive ways that there is to share attunement.

Chair Attunements

Sharing attunements in a chair is probably the easiest way of sharing attunements with others if you don't have a massage table. You can try having your client lie on a sofa, but this may not be the best position for your arms and back. I have found that it is better to have your client sit in a chair, especially if you are going to be sharing a representational object attunement without a massage table. The best types of chairs to use are the big, comfy ones or easy chairs or recliners which fold back. A straight-back chair works okay too, but this should be your last choice. If you use a straight-back chair, you may wish to place a pillow at your client's back and have her put her feet up on another chair for added comfort. Follow these next guidelines when using a chair to share attunements:

- Have the primary practitioner stand behind the seated client, or be seated at the side of the client in the chair. Have the secondary practitioner sit on a stool and share attunement through the feet. Both should keep in mind practitioner self-care guidelines (see *Chapter One* for review).

- Your client may choose to use a representational object for greater release of love energy into a particular situation. If you use an object, make sure your grouping first shares its meaning with each other, and if your object represents someone else, you may wish to contact that person prior to the session so that they can be 'on line' with you in consciousness and receive your love energy.

- Make sure that you trade places and share attunements with each other to allow a full healing release to occur in all people involved.

- To establish a collective conscious connection to higher power, someone may choose to read passages from a inspirational book while you share the attunement and/or representational object session. Low light and soft instrumental music may help to fill your healing space with spirits of warmth and nurturing assurance.

Chapter 21 Notes

[1] Dr James Oschman, 'What is healing energy? Energy entrainment, Energy Review Part 3B,' p. 190.

[2] Stephan Rechtschaffen, 'Time Shifting, How to Pace Your Life to Natural Rhythms,' *Noetic Sciences Review*, p. 20.

22. Radiant Gatherings

The most dramatic world healing event in which I ever had privilege of participating took place in the fall of 1989. I was attending the *Emissary World Assembly* in British Columbia, Canada. This was an assembly attended by 30 people from around the world and was a coveted event which occurred only twice a year. Our focus of consideration was on personal expression of spiritual divinity and world attunement. Because we were all from different parts of the world, our spiritual clarification processes occurring during that time carried larger ramifications and influence into world affairs than could be seen on the surface. Underneath our collective exterior ran the vibrational connections to people and situations present in Europe, the Middle East, the Americas and the Far East. Each person present had already attended all the Emissary classes and was well aware that they each represented a larger portion of the earth's population. Coming into this intense experience, we knew that we were expected to be as open as possible and were to be used by spirit as contact points into the earth.

For two weeks, I sat with 25 other people plus four faculty members in a warm log cabin in the middle of the Canadian Caribou, and we considered our individual relationships with the world at large. We placed a large globe within our circle each day, and from time to time during our discussions and attunement sharing, focused our attention on specific areas in the earth which needed our loving focus.

One representational object exercise in which we all participated was particularly intense. One of the facilitators brought forth a large platter carrying a loaf of freshly baked bread. We were asked to keep in mind, during this exercise, someone whom we loved. In fact, we were to imagine that this loaf of bread was the very love that we shared with this person. In our own time, we were asked to come up to the bread, break off a piece, and 'eat our love.' In other words, we were to swallow and digest that love which we held for our friend. We were also given a small cup of wine. This exercise was apparently a modern day version of Jesus' admonition during the Last Supper to eat his body and drink his blood. We were asked to re-enact the Last Supper as modern-day disciples of the Master's healing ministry, and recognize for ourselves just what was the nature of the love we carried for each other.

This exercise was very telling of the quality of love I brought to a loved one, for I found it very hard to swallow that piece of bread. While chewing, I realized that I carried unclear thoughts for my friend, whom I thought I loved, and in actuality my actions towards him were hypocritical. On the surface I professed unconditional love, but underneath, in what I kept secret from him, I wanted more from him than he cared to give me. I swallowed my own resentments toward him with each bite. The bread tasted stale and hard to swallow. This exercise is only one example of the quality of attunement exercises we shared together during that time. All of these exercises, as well as our heated discussions, allowed me to clarify the way I expressed love into the world.

We shared many attunement exercises during those two weeks, using representational objects and traditional attunement technique to send love to our personal and collective worlds. A few days into our assembly time, I recall one of our discussions in which a man from Germany spoke at length about his life there, about communism in East Germany and the recent unrest. A couple days later, during lunch, we heard that the Berlin Wall had fallen. We looked at each other with amused surprise, knowing personal connection to that outworking because of the contact point connection we had carried for this man who lived in Germany.

In usual synchronistic fashion, our Emissary Director was traveling to Hungary at the end of the week, and for the first time he was going behind the eastern block to offer attunement and spiritual leadership classes. With the fall of the Berlin wall, his path was now vibrationally clear to offer his public talks without communistic constraint. We felt sure that our assembly time had helped set in motion larger openings in the spiritual fabric of humanity, allowing a clearer focus of spirit to move through the world.

Radiant Gatherings

> *When the second Buddha comes,*
> *(he) will come not as an individual but as a community.*
>
> —*Thich Nhat Hanh*

Radiant gatherings, or attunement prayer circles have been used by many people as a collective gathering place to rekindle spirituality, and specifically to celebrate a season or event, or to offer a larger focus of love energy to a specific area of humankind and the earth. At its heart, a prayer circle represents factors of consciousness associated with the divine, which then imbues and empowers a larger population of people. From backyard drumming circles to yearly harmonic convergence gatherings, people choose to congregate their bodies and minds for worship, pleasure and a renewed sense of faith in the universal order.

Robert C. Beck is a scientist interested in discovering why and how healing phenomena occurred in groupings of people, and conducted ten years of experiments. His results may give us more understanding as to how collective radiant gatherings heal. Beck found that all the healers he had tested registered similar brain wave patterns when they were performing a healing. These wave patterns were apparently connected to the altered states of consciousness produced by the healer during a healing ritual. Beck notes: "It did not matter what the healers' belief and customs were, all registered brainwave activity averaging about 7.8–8 cycles/second while they were in their healing state." Among those tested in Beck's experiments were so-called 'sensitives,' psychics, dowsers, shamans, charismatic Christian faith healers, seers, wicca practitioners, Hawaiian kahuna, etc. Beck found that in all of these healers, they "produced nearly identical EEG signatures, which lasted from one to several seconds."[1]

What was also found to be significant was that during their healing moments, the healers' brainwave patterns "became phase and frequency synchronized with the earth's geoelectric micropulsations." These micropulsations are known as the Schumann resonance. The Schumann resonance is a theory postulated by W.O. Schumann, a German physicist, who suggested that the ionosphere of the earth and the surface of the earth act together to form a resonant cavity which contains electromagnetic pulsations created by lightening activity. Schumann's theory demonstrates that lightning creates electromagnetic standing waves which travel around the globe, and affect human activity through their electromagnetic pulsations, moving in the range of 1–40Hz. This resonance field is affected by solar and lunar positions, sun spots, planetary positions, etc.[2] Given this information, we may see that the entrained brainwave and cardiac rhythms experienced by healers are actually connected with and affected by the earth and its surrounding celestial astronomy. This is apparent confirmation of ancient mystical knowledge that we are one with all things in the known and unknown universe in vaster ways than we can realize. Given that the healers tested in Beck's experiments produced therapeutic results in their clients, we may also delight in knowing that the entrainment we experience in mind and heart during our attunement sessions is a part of the unifying pulsations and purposes of life.

Radiant Gathering Guidelines

Follow these gathering guidelines to help you establish your radiant gathering partnerships:

- Radiant gatherings should only be initiated after first thinking through the ramifications of their offering. The group may be large or small. You may start with only two members trading full-body attunements and let your membership grow, or begin with a larger grouping of people, each offering prayer and attunement and/or other energy practices with each other.

- Members should agree on how often they will meet. They should plan to spend 1 – 2 hours once a week, or every two weeks, or once a month or at solstice and equinox times in order to send a committed and continuous spirit of recollection amongst the members and into the earth.

- Circles should be membered by mature individuals who maintain a sense of spiritual adventure and a willingness to move together as a group without placing constraints on each other or themselves.

- You may wish to establish a leadership group within the larger sphere to determine the focus for each gathering, and to handle practical needs such as who brings what food (if you include a meal), etc.

- Personal issues should not be brought into a prayer circle time, but may be discussed afterwards in a different setting. Your guidelines should be clearly stated for all members to agree to before they decide to join up. Try to keep personal and bureaucratic affairs outside the time of the circle gathering to maintain vibrational clarity of the space.

- If a member has a relative or friend in need of healing, this person may be brought into the healing circle either in person, or through long distance attunement. Bringing other people into the shared space should be an agreed upon practice by members of the group. If the group decides not to include others, other peoples' names may be placed on a group long distance attunement list, and each member may receive a copy for their own keeping and practice.

- The heart of a radiant gathering is its self-organizational dynamic. Persons should refrain from trying to 'run' the group, organize its purpose or change its members. If prayers are verbally requested from each member to another, the prayers should focus on positive outcome, without trying to change the prayer's original intent, or sway spirit's directing power. If at times your group's dynamic is 'messy', you may wish to view this energy as simply life's way of experimenting with itself, of changing patterns emerging within the whole. Focus your group's intent on what works, not on who is right. Focusing on what works tends to shift the energy of the group away from disorder into creative potential.

- Establish a set time, maybe at the beginning of your time together, for individual members to share what doors have opened, how healing has taken place in the lives of loved ones, etc. This will establish a sense of camaraderie and empowerment which is supportive and nurturing for each person and the group as a whole.

Defining the Purpose

Beyond the support group environment, radiant gatherings provide their members with many beneficial attributes for personal and societal enrichment. These include a personal sensing of:

- responsibility and care for Self and others,

- healing potential and power for Self and others,

- consistency in offering prayerful activities to Self and others,

- affiliation with a like-minded and divinely inspired grouping of people,

- inspiration to assist in further community-based activities,

- exploration and specific hands-on experience in specific attunement practices, and

- achievement within a positive, limitless, spiritually-based outreach program.

Attunement-based prayer circles are seed planting times. Much like other spiritual events, each radiant outflow of spiritual energy attracts its own kind, across the miles eliciting a healing response within its scope of service. As mentioned before, when you send out radiant love energy, this flow of energy travels within its own boundaries and throughout its territory, touching all things and people in its wake. Since we are all connected to each other through the spirit of love, all those people who have heart-felt connection to those on your prayer list are touched. All situations adjoining those people are touched. You do not need to know the full extent to which your radiant flow of love travels, although you may sense its grand design. You may rest easy in the awareness that the love energy you are sending out is traveling to, and healing, those in need, and that all is well.

Beyond the gathering itself, other off-shoots of your group may naturally emerge. Often friends who pray together gather afterwards at a person's home or a nearby café for socializing on a regular basis. Prayer group members have been known to organize their own meetings and attunement classes based on the principles offered through their circle times.

Attunement radiant gathering times are pivotal in establishing a spirit of *transformation* within any grouping of people. The work itself brings about a spiritual transformation within its core and beyond. As long as the rules are clear, that no one person leads the group and that the energy of the group is free to do what it needs and to go where it needs, then those who attend may feel safe in traveling the transformational journey together, knowing that spirit is guiding the way.

Creating the Setting

It is usual to create within your midst an atmosphere of healing grace and sanctuary. Some useful tools include candles, low lights, incense, soft lyrical music, inspirational books (portions to be read during attunement time), a world globe and representational objects signifying the area of the earth on which you will be focusing. Some people may even choose to play musical instruments. Several professional attunement practitioners I know enjoy chanting together for their circle time, focusing their consciousness on a world event while enlivening the air with overtone sounds.

Choosing the Form

There are many forms of prayer circles or radiant gatherings. Some forms are offered in a listing below. The term *radiant gathering* has always been associated with collective attunement gatherings; however, I choose to use the two terms, *radiant gatherings* and *prayer circles* interchangeably, to allow you the freedom to choose the appropriate form of collective assembly which best suits your group's needs and desires. You may wish to experiment with several forms at once, or one at a time, to give you a full flavor of the rich spiritual potential available for experience and release by your collective. Consider using the following:

- Long distance attunement practices: the paper dot exercise, creative triangle exercises, representational object exercises, and simple radiant energy practice.

- One-on-one attunement practices: chair attunements, full body attunements, cervical pattern and endocrine gland attunements, spinal cord and lymph/immune system attunements, foot attunements, and team attunements.

- Group meditation exercises prior to radiant energy time: Inner Healing Meditation, Sanctification, Seven Levels of Spiritual Expression Meditation Exercise, and Visualizing Health Meditation.

- *Teleconferencing.* Some of the most powerful radiant gatherings I've attended have been peopled by thousands of people at one time through satellite teleconference. If your grouping is a large organization (religious or otherwise), you may choose to share both on-site one-on-one attunements and long distance attunement simultaneously. In each radiant setting, place a speaker phone in the center of your circle. As technology advances, you may choose to utilize video conferencing equipment.

- *Internet teleconferencing and chat rooms.* Certainly the Internet carries the potential to creatively affect lives through right use of digital systems. At the time of this writing three attunement sites are up and running (see *Appendix C* for more information). These sites offer a variety of linked attunement resources to the world. We may eliminate international boundaries by connecting online with each other.

During my participation in teleconferencing events, I have always felt an overwhelming sense of having positively influenced the world simply by focusing my energies on attuning the person right in front of me. In these types of gatherings, the person in front of you *is* the world, and represents to you a contact point for directing radiant love energy. Looked at in this way, all people and places are potential contact points for you to share world radiation in a loving and thoughtful manner.

Freeing the Spirit

As I continue to participate in attuned radiant gatherings, I am continually impressed by the creative potential unleashed through participants, as spirit is allowed to flow freely through the open hearts and minds of those present. We breathe in our connection with the divine and breathe out our healing power, acting together as one intelligent organism feeding its world. During these times, we exist *"in the world but not of it,"* free of worldly constraints and attachment. We are of one mind and with one purpose, yet separate individuals. Analogous to a natural symbiotic environment, a healing prayer or attunement circle works best when its members maintain themselves with mature integrity, not organizing each other, but allowing the sense of the whole to emerge in its own season. As Margaret Wheatley, author and spiritual advisor writes, "There's nothing out there to save. There is a lot to be engaged with."[3]

Just as a system organizes itself around its identity, so too we may see our prayer circle times as indispensably linked to ourselves. We are, after all, that which creates the space. Our being informs the earth of our presence. Our healing power infuses the air. Our consciousness pours itself through space and time with purposeful creative intention. Our interactions transform ourselves and others with healing grace. When led with self-organizing power, prayer circle members realize that we as a species are one and are capable of affecting each other with tremendous subtle energy power. Wheatley suggests:

> *In a self-organizing world, one of the things that works on our behalf is not only that we have a natural tendency toward change, that we can constantly reorganize, or that we can structure ourselves without leaders (as long as we're well connected and informed and focused), but that, underneath it all, what we're doing is discovering our connections.*[4]

When allowed to work in its own natural way, prayer circles act as a midwife, stewarding the changing patterns of relationship, consciousness and order with healing intent.

Chapter 22 Notes

[1] Dr James Oschman, 'Therapeutic entrainment, Energy Review Part 3B,' p. 189.

[2] Dr James Oschman, 'What is Healing Energy? Part 3: silent pulses,' p. 185

[3] Margaret Wheatley, 'The Unplanned Organization,' *Noetic Sciences Review*, Spring, 1996, p. 20.

[4] Ibid.

Attunement Overview

Sharing an Attunement from Start to Finish

Now that you are familiar with attunement practice, simply follow these guidelines to share a traditional, full body attunement. Check back to Part 2 of this book for specific directions and attunement anatomical charts:

1. Establish sacred space in heart and mind.
2. Sitting at the head of your client, balance the cervical pattern.
3. Open the Portals of Light by attuning the endocrine glands, in order, from pineal to gonads. When you get to the thyroid and thymus, stand to the left of your client for the main portion of the attunement.
4. Attune the digestive system by using the face contact points:
   - begin with the cecum and its corresponding contact point on the base of the left wrist to establish the flow into the digestive system;
   - then do the ascending colon, transverse colon, descending colon;
   - small intestines;
   - stomach;
   - liver; and
   - gall bladder.
5. Attune the circulatory system (heart).
6. Attune the excretory system (kidneys).
7. Attune the respiratory system (lungs).
8. Attune other areas needing specialized attention:
   - spinal cord,
   - lymph system,
   - long bone technique,
   - pregnancy, terminal illness and/or injury, and
   - feet and hand attunements.
9. *Perform a body scan.* With your hands, feel over your client's entire etheric body. Beginning with your client's hands, bring your hands over their arms, shoulders, come down their chest region, over stomach and torso, down their legs and end your scan by moving the energy off of their feet. If at any time you feel any energy draws, distortion or dissonant energies or hot spots, stop your scan for a moment at that area and sweep away the dissonant energies, before continuing on. This sweep motion is actually a Therapeutic Touch technique.

10. Moving to the head and once again seating yourself there, attune the Central Sulcus, in the head region of the brain
11. Balance the Cervicals again.
12. With prayer, give thanks for your client and for the healing time you've spent together.
13. Discuss your findings with your client, and document the session as appropriate.

Documenting Attunement Therapy Sessions

Documenting energy medicine sessions is an important information-gathering tool. If you are an alternative or healing arts practitioner, you probably already use some form of writing documentation which helps you maintain a diary of each of your client's progress. Documenting your client's feedback can also help you see how your work subjectively affects your client. You may choose to use standard SOAP charts (Subjective-Objective-Assement-Plan) to document your attunement sessions, or purchase a set of my Energy Medicine Documentation Forms (please contact Findhorn Press). SOAP charts provide a practical means for maintaining a record of your client's energy medicine progress, and may serve to bring further evidence of the powerful healing effectiveness of energy medicine within mainstream medical practice.

If you choose to purchase a set of my Energy Medicine Documentation Forms, you may order them from Findhorn Press. Each set comes with a limited copyright warranty which entitles you, the purchaser, to make copies of these forms for your own use. Each set contains the following:

- *Instructional Guidelines;*
- *Inner Guidance Intake Forms,* a Mind-Body intake form;
- *Client Personal Report,* a one page report for the client to fill out prior to each session,
- *Attunement Questionnaire,* a subjective short form for the client to fill out at various times throughout their treatment cycle to give you a better idea about how they feel their sessions are helping them; and
- *Attunement/Energy Medicine SOAP Charts,* a standard Subjective-Objective-Assessment-Plan, charting tool for you to fill out at the end of each session.

Attunement Therapy Training, Home-Study and Certification Programs

Healing arts professionals and interested lay-persons may learn attunement therapy technique and its associated spiritual cosmology by attending three weekend training intensives, and their consecutive home-study modules. Level I — III weekends are offered throughout the year at various places throughout the USA, Canada and abroad.

Each Level of training includes 32 hours of Continuing Education — 16 hours of weekend training and 16 hours of home-study. Home-study training lasts from 2 – 3 months between weekend intensive cycles, and are monitored through instructor mentoring. The entire certification process takes one year to complete. Just as all life systems require time, nurturing space and care to gestate, grow, blossom and harvest, so too may you re-create your life through this year of committed service to spiritual expression and practice.

For another alternative, students may opt to purchase a separate home-study course, which has been created to go along with this book, as part of the certification home-study requirements. Or, they can simply complete this new home-study course by itself to receive 25 Continuing Education credits. (Please contact Findhorn Press for more information).

Attunement Training — Objectives

The Attunement Therapy Certification Program will teach the student all of the techniques and healing practices presented in this book. With the addition of hands-on training, each student will learn:

- how to work within a team approach to healing, both giving and receiving attunement;
- how to balance, clarify and stimulate the light path on the body;
- how to assist healing processes by expressing non-directed prayer;
- how to offer non-local transference of attuned healing energy;
- the spiritual path of the endocrine gland system (portals of light);
- how to clear vibrational dissonance patterns from anatomical systems; and
- how spiritual expression may enhance personal processes of attitudinal healing.

Attunement Training — Level I

Level I topics include:

- History of Attunement Therapy
- How Attunement is different
- Non-Directed Prayer
- Pneumaplasm and Intercessorship
- Non-local transference of attunement energy
- Spiritual orientation video
- The spiritual path of the endocrine gland system
- The attunement contact point system
- Team attunements
- Foot attunements
- Self attunements, car attunements
- Wound Healing and injury treatment (beginning), and
- Course evaluation and practical exam.

Levels I – III home-studies come with two options.

1. The student may purchase the separate home-study program, and receive 25 CE certification credits in partial fulfillment of the certification course's home-study requirements. The student must then fulfill the other 23 home-study credits through the certification course's format; or

2. The student may choose to follow the Certification course's home-study guidelines which include completing: 6 charted attunements, required reading, take-home exam, personal essay, 2 non-local attunement exercises and write-ups, and 2 handbook exercises per each level of study.

Attunement Training — Level II

Level II students will review:
- all anatomical contact points;
- non-local transference of attunement energy;
- team attunements;
- representational objects; and
- terminology.

Students will then learn specialized techniques for healing:
- the lymph and immune system;
- long bones;
- spinal vertebrae and nervous system;
- SOAP charting and documenting attunement sessions;
- hand and knee contact points; and
- course evaluation and practical exam.

Attunement Training — Level III

Level III students will review the course contents and then learn about:
- radiant gatherings / prayer circles
- attunement with animals and nature;
- how to begin an attunement practice;
- hospital on-site attunement practice, including surgeries, terminal illness, birth and death.

During the Level III weekend intensive, students will take a practical exam which will confirm their knowledge of all the contact points and required information. Students who have attended each weekend and who have successfully completed all necessary home-study work will receive their certification in attunement therapy.

When you choose to complete the Attunement Therapy Certification Program, you will enjoy being at a massage school or retreat site facility in a small group environment (up to 24 people), and will receive personal and professional attention to your training needs within a peer-supported environment.

Please write, call or e-mail me to receive scheduling information on attunement training and home-study. I am also available to speak to you regarding any of the following possibilities:
- If you represent a health care facility, center or school, and you are interested in hosting one of my attunement classes or the entire certification program;
- If you would like to have me speak to your group or assist you in setting up a radiant gathering in your area;
- If you would like to consult with me regarding any health concern you may have (on a fee per hour basis); and/or
- If you would like me to share long distance attunement with you (on a fee per hour basis).

I look forward to expanding this attunement program into your world, in whatever creative ways seem suitable to us both.

Jaclyn Stein Henderson is approved by the National Certification Board for Therapeutic Massage and Bodywork as a Continuing Education Provider in Category A.

Jaclyn Stein Henderson, NCTMB, RC
The Right Touch Healing Arts Center
6811 Phillips Rd., S.E.
Port Orchard, WA 98367
jaclynh@oz.net   www.oz.net/attunement
(360) 895-8589
Please call between normal business hours:
9 a.m. - 5 p.m., Monday - Friday.

Crossroads

More Light!
—Goethe's final words

It seems that we've come to the end of our journey together, only I have a feeling that this end is only a beginning of a new path for both of us. Your attunement experience thus far has been an opportunity for you to open your heart and mind with acceptance to the influences of love in your life, in a much greater manner than you knew before. Now that you've been introduced to and have practiced these attunement exercises, I know that something has shifted in your perspective. A new path has emerged for you to solve a particular problem, a different kind of light now fills your being, a soft and tranquil hush has fallen over your life, your fears are less intense, and your body is more attuned. Perhaps you are now inspired to offer attunement to yourself, your family and loved ones on a regular basis. Or maybe love has now opened and inspired you to take that job, join that healing arts profession, or carry out that creative task which resistance caused you to put off. All things change with love's upward motion. Love changes things because of its ascending movement in life's spiral dance. Your identification with love's intent changes you as you move forward and upward, drawn to higher purpose by love's creative action.

I leave you with a few closing thoughts. The first has to do with forgiveness. I think that the fine art of offering and receiving forgiveness is a sorely underestimated practice in our world. Forgiveness is just what it sounds like — it's for giving something. It's for giving of yourself to something or someone. It's for giving of yourself in a multitude and variety of ways you haven't chosen to give of yourself before. Forgiveness energy can provide you with a profound shift in life perspective as you move with the radical changes which it creates. *Life is for giving, share attunement.*

Forgiveness has the energy of a double-edged sword. It's for giving of yourself to yourself or another, and it's also for receiving that giving energy, which has been extended to you by God or another, back into your world. Oftentimes I've found that people don't complete the cycle, and forget to receive back again that which was first given out. You need to wield both sides of the sword in order for forgiveness to have any lasting impact. You may forgive someone of their errors, but until that person receives and accepts your forgiveness, it feels as though the forgiveness never happened. In this way, forgiveness is a useful reminder to us that we need to communicate our feelings to keep each other up to date with our rapidly changing emotional patterns, and to let each other know our new perspective.

I'd like to leave a gift with you now. I think that gift giving is also a sorely underestimated and untapped means of exchange that our society hasn't fully explored or mastered. We exchange money for goods, but those funds, at its heart, represent our love substance. If we each gave someone one gift each day, even if it's just in a hug or in a little "I'm thinking of you" note, then our world would attune itself to a more loving and harmonious vibration very quickly.

The words which follow were a gift given to me by a complete stranger while I was waiting for a bus. I don't know who wrote these words, because the man who gave them to me didn't have the author's name. The words were given to him by someone who also didn't know the author. So the cycle of giving anonymously continues here. These words are printed on a piece of paper I keep taped to my business filing cabinet, within eye-shot of my computer where I spend most of my time writing. The words have served as a means of attuning my consciousness to the spirit of integrity, which serves as the core nature of divine spirit.

At these crossroads, I offer you these words in the spirit of universal love, without beginning or end, and in likewise fashion, you may choose to pass them on to someone else. I am Alpha and Omega, the beginning and the end. So heard Saint John while experiencing his vision on the Isle of Patmos. Our life is God's gift, and in between the beginning and the end points of this gift experience, we have opportunity to discover the totality of what that gift means. We may discover the gift of ourselves by truly giving of ourselves to others. In doing so, I believe that we begin to know each other's gifts of being in a more purposeful and resonant manner.

My life continues to move with this current — giving to others those gifts which were first given to me. Certainly that is what this book is all about — giving to each other the beginning and the end points of ourselves, and all the cherished beauties that lay between. I am tremendously thankful to be able to bestow on you these gifts from my life. It is from that generous flow that my life's purpose has emerged, and from which all of life's greater gifts have been and continue to be born. It has been my privilege to have shared these gifts with you during our time together. Be well.

Be careful of your thoughts,
for your thoughts become your words.
Be careful of your words,
for your words become your actions.
Be careful of your actions,
for your actions become your habits.
Be careful of your habits
for your habits become your character.
Be careful of your character
for your character becomes your destiny.

About the Author

Jaclyn Stein Henderson has 17 years experience in massage, bodywork, and attunement. Having practiced professional massage since 1981, she graduated from the University of Oregon's Robert D. Clarke's Honors College in 1990 with a B.A. in Independent Study. She then received a 1,000 Hour Certificate in Massage from the Colorado School of Healing Arts in 1992. Having attended initial naturopathic medicine study at Bastyr University, Seattle, WA, Jaclyn now co-owns and manages her home-based business, *The Right Touch Healing Arts Center* in Port Orchard, WA. A former Instructor at *Seattle Massage School*, Jaclyn now teaches Attunement Therapy courses worldwide, and writes for *Massage and Bodywork Magazine* (the trade journal of Associated Bodyworkers and Massage Professionals) and other bodywork and new age journals. She loves to sew, quilt, garden, cook, travel, write and share attunement, and lives with her husband, Dick Henderson and their two cats on a 4.5 acre sacred site on the Kitsap Peninsula, in Washington.

Appendix A: Histology Notes on the Endocrine Gland System

The following histological descriptions of the endocrine gland system may give you a fuller understanding of how the endocrine glands function within the human anatomy. Most of these notes were taken during my first year of medical school training while I was a student at Bastyr University. They may serve you as an outline of their purpose and function. For more in-depth information, please see other medical reference material. Attunement students would do well to read this section, and correlate the physical aspects of these glands to their spiritual counterparts discussed in *Chapter 11*.

1. Pineal Gland

Usually ignored as 'useless' by most medical studies, this small gland, which is located in the center of the brain, is thought to regulate melatonin production and secretion (a neurohormone), internal adjustments to light and dark and, as has been recently discovered, production and secretion of pinoline, a beta-carboline thought to influence psychic sense, intuition, clairvoyance, pre-cognition and out-of-body experience.[1]

Since the pineal produces melatonin, which regulates the activities of the pituitary gland (the master gland of the body), some consider the pineal gland be the 'super master gland,' describing it alongside its metaphysical properties as the 'third eye.'[2] Jacob Liberman, OD, PhD, discusses the role of the pineal in modern and post-modern man:

> [I]n humans, as well as in all hairy creatures, light stimulates the pineal exclusively by way of our eyes, therefore making it an integral part of the visual system. The technical name of the pineal is epiphysis cerebri, which literally means "top of brain." It is my belief that humans originally also received light stimulation through the top of the head… This indicates that at one point in human evolution… the pineal may have actually been positioned at the top of the human brain.[3]

Dr Liberman states that the size of the pineal gland directly correlates with where living creatures live, and the degree to which they are in touch with their environment. This is because he believes that the pineal is responsible for regulating the entire physiology of organisms with their environment. Since our present pineal size resembles that of a pea, Dr

Liberman suggests that a "change in our consciousness, and a closer connection between us and nature" may increase the size of our pineals.[4]

A long known spiritual philosophy to attunement servers, the pineal gland is thought to anchor the silver cord of life in an individual, which is broken at death.

2. Pituitary Gland

Located close to the pineal and directly in back of the eyes, this pea-sized 'Master Gland' of the body, affects the regulation of all endocrine glands except the islets of langerhans, located in the pancreas, and is itself regulated by the hypothalmus, part of the nervous system (which, in turn, is regulated by melatonin, secreted by the pineal).

The pituitary is divided into anterior and posterior divisions. The anterior division is responsible for producing and secreting:

- Growth hormone (GH also known as somatotrophin) which controls and regulates growth of bones and muscles, and stimulates cellular uptake of amino acids and protein synthesis, carbohydrate and fat breakdown;
- Prolactin (LTH) which stimulates development of mammary glands during and after pregnancy and stimulates milk production;
- Thyroid stimulating hormone (TSH or thyrothrophin) which controls growth of the thyroid gland, uptake of iodine, and synthesis and release of thyroid hormones;
- Follicle stimulating hormone (FSH) which stimulates growth of the ovarian follicles in the female, and stimulates spermatogenesis (new sperm production) in the male;
- Lutinizing hormone (LH) which stimulates the maturation of follicle cells, promotes ovulation, and stimulates the corpus luteum (surrounding egg) to secrete estrogen and progesterone in the female, and in the male, stimulates interstitial cells to secrete testosterone; and
- Adrendocorticotrophic hormone (ACTH) which stimulates growth of the adrenal cortex and secretion of glucocorticoids (cortisol) which regulates metabolism.

The posterior division secretes neurohormones produced in the hypothalmus located near by. These hormones include:

- Oxytocin which stimulates uterine contraction of smooth muscle and secretion of milk from the breast; and
- Vasopressin (ADH) which promotes water absorption in the kidney, concentrating urine and increasing blood volume (of physiological importance).

3. Thyroid Gland

Located in the neck, on the ventral or frontal portion of the trachea, these two large, lateral, butterfly-shaped lobes are responsible for producing and secreting several hormones. Together with the pituitary, these two glands participate in a negative feedback loop, meaning that when the pituitary (for example) produces too much of one hormone (found circulating in the blood), the thyroid produces another hormone which shuts-off production of the pituitary's hormone (and vice-versa). Thyroid function and hormone production includes:

- the uptake of iodine into the thyroid (an important element for all the thyroid hormones produced);
- production of thyroglobulin (a glycoprotein containing several amino acids);
- production of thyroxine and triiodothyronine. These are hormones which maintain normal metabolic levels in all body cells, increase the rate of protein synthesis, are responsible for nervous system maturation and increase energy utilization; and
- production and secretion of calcitonin (thyrocalcitonin) which regulates calcium levels in the blood.

The parathyroid are four pea-sized glands located in back of the thyroid gland. They produce and secrete parathormone (PTH) which increases the presence of calcium in the bloodstream by various means.

4. Thymus

Located a few inches lower than the thyroid, behind the sternum, this large gland is most productive prior to puberty. This gland produces and secretes t-cells, helper t-cells and killer t-cells which play major roles in immune function, ridding the body of viruses. Once produced in the thymus, these important viral fighting cells migrate to specific regions of the body: largely to lymph nodes and the spleen where they do most of their work to fight off harmful viral infection (bacteria are fought off by b-cells produced in bone).

5. Islets of Langerhans

Located in the pancreas, these ductless glands are completely interspersed throughout the pancreas, and produce the following polypeptide hormones:

- Insulin, which signals the 'fed state' in the body, and clears the blood of sugar, storing it as fuel, stimulating glycogen synthesis and glucose breakdown;

- Glucagon, which acts opposite that of insulin by stimulating glycogen and lipid breakdown (putting sugar in the bloodstream), and production of gluconeogenesis (new sugar); and
- Somatostatin, which acts to block insulin and glucagon secretion (as well as other enzyme and hormone secretions). It also inhibits production and release of pituitary growth hormone and thyroid stimulating hormone. These changes lead to a decrease of nutrients in the bloodstream.

6. Adrenal Glands (Suprarenal Glands)

Capping the superior border of the kidney, these two glands are pyramidal in shape, and secrete the following hormones:

- Corticosteroids. Derived from cholesterol. The most important hormone being a mineralcorticoid called aldosterone, which regulates electrolyte concentration in the blood, and increases re-absorption of sodium in the kidney. An important glucocorticoid hormone (one of the corticosteroids) is cortisol, which regulates metabolism of sugar, fats and proteins in all cells.
- Epinepherin and norepinephrine (adrenaline) which, when released into the bloodstream, mimics the sympathetic nervous system's reaction to fight or flight.

7. Gonads

Known as the testes in the male and ovaries in the female, these glands produce testosterone (male) and estrogen and progesterone (female) which assist in giving each sex its differential characteristics, and assist in the maturation and development process of each sex. The production of these hormones are regulated by hormones produced and secreted by the pituitary. Together, they function to promote procreation and continuation of the human species.

Appendix B:
The History of Attunement Therapy

Attunement (*At-one-ment*) was first created in the 1920's by Lloyd Arthur Meeker, pen name *Uranda*, in North America. He used the attunement technique, a hands-on method of balancing vibrational energies in the body, to help people live in constant attunement with God's life force, as he helped to facilitate their spiritual awakening. Uranda had a vision of restoring humankind to its original garden state consciousness, and he devoted his adult life to this end. In 1940, he established the Emissaries of Divine Light Ministry, a legal church, to accomplish that goal. Until his death in 1954, Uranda offered weekly services, public talks, classes and written literature to the thousands of followers who flocked to be with his spiritual focus.

In the early 1950's, Uranda met George Shears and Albert Ackerley, chiropractors, who were Palmer College graduates. Palmer College advocated a spiritual approach to healing and taught its students that adjusting the spine released the flow of 'Innate Intelligence', or Positive Center from within the body. By adjusting the spine, chiropractors could clear interference from within the nervous system. Dr Shears developed Palmer's approach into a principle he referred to as the 'One Law of Life'. He stated:

> The one law is the law of positive action and negative response. The law controls the universe and everything in it, including man and the healing of what is called illness. The healing process is set in motion by the positive expression of the power of God's love and the response to it by the one served. The main contribution of the spinal adjustment is that it helps increase the response in the one served in compliance with the requirement of the One Law.[1]

Shears discovered that he could effect change in his clients without the need of forceful manipulation, and began to base his treatments on principles based on the One Law, sending radiant love energy through his hands to his client's body. His story reads as follows:

> I realized that there was something else in the picture which was producing the results. Many people started improving after the examination period before I got the first adjustment. To find out what it was, I started a research program as follows: I decided to take the first 25 new cases which came in, regardless of the nature of their trouble, make my usual examinations and then only simulate the

giving of an adjustment, being careful not to contact any specific vertebra of the spine.

I used this procedure with these 25 cases three times a week for thirty days, then took new x-rays and repeated the examination for comparison. At the end of the thirty-day period, 24 of them had received results as good or better than we had ever experienced before.

Then the time came when my co-researcher, Dr Albert Ackerley, and I wanted to start a school to teach this wonderful truth to others, so that the blessings contained in the principle could be preserved for all mankind.[2]

With the addition of Dr Shears' non-touch technique, attunement changed its focus from being a hands-on technique to a non-touch technique. This approach coincided with Uranda's perspective on healing, and in 1952 the three men began offering classes at Sunrise Ranch, the Emissary International headquarters, in Loveland, Colorado, under the name of 'Server's Training School.' Many Palmer students, graduates and chiropractors from other institutions attended the Emissary's 'G-P-C' (God-Patient-Chiropractor) Server's Training School to learn attunement for their own lives and practices.

With Uranda's death in 1954, the training school and Emissary ministry continued under the direction of Martin Exeter (1954 –1988), and later, his son, Michael. Exeter leadership brought new dimension and scope to the Emissary program. During this time, thousands of people with differing spiritual faiths were attracted to and began association with the Emissaries, including those associated with Christian, Jewish, Native American Indian, Hindu, Won Buddhist (Korea) and Joh Rei Fellowship (Japan) faiths. Since at one time the Emissary program reached every major country of the world, it may be said that the attunement current touched many different faith systems, welcoming in all to share in the focus of spiritual leadership offered through attunement orientation. The divine current moved as one tide of awakening and people responded to their own inner light, regardless of their personality or earthly identification. Individuals drawn into the Emissary program were invited to pay attention to the presence of the *One Who Dwells Within*, awakening their consciousness to the commonality amongst themselves instead of that which isolated or divided. The attunement current became an uplifting beacon of light moving silently through the lives of many, integrating, clarifying, balancing, making whole.

Attunement practitioners also served the needs of the critically and terminally ill, those going through the birth process, and those at life' termination. During these more stressful times, attunement provided a rich solace of spiritual energy flow which always brought about a sensation of inner peace and tranquillity, and quickened the healing process for all concerned. Even though no one really knew how it worked at the physical level, everyone knew that sharing an attunement would assist their healing, no matter at what level of being the illness resided. Body, mind, heart or spirit — attunement opened doors for divine light to work its magic in the minds and hearts of those who responded to its gentle flow. (Today, of course, scientific research affirms the healing power of many different kinds of energy practice, and many hospitals and health care centers offer energy therapies as a viable form of health care service.)

The Future of Attunement Therapy

There is now scientific evidence to support what had previously been recognized anecdotally, namely the phenomenon that people who have been influenced by one spirit develop non-local thought and behavior patterns identical in nature, time and space.[3] This means that twins who emerge from the same ovum, or groups of people who have been deeply touched by one spirit, appear to move in the same lifestyle rhythms, thought processes and change patterns, regardless of their conscious connection with each other.

This phenomenon takes on deeper meaning for those associated with the attunement process, and for humanity as a whole. As the one spirit of love continues to move deeply through the lives of those open to spiritual awakening, these individuals become aware of the common oneness between themselves, others and all life systems on earth. The ramifications of this higher consciousness, in terms of increasing respect for the animal, vegetable and mineral kingdoms, takes on new significance. The futuristic 'human potential' movement, which once appeared during the 1960's and 70's as a vision for the future, now appears active and thriving with holographic consequences. This means that my personal awakening process affects yours in every way. My personal assurances, set backs, opening destiny paths, etc. affects yours, and vice-versa. The awakening process, stimulated into action by attunement and facilitated by countless other spiritual faiths, energy and light work practices, brings with it the recognition that we are indeed each other's keeper, and are of one body. Spirit makes us one. This is how we know each other, and this is how we serve each other in truth.

Many recognize that humanity is now leading itself through a self-created paradigm shift in consciousness. This book salutes those services, faiths, energy practices, and committed individuals who seek to attune themselves to their own inner divinity, thus creatively affecting the whole. For those who share attunement with Source, the mystery of how God acts through human beings is finished on earth, as the light shines brightly through the eyes of each one who sees a new world.

Appendix B Notes

[1] Garry Diggins, Introducing the Attunement Process (Self-Published. Toronto: Toronto Attunement Center, 1989), p. 4.

[2] Ibid.

[3] Dossey, Larry, MD, 'Lessons from Twins: Of Nature, Nurture and Consciousness,' *Alternative Therapies*, May, 1997, Volume 3, No. 3, pp. 8–15.

Appendix C: Attunement Practitioners and Conference Facilities

The following is a partial listing of Attunement Practitioners who have been working in the field of attunement for many years. Also listed are some Emissary conference facilities and businesses which offer attunement services. Prices for private on-site and long distance attunement therapy sessions and classes vary with each practitioner and location. Since every practitioner and teacher has his or her own expertise, style and scope of practice, you may wish to find the right teacher or practitioner who best suits your needs and/or fits your pattern of resonance.

USA

California

> Glen Ivy
> 25000 Glen Ivy Road, Corona, CA 91719
> (909) 277-8701 General Reception; 277-8700 (fax)
> Barbara Lurgos, Retreat Center Coordinator, (909) 277-8711

Glen Ivy is an international spiritual community and Emissary affiliate, 20+ years old, offering attunement sessions and an attuned retreat sanctuary for other faith groups and non-profit organizations.

> William H. Tolhurst, DC
> 409 Alberto Way, Suite 3, Los Gatos, CA 95032
> (408) 356-9459

Private attunement sessions, classes and seminars. Call for details.

> Steve Tashiro, DC
> 7960 Patricia Court, Sebastopol, CA 95472
> (707) 823-2271

Private attunement sessions and classes. Call for details.

Colorado

> Sunrise Ranch
> 5569 N County Rd. 29, Loveland, CO 80538
> (970) 679-4200 General Reception; Fax (970) 679-4233
> Events Coordinator (970) 679-4238
> Ted Black, Literature Department, (970) 679-4221,
> Fax (970) 679-4233, E-mail: tblack@emnet.org

Long Distance Attunement and Radiant Gatherings, 'Spirit in Action' Correspondence Course in the Art of Living based on Emissary principles.

Sunrise Ranch is the International Emissaries headquarters, and was founded in 1946. As one of the largest spiritual communities in the world, Sunrise Ranch hosts large public events, retreats, seminars and offers daily attunement practice.

Cynthia Kay Pilmore, Counselor
1526 Spruce Street, Suite 101, Boulder, CO 80302
443-2230 Voicemail

Long Distance attunement and on-site practice by appointment.

Florida

Laurence Layne, LMT
Healing Waters Clinic
2200 N. Ponce De Leon Blvd. #3, St. Augustine, FL 32084
904-826-1965; E-mail: llayne@aug.com;

Licensed Massage Therapist, Herbalist, Practice of Natural Healing, Attunement Classes. Author of 'Attunement: The Sacred Landscape' (self-published, 1997).

Georgia

South Garden Center for Education and Attunement
1411 Dresden Drive, Atlanta, GA 30319
(404) 231-1470; E-mail: sgarden@onestory.com
URL: http://www.onestory.com
Spritual Coordinators: Grant Clarke (706) 864-6270; Fax (706) 864-1262;
E-mail: grantclarke@mindspring.com

Private attunement sessions, worship services Sundays and Wednesdays. Introductory classes Tuesday nights. All offerings on donation basis. Call for details.

Indiana

Oakwood Farm Retreat Center
3801 S. County Rd. 575 E., Selma, IN 47383-9604
Retreat Center Office (765) 747-7027

Oakwood Farm is a unique retreat center surrounded by a lush wildlife sanctuary. The vision of this 28 year old community includes a love and reverence for life, creative collaboration, and the provision of an attuned atmosphere for personal and planetary transformation.

Louisiana

Anthony J. Palombo, DC
Healing and Attunement Center
910 Eighth Avenue, Suite 3, Lake Charles, LA 70601
(318) 437-3991; Fax (318) 439-1526

Dr Palombo offers harmonic toning to facilitate the attunement current. He also offers Bio-Energetic Synchronization Technique (BEST) and Contact Reflex Analysis (CRA) for nutritional profiling.

Missouri

Dr Larry Herbig, DC
Chiropractic Wellness Center
3611 Main Street, Suite 103, Kansas City, MO 64111
(816) 561-7035; Fax (816) 561-3851

With 16 years experience, Dr Herbig offers a 150 hour Energy Studies, Vibrant Healing and Attunement Certification Program, which has been approved by the Missouri Nursing Association, AMTA and many other alternative therapy associations. He also offers private sessions by appointment and long distance attunement.

Chris Jorgensen, Attunement Master Teacher
1600 Genessee, Suite 524, P.O. Box 014064, Kansas City, MO 64102
(816) 221-7123; Fax (Same)

Private sessions, on-site and long distance, and seminar classes in Attunement, Reiki, and Cranial-Sacral Therapy. Author of 'Attunement: Love Made Visible' self-published, 1996.

Montana

Bill and Joanne Comer
Montana Center for Healing Touch
601 Nikles Drive, Suite 9, Bozeman, MT 59715
(406) 586-1188, (800) 200-3735; E-mail: healing.touch@usa.net

New Jersey

Lawence Bakur, DC
278 Green Village Road, Green Village, NJ 07935
(973) 822-2234

Wednesday Night Attunement Circles, 7 – 8p.m. — an hour of attunement education, attunement private sessions.

Wallace Lauder, RRPT
Princeton Center for Yoga and Health
113 Commons Way, Princeton, NJ 08540
(609) 279-0550

Attunement and Polarity Therapy; private sessions by appointment.

New York

Lenny Izzo, DC, Attunement Master Teacher
Center for Health, Healing and Attunement
202 East Main Street, Huntington, NY 11743
(516) 547-5433; Fax (516) 547-5434; E-mail: lendoci@aol.com

Private attunement therapy sessions and classes. Dr Izzo specializes in nutritional evaluation and guidance.

Oregon

Still Meadow Community
16561 S.E. Marna Road, Clackamas, Oregon 97015
David Reis, Events Coordinator and Attunement Practitioner (503) 658-8793,
Fax (503) 658-4799; E-mail: david_m_reis@emnet.org

Still Meadow Community hosts personal and group retreats, and resonant group activities in a sacred woodland setting.

Washington

Jaclyn Stein Henderson, NCTMB, RC
The Right Touch Healing Arts Center
6811 Phillips Rd. SE, Port Orchard, WA 98367
(360) 895-8589; E-mail: jaclynh@oz.net;
URL: http://www.oz.net/attunement

Personal and group attunement sessions, on-site and long distance, public speaking. Attunement Certification, Home-study and Training Program, author of 'The Healing Power of Attunement Therapy, Stories and Practice,' Findhorn Press, 1998.

Wisconsin

Larry Johansen
Heart & Health, SC
1011 North Mayfair Road, Suite 301, Wauwatosa, WI 53226
302-1011; E-mail: larryj@execpc.com

Private attunement sessions and classes, including stress management and nutritional counseling.

CANADA

British Columbia

The Lodge Conference and Retreat Centre
P.O. Box 9, 100 Mile House, BC V0K 2E0 Canada
150 North Cariboo Hwy 97, 100 Mile House, B.C.
Anne Blaney and David Barnes, Retreat Coordinators (250) 395-4077, ext.
23 & 21
E-mail: ebclodge@bcinternet.net
Dorothy Hughes (250) 395-4077, ext. 27; E-mail: ebclodge@bcinternet.net

On-site and long distance attunements offered weekdays by appointment.
Hugh Duff (250) 395-4077, ext. 27; E-mail: ebclodge@bcinternet.net

On-site attunements offered weekends by appointment. Radiant Gathering Thursdays at 6:00 p.m., PST (call first to be included).
Jim and Grace Moore (leave message at 250-395-4077)

Radiant Gatherings, Thursdays, 10:00 – 10:30 a.m., PST.

Edenvale Retreat Centre
4330 Bradner Road, Abbotsford, BC V4X 1S8 Canada
856-3388; Fax (604) 856-3298

Edenvale offers personal and group retreats in a luscious country setting. Vegetarian dining offered. Attunement Seminars offered. (Capacity: meeting rooms 30 – 70; overnight 1 – 35; dining 70.)

FourWinds
5055 Connaught Drive, Vancouver, BC V6M 3G2
Jude Repar (604) 263-1990; E-mail: juderepar@hotmail.com

Jude holds weekly attunement circles classes and spiritual retreats, entitled 'The Quickening,' locally and abroad, that have attunement as the foundation.
Jonathan Beals (604) 263-3797; E-mail: jonathan_beals@emnet.org
Jonathan offers private attunement sessions weekly, from 9a.m. – 9p.m., and teaches attunement classes.

Victoria Attunement Center
1-2727 Quadra Street, Victoria, BC, V8T 4E5 Canada
Phone: (250)   920-4438,   Fax: (250)   920-4458;   E-mail: edlvicbc@islandnet.com
URL: http://www.islandnet.com/~edlvicbc
Gary Courtland Miles and Desmond Michael, Attunement Practitioners
Sunday Radiant Meditations, 11a.m. Attunements offered during the week by appointment, on-site and long distance. Classes to be scheduled. Please see internet site for current information.

Montreal

Judie Diamond (two addresses)
4493 Marcil Avenue, Montreal, H4A 2Z9 Canada
(514) 486-0466; *and*
Long Lake Road, Parham, Ontario, Canada K0H 2K0
(613) 375-6772

Attunement Therapy and Life Purpose Counseling, attunement workshops. Instructor at the Institute for Natural Health Consultants, Montreal, Canada.

Ontario

King View Conference and Hospitality Center
P.O. Box 217, Aurora, ON L4G 3H3 Canada
(905) 727-9171; (905) 727-7031

King View hosts personal and group retreats, workshops, attunement services and classes in a restful, country setting.
Diane Hoover (905) 726-1460
Paul Price (905) 727-8497, Fax (905) 727-7031

Attunement Certification Training Program, personal attunement sessions on-site and long distance.

ISRAEL

Jeff Goldstein
P.O. Box 10649, 91104 Jerusalem, Israel

Private attunement sessions, local and long distance, radiant gatherings, attunement classes.

SOUTH AFRICA

Judy Bekker and Valerie Morris
P.O. Box 245, Constantia, Cape 7848, South Africa
Tel: 27 21 794-4646; Fax: 27 21 794-5088
E-mail: Valerie_Morris@emnet.org

Vision Quest: An 11 day process that includes ritual, ceremony, prayer, attunement with nature, and 4 days and nights solo, fasting in the African wilderness. A time for deep, undistracted reflection and renewal. Based on indigenous peoples rites of passage. An opportunity to mark a life change, be it a beginning, an ending or a transition.

The Virus Diseases of the Nervous System
(editors) Cxon Whitty, J.T. Hughes and F.O..
MacCallum (Blackwell Scientific Press, Oxford)

Bibliography

Bendit, Lawrence and Phoebe. <u>The Etheric Body of Man</u>. Wheaton: The Theosophical Publishing House, 1977.

Brennan, Barbara Ann. <u>Hands of Light</u>. New York: Bantam Books, 1993.

Burghley, Michael, and Nancy Burghley. <u>The Rising Tide of Change</u>. Loveland, CO: Foundation House Publications, 1986.

Cecil, Martin. 'The Preservation of Essences.' <u>The Third Sacred School</u> Volumes. Loveland, CO: Eden Valley Press. Vol. 5, No. 56: 321.

Diggins, Gary. <u>Introducing the Attunement Process</u>. Toronto: Toronto Attunement Center, 1989.

Dossey, Larry, MD <u>Healing Words</u>. New York: HarperCollins, 1993.

Dossey, Larry, MD 'Prayer, Old Approach, New Wonders.' <u>The Quest</u>. Summer, 1990: 43-44.

Editor. 'Practitioner Profile: Stephen A. Nezezon, MD.' <u>Flower Essence Society Newsletter</u>. Summer, 1995: 14-15.

Exeter, Martin. <u>As of a Trumpet</u>. Loveland, CO: Eden Valley Press, 1968.

Exeter, Michael. 'Entrainment of Capacity.' Extemporaneous Worship Service. Loveland, CO: Eden Valley Press. December 9, 1990: 1.

Gerber, Richard, MD <u>Vibrational Medicine</u>. Santa Fe: Bear & Co., 1988.

Gray, Eden. <u>A Complete Guide to the Tarot</u>. New York: Bantam, 1970.

Heinberg, Richard. <u>Memories and Visions of Paradise</u>. Los Angeles: Jeremy Tarcher, 1989.

Herman, Judith Lewis, MD <u>Trauma and Recovery</u>. BasicBooks, a Division of HarperCollins Publishers, 1992.

Hurley, Thomas J. III. 'Placebos and Healing: A New Look at the 'Sugar Pill'' <u>Noetic Sciences Collection</u>. Summer, 1985: (no pages no.)

Jorgensen, Chris. <u>Attunement, Love Made Visible</u>. Kansas City, MO: Self published, 1996.

Kaminski, Patricia and Richard Katz. <u>Flower Essence Repertory</u>. Nevada City: Earth-Spirit, Inc, 1994.

<u>Kundalini Yoga, Guidelines for Sadhana (Daily Practice)</u>. Los Angeles: Arcline Publications. 1974.

Leskowitz, Eric, MD. 'Metaphors in the Teaching of Holistic Medicine.' <u>Alternative Therapies</u>. July, 1997, Vol. 3, No. 4:111-112.

Levin, Jeffrey, S., PhD, MPH. 'How Prayer Heals: A Theoretical Model.' <u>Alternative Therapies</u>. January, 1996, Vol. 2, No. 1:66-73.

Liberman, Jacob, OD, PhD <u>Light: Medicine for the Future</u>. Santa Fe: Bear & Co., 1991.

Maynard, Joseph, DC, PhC 'Dr George Shears and the GPC Movement.' <u>Today's Chiropractic</u>. July/August, 1996: 40-45.

Moore, Keith L., PhD <u>Clinically Oriented Anatomy</u>, Third Edition. Baltimore: Williams & Williams, 1992.

Netter, Frank H., MD <u>Atlas of Human Anatomy</u>. New Jersey: CIBA-Geigy Corporation, 1989.

Northrup, Christiane, MD <u>Women's Bodies, Women's Wisdom</u>. New York: Bantam, 1994.

Oschman, James. L., PhD 'What is healing energy? Part 3: silent pulses.' <u>Journal of Bodywork and Movement Therapies</u>. April, 1997, Vol. 1, No. 3: 179-189.

Oschman, James. L., PhD 'Therapeutic entrainment, Energy Review, Part 3B.' <u>Journal of Bodywork and Movement Therapies</u>. April, 1997, Vol. 1, No. 3: 189-194.

O'Regan, Brendan. 'Placebo — The Hidden Asset in Healing.' <u>Investigations, A Research Bulletin</u>. Sausalito: Institute of Noetic Sciences, Vol. 2, No. 1: 4.

O'Regan, Brendan and Caryle Hirshberg. <u>Spontaneous Remission, an Annotated Bibliography</u>. Sausalito: Institute of Noetic Sciences, 1993.

Pert, Candace, PhD 'Candace Pert, PhD: Neuropeptides, AIDS and the Science of Mind-Body Healing.' <u>Alternative Therapies</u>. July,1995, Vol. 1, No. 3: 70-76.

Price, Paul. 'The Long Bone Attunement Technique.' <u>The Capstone</u>. New York: Center for Health, Healing and Attunement. January,1993: 2.

Rechtschaffen, Stephan. 'Time Shifting.' <u>Noetic Sciences Review</u>. Summer, 1997, No. 42: 16-20.

Roney-Dougal, S.M. 'Recent Findings Relating to the Possible Role of the Pineal Gland in Affecting Psychic Ability.' <u>Journal of the Society for Psychical Research</u>. April, 1989. Vol. 55, No. 815: 313-328.

Russek, Linda G., PhD, & Schwartz, Gary E., PhD. 'Dynamical Energy Systems and Modern Physics: Fostering the Science and Spirit of Complementary and Alternative Medicine.' <u>Alternative Therapies</u>. May, 1997, Vol. 3, No. 3: 46-56.

Russek, Linda G., PhD, & Schwartz, Gary E., PhD. 'Energy Cardiology: A Dynamical Energy Systems Approach for Integrating Conventional and Alternative Medicine.' <u>ADVANCES: The Journal of Mind-Body Health</u>. Fall, 1996, Vol. 12, No. 4: 4-24.

Russek, Linda G., PhD, & Schwartz, Gary E., PhD. 'Perceptions of Parental Caring Predict Health Status in Midlife: A 35-Year Follow-up of the Harvard Mastery of Stress Study.' <u>Psychosomatic Medicine</u>. 1997, 59:144-149.

Scheffer, Mechthild. <u>Bach Flower Therapy Theory and Practice</u>. Rochester: Healing Arts Press, 1988.

Schlitz, Marilyn, PhD 'Intentionality in Healing: Mapping the Integration of Body, Mind, and Spirit.' <u>Alternative Therapies</u>. November, 1995, Vol. 1, No. 5:119-120.

Smith, Stretton, Rev. <u>4T Prosperity Program</u>. Carmel: The 4T Publishing Company, 1993.

Tiller, William A., PhD <u>Energy Fields and the Human Body, Part II</u>. Phoenix: Edgar Cayce Foundation, no date.

Tiller, William A., PhD. Preface. <u>The Science of Homeopathy</u>. By George Vithoulkas. New York: Grove Weidenfeld, 1980.

Uranda. 'A Clean Heart.' <u>Behold I Create</u>. Loveland, CO: Eden Valley Press, 1985. Vo. 4, No. 11: 15.

Uranda. 'Belonging to God.' <u>The Third Sacred School Volumes</u>. Loveland, CO: Eden Valley Press. January 25, 1953: 4-8.

Uranda. 'The Creative Life #8.' Extemporaneous Service. Loveland, CO: Eden Valley Press. January 27, 1954: 9.

Uranda. 'Forgiveness.' The Third Sacred School Volumes. Loveland, CO: Eden Valley Press. August 2, 1953: 3.

Uranda. 'The Four Forces.' Behold I Create. Loveland, CO: Eden Valley Press, 1985. Vol. 2, No. 5: 17.

Uranda. 'Instantaneous Manifestation.' The Third Sacred School Volumes. Loveland, CO: Eden Valley Press, 1933. Chapter Six: 32.

Uranda. 'Learning to Welcome Changes.' The Third Sacred School Volumes. July 21, 1954: 8.

Uranda. Letters to You. Loveland, CO: Eden Valley Press, 1941.

Uranda. 'The Necessities of Correction to Maintain Balance.' The Third Sacred School Volumes. Loveland, CO: Eden Valley Press. Vol. 5, No. 31: 173.

Uranda. 'Perfection and the Use of Substitute Patterns.' Behold I Create. Loveland, CO: Eden Valley Press, 1985. Vol. 3, No. 7: 8.

Uranda. 'A Personal Message.' The Third Sacred School Volumes. March 24, 1938: 2.

Uranda. 'A Personal Message.' The Third Sacred School Volumes. June 30, 1945: 1.

Uranda. 'The Primary Key to the Triune Chart of Manifestation.' The Third Sacred School Volumes. February 2, 1938: 2.

Uranda. 'The Reality of Letting Go.' The Third Sacred School Volumes. December 6, 1952: 4.

Uranda. Seven Steps to the Temple of Light, Fourth Edition. Loveland, CO: Eden Valley Press, 1977.

Uranda. 'Your Place in the Midst of the Garden.' Behold I Create. Loveland, CO: Eden Valley Press, 1985. Vol. 2, No. 6: 42.

Uranda. The Triune Ray. Loveland, CO: Eden Valley Press, 1936.

Uranda. 'Understanding the Principle of Absence.' The Third Sacred School Volumes. Loveland, CO: Eden Valley Press, Vol. 7: 333.

Van de Castle, Robert L., PhD Our Dreaming Mind. New York: Ballantine, 1994.

Van Duzen, Grace. The Vibrational Ark. Loveland, CO: Eden Valley Press, 1996.

Weinstein, Marion. Positive Magic, Revised Edition. Custer, WA: Phoenix Publishing, Inc., 1981.

Wheatley, Margaret. 'The Unplanned Organization.' Noetic Sciences Review. Spring, 1996, No. 37: 16-23.

White, Stuart, DC 'Immune-Lymph System Awareness.' The Capstone. New York: Center for Health, Healing and Attunement, February, 1994: 3.

Wilber, Ken. A Brief History of Everything. Boston: Shambhala, 1996.

Wilber, Ken, Ed. The Holographic Paradigm and Other Paradoxes. Boulder: Shambhala, 1982.

Index

Albert Ackerley 255
acupuncture 26, 32, 73, 143
adrenal glands 122, 207, 254
AIDS 32, 121, 155
Air phase 199, 204
anjali 116
anorexic/bulimic 91
aorta 170
ascension process 83, 85, 169, 189
Atlas Balancing 119
atlas point 177
attitudinal healing 31, 32
attitudinal release 66, 194
Attunement and Massage Sessions 176
Attunement and Pets 196
Attunement Ascension Theory 85
attunement babies 195
Attunement Intensive 81
Attunement Master Server 35, 41, 135, 173
Attunement Overview 241
attunement prayer circles 235
Attunement Sanctuary 81
Attunement Therapy Training 17, 222, 243
Attunement through the Eyes 171
attunement with Source 197
Attunement-based prayer circles 237
Attuning the adrenals 132
Attuning the brain 166
Attuning the colon 141
Attuning the gallbladder 142
Attuning the gonads 133
Attuning the heart 148
Attuning the islets of langerhans 132
Attuning the kidneys 150
Attuning the liver 142
Attuning the lungs 154
Attuning the pancreas 142
Attuning the pineal 132
Attuning the pituitary 132
Attuning the small intestines 141
Attuning the spleen 161
Attuning the stomach 142
Attuning the thymus 132
Attuning the thyroid 132
autonomic nervous system 167
Axillary Lymph Nodes 161

Bill Bahan, DC 11, 145
Bailey Boushey House 32

Balancing the Body through the Feet 120
Balancing the Cervical Pattern 116, 241
Bastyr University 28, 32, 101, 251
Robert C. Beck 235
birth cycle 194
brainwave oscillation 115, 119
breast cancer 41, 91, 162
breast implant syndrome 159
breast tissue 162
Barbara Brennan 25

cancer 31, 43, 159
cancer remission 42
capacities of heart and mind 165
capacities of mind and heart 45, 61, 171, 200
Car Attunements 80
cardiovascular system 217
carotid or femoral artery points 148
cataracts 172
Central Sulcus or Fissure of Rolando 166
Cervical Lymph Nodes 161
cervicals 111
Chair Attunements 28, 230
chakras 31
chi 26
Children and Foot Attunements 196
chiropractic 11, 32, 143
Depak Chopra, MD 77
chronic fatigue syndrome 143, 159
Circulatory Attunement Practice Guidelines 148
Circulatory, Excretory and Respiratory Systems 145
Circulatory System Attunement Practice 146
Bill and Joanne Comer 207, 261
Conception and birth 194
Contact point long distance attunement 79
contact points 138, 139, 141, 149, 151, 153, 213, 214, 215
counseling 32, 73, 144
Norman Cousins 46
cranial nerves 140
Cranial-Sacral Therapy 115
Creative Process Guidelines 202
Creative Triangle Exercises 96

Guru Ram Das 152
Death Transition Attunement Guidelines 211
Denver Nursing Center for Human Caring 32

The Digestive System 137
dissonant energy 28, 158
dissonant pattern 30
distortion patterns 29, 30, 137, 171
Documenting energy medicine sessions 242
Larry Dossey, MD 43, 55, 77

Emissaries of Divine Light Ministry 16, 255
Emissary Ministry 194
Emissary World Assembly 233
Endocrine Gland Attunement Guidelines 129
endocrine gland system 28, 31, 122, 127
Entering in 24, 37, 45, 49, 92, 186
Entrainment 114, 165, 166, 183
etheric body 21, 23, 122, 219
excretory system 145
Excretory System Attunement Practice 150
Martin Exeter 81, 150, 171, 256
Eye Attunement Technique 172

faith 66, 67, 75, 105, 163
Tom Fallon 119, 167, 169, 174
fibromyalgia 159
Fire phase 200, 204
Fissure of Rolando or Central Sulcus 166
Foot and Hand Attunement Practice 211
Foot Attunement Technique 213
foot attunements 196
Matt Frazer 197
Frontal Lobe 167
full body attunement 79, 81, 112, 116, 145

G-P-C (God-Practitioner-Client) pattern of
    agreement 94
G.P.C. (God-Patient-Chiropractor) Servers
    Training 94
gall bladder 138
Generation X 197
Richard Gerber, MD 26
Getting to Yes program 228
Ghandi 126, 188
God Being 88, 104
Gonads 254
Guillian Barre 63
Richard S. Gunther 210

Hand Attunement Technique 215
Hand attunements 211
Harvard Mastery of Stress Study 196
Harvard Negotiation Team 228
Healing Touch 115
Heart 146, 148

heart disease 146, 201, 217
Higher Power 23, 24, 44, 67, 164, 186
Higher Source 54, 94, 121
Hirschberg and O'Regan's Inner Healing
    Mechanism 66
Caryle Hirshberg 45
Histology Notes on the Endocrine Gland System
    251
history of attunement therapy 16
HIV 32, 155
holding pattern 163, 164
holon 84
Holy Place 36, 37, 43, 198
Home-study training 243
homeopathic remedies 143
Hospital Settings and Surgery 219
human anatomy 27

Dr Yujiro Ikemi 43
iliocecal valve 141
immune system attunement 158
Inferior Venacava (IVC) 150
inhalation and exhalation prayer 152
Injury Treatment Attunement Guidelines 185
The Inner Healing Meditation 48
inner divinity 44, 66, 69, 200
inner faith 209
Inner Guidance Intake Forms 242
The Inner Guidance System 66
inner healing 66
Inner Healing Mechanism 45
Inner Healing Meditation 51
inner wisdom 21, 117, 163
Institute of Noetic Sciences and Fetzer Institute
    45
integrity 27, 61, 66, 209
intercessor 82, 94
Intercessory Prayer 55
International Emissaries 16
Internet 239
intuition 27, 66
Islets of Langerhans 253

Jesus 124, 172, 189
Jesus Christ 85, 92, 188, 203
Tom Johnston 183
Chris Jorgensen 185, 210, 211, 220, 195,
    260

kidneys 75, 122, 150
Kitsap Peninsula 102
Elisabeth Kubler-Ross 157

Kundalini Yoga 152

large colon 137
large intestine 138
Eric Leskowitz, MD 165
Jeffrey S. Levin, PhD, MPH 54
Dr Judith Lewis Herman, MD 182
life force 11, 15, 17, 61, 64, 109, 155, 207
liver 138
Long Bone Technique 174
Long Distance (Non-local) Attunement Practice
    78
lupus 143, 159
lymph and immune systems 31
Lymph and Immune Systems Attunement
    Practice 157

Manifestation Guidelines 104
Master Attunement Server 81
meditation 31, 36, 42, 47, 73, 152
Medulla Oblongata 167, 170
Lloyd Arthur Meeker 255
memory trace 69, 182, 183
Meridian System 26, 30
migraine 143
Eddie and Gladys Miller 170
Carol Leppanen Montgomery, RN, PhD 56
Dr Michael J. Moore, Chiropractor 193
Morphogenetic Human Fields 25
morphogenetic/etheric body field 83, 87
Mother Teresa 126
Julie Motz, MPH, MFA 219
Caroline Myss, PhD 187

Native American Indian drum music 226
Naturopathic Medical School 25, 28, 101
ND program 101
negative contact points 130
negative emotional patterns 158
negative energy 29
negative entropy 84
nervous system 123, 168
Non-Directed Prayer 53, 164
Non-local Agreement 77, 170
Northern Blackfoot Indians 147
Christiane Northrup, MD 67

Occipital Lobe 167
One Law of Life 255
Open the Portals of Light 241
opening the endocrine glands 123
Brendan O'Regan 45

O'Regan and Hirschberg's Inner Healing
    Mechanism 66
Dr James Oschman 183

palm chakras 27, 172, 186
Palmer College of Chiropractic 11, 255
Anthony J. Palombo, DC 75, 260
parasympathetic nervous system 168
parasympathetic response 31, 122
Parietal Lobe 167
The Path of Spiritual Expression 127
pernicious anemia 143
Dr Ronald Pero 47
Candace Pert, PhD 26, 77, 96
pineal gland 76, 123, 171, 251
pineal, pituitary and thyroid glands 159
Pituitary Gland 150, 171, 252
placebo effect 46
Pneumaplasm 25, 220
Pons 167
portals of light 124, 129
positive contact points 130
Positive Entropy 84
post-traumatic stress disorders 31, 182
posterior pituitary gland 150
prayer circle 235
Pre-Surgery Self-Attunement 186
pregnancy 195
Paul Price 174, 263
Principles of Manifestation 102
prostate cancer 207

Qi 85
Qi Gong 29, 73, 115

radiant energy 22, 23, 30, 45, 46, 57,
    64, 69, 78, 82
Radiant energy exercises 57, 58
Radiant Gatherings 78, 229, 235
Stephan Rechtschaffen 115, 229
rectum 138
William Redpath 183
reflexology 30, 143
Reiki 29, 73, 217
relaxation 15, 73, 164, 182, 201
Remission 42
representational object exercise 225, 233
Representational Object Practice Guidelines
    229
respiratory system 145
Respiratory System Attunement Practice 152
The Returning Cycle 61

rheumatoid arthritis 32
The Right Touch Healing Arts Center 246
Rising up to Reawaken 117
Robe of Radiance Practice 87
Russek and Schwartz 228

sacral nerve plexus 168
sacrum 168
Sanctification 29, 61, 70, 73, 186
Schumann resonance 235
self-attunement 179
Self-Care 21, 28
Seven Levels of Spiritual Expression 31
sexual abuse 31, 194
Sharing an Attunement 23
George Shears 255
Shears, Ackerley and Uranda 94
Rupert Sheldrake 25
Shinto religion 43
short attunement 131
the Silver Cord 125
Simian AIDS 155
singular representational object exercise 230
sjogran's syndrome 143
Skeletal System Attunement Practice 174
Sloan Kettering Memorial Hospital Cancer
      Research 47
small intestines 135, 138
Dr Justa Smith 85
SOAP charts 242
solar plexus 39, 148, 207
Source 22, 24, 30, 36, 40, 46, 51, 5
      7, 68, 70, 73, 91, 165, 171, 189, 200
The spinal column 31, 168
Spinal Cord Ascension Technique 169
Spinal Cord Attunement Practice 168
The Spindrift organization 55
spiritual agreement principle 94
spiritual awakening 113
Spiritual Chiropractic 107
Spiritual expression 24, 146, 210
Spiritual Leadership 111
spiritual orientation 144
Spiritual transcendence 54, 56
spiritual transformation 238
Spirituality 23
spleen 158
Spleen Attunement Practice 161
spontaneous remission 44, 45
Jaclyn Stein Henderson, NCTMB, RC 246, 262
steroid hormones 194
stomach 138

Stress 38, 158, 200, 202
structural integrity of the body 174
subtle energy 23, 26
Sunrise Ranch 41, 81, 94, 256
Superficial Inguinal Lymph Nodes 161
superior vena cava 170
Superior Venacava (SVC) 150
surgery 82, 182, 183, 219

t-cells 157
team attunement 217
Team Attunement Guidelines 222
Temporal Lobe 167
thalamus 114
Thankfulness 36, 105
Thankfulness Exercises 39
The Endocrine Gland System 123
The Four Forces of the Creative Process 198
The Greater Release Pattern 209
The Path of Spiritual Expression 127
The Seven Levels of Spiritual Expression 124
Therapeutic Touch 29, 115, 219
Thermodynamics 84, 96
Thoracic Duct 161
Thymus 144, 253
thymus gland 157, 159, 207
thyroid 157, 253
Dr William Tiller, PhD 124
Professor William Tiller, PhD 83
Tom Fallon 119, 167, 169, 174
Tom Johnston 183
transcendental meditation 47

Unity Church 101
Uranda 19, 81, 86, 102, 117, 146, 169,
      171, 174, 201, 255

Vasopressin hormone regulation factor 150
venal portal systems 146
visualization 29, 39, 73, 104, 159
vital energy 28, 67

Water phase 199, 204
Margaret Wheatley 240
Dr Stuart White, Chiropractor, 158
Ken Wilbur 84
Stacey Ann Wolf 198
World Service Class 114, 225

Yin and Yang 86

Attunement Therapy Materials Order Information

Energy Medicine Documentation Forms

A full set of new SOAP charts and other record-keeping forms for all your energy medicine needs. Includes: Inner Guidance Intake forms, Attunement Subjective Questionnaire, and Client Record Notes, plus state-of-the-art energy SOAP charts. Documents are copy-ready to meet all of your insurance and L&I billing needs. Limited Copyright agreement included. Cost: $19.95.

Attunement Anatomical Charts.

This 8.5 x 5.5", color-coded booklet is the perfect addition to any attunement student's library, giving easy reference to the attunement contact point system. Simply lay this booklet alongside your client while you share attunement. Lightweight and transportable. Cost: $12.95.

The Attunement Therapy Home-study Course.

Through a mentoring process, you can receive 25 CE credits by simply completing chapter exercises, and then sending them in for credit. This course may be completed by itself or as part of the Certification home-study program. Cost: $15.00 plus love offering ($5 – $10 suggested donation for each CE credit).

Please inquire with Findhorn Press or with myself for discounts, tax and shipping charges.

Findhorn Press, Inc.
P.O. Box 13939
Tallahassee
Florida 32317-3939
USA
tel (850) 893-2920
fax (850) 893-3442

Findhorn Press Ltd
The Press Building
The Park, Findhorn
Forres IV36 0TZ
Scotland, UK
tel 01309-690582
fax 01309-690036

email: info@findhornpress.com
url: http://www.findhornpress.com

to:

FINDHORN PRESS

P. O. Box 13939
Tallahassee
Florida 32317-3939
USA

- -

to:

FINDHORN PRESS

The Press Building
The Park, Findhorn
Forres IV36 0TZ
Scotland

FINDHORN
Press

Tel (850) 893 2920
Fax (850) 893 3442
e-mail info@findhornpress.com
http://www.findhornpress.com/

Thank you for choosing this book. We appreciate your interest and support.

If you would like to receive our full catalogue of books and other inspirational material, please fill in this card and mail it to us.

❏   Please send book and music catalogue

❏   Please send information about the Findhorn Foundation in Scotland

In which book did you find this card? _____

Where did you buy this book? _____

Please write
your name and
address here
(please PRINT)   }

FINDHORN
Press

Tel +44 (0)1309 690582
Fax +44 (0) 1309 690036
e-mail books@findhorn.org
http://www.findhornpress.com

Thank you for choosing this book. We appreciate your interest and support.

If you would like to receive our full catalogue of books and other inspirational material, please fill in this card and mail it to us.

❏   Please send book and music catalogue

❏   Please send information about the Findhorn Foundation in Scotland

In which book did you find this card? _____

Where did you buy this book? _____

Please write
your name and
address here
(please PRINT)   }